Motherhood in Ireland

Class No. 306-8743   Acc No. C/16310)

Author: MOTHERHOOD.. Loc: _____

6 – FEB 2009

**LEABHARLANN
CHONDAE AN CHABHAIN**

1. **This book may be kept three weeks. It is to be returned on / before the last date stamped below.**
2. **A fine of 25c will be charged for every week or part of week a book is overdue.**

1 3 NOV 2009

– 9 AUG 2010

7 JUN 2011

D0542342

This book is dedicated with love
to the memory of
my lovely sister, Arie

Motherhood in Ireland

Creation and Context

edited by
Patricia Kennedy

MERCIER PRESS

CAVAN COUNTY LIBRARY
ACC No. C/163105
CLASS NO. 306.8743-1R
INVOICE NO 5969 O'M
€16.00

Acknowledgements

I would like to thank Mick, Conor, Dylan, Fionn and Millie for their love and support always. To my friends, who I need not name, who are always there for me. Thanks to Professor Gabriel Kiely and all of my colleagues and students in the Department of Social Policy and Social Work at UCD for their interest and encouragement. I would like to thank the Women's Studies students I have met over the years, many of whom have become close friends. Thank you to Angela Bourke, Margaret Mac Curtain, Seamus Cashman and Theo Dorgan for their belief in me and their generous and good advice. Finally, thank you to all of the contributors who have given their time and energy so enthusiastically to this project and to Aisling and Mary at Mercier Press.

The author and publisher wish to thank all those who have kindly given them permission to make use of copyright material: Seamus Heaney and Faber & Faber for 'St Kevin and the Blackbird'; Louis de Paor for 'Ceas Naíon'/'The Pangs of Ulster'; Eavan Boland and Carcanet Press for 'Night Feed'; Theo Dorgan for 'Rosa Mundi'; Mary O'Donnell for 'Antartica'; Nuala Ní Dhomhnaill and New Island Books for 'Ag Cothú Linbh'/'Feeding a Child'; The Gallery Press for permission to use Michael Hartnett's 'The Creatrix'; Mary Dorcey and Salmon Publishing for 'Each Day Our First Night'; Paula Meehan and The Gallery Press for 'Ard Fheis' and 'The Statue of the Virgin at Granard Speaks'; Paul Durcan for 'A Catholic Father Prays For His Daughter's Abortion'; Pearse Hutchinson and The Gallery Press for 'She Fell Asleep in the Sun'; Freddie White for permission to use Don O'Sullivan's 'Treasure'; John Montague and The Gallery Press for 'The Locket'; Tony Davis for 'Song for Christy'; Chris McCarthy for 'How do you Sleep?'; Dermot Bolger and New Island Books for 'Dublin Girl, Mountjoy Jail, 1984'; Dennis O'Driscoll and Anvil Press for 'Out of Control'; Austen Greene for permission to use Angela Greene's 'A Young Woman with a Child on each Hand'; The Bucks Music Group for permission to use Ewan McColl's 'The Moving On Song'; Billy Kennedy for 'Horizon'; The Gallery Press for Ó Bruadair extracts as translated by Michael Hartnett; Caroline Canning for 'Despairing Couple', 'St Kevin's Hand' and 'Mother of Emigrant Children'; Imogen Stuart for the photograph of her sculpture; Mary Moynihan for the photograph of her and her mother, Helen; Helen S. Callary for the image of the crucifix and the photograph of the convent building; Caroline Mullen for the photograph of Molly Collins in Cork; Mick Kennedy for the photograph of the 1950s mother.

First published in 2004 by Mercier Press
Douglas Village, Cork
Email: books@mercierpress.ie
Website: www.mercierpress.ie

Trade enquiries to CMD Distribution
55A Spruce Avenue
Stillorgan Industrial Park
Blackrock, County Dublin
Tel: (01) 294 2560; Fax: (01) 294 2564
E-mail: cmd@columba.ie

© Patricia Kennedy 2004
ISBN 1 85635 422 9
10 9 8 7 6 5 4 3 2 1

A CIP record for this title is available from the British Library

Cover design by mercier vision

Printed in Ireland by ColourBooks, Baldoyle Industrial Estate, Dublin 13

This book is sold subject to the condition that it shall not, by way of trade or otherwise, be lent, resold, hired out or otherwise circulated without the publisher's prior consent in any form of binding or cover other than that in which it is published and without a similar condition including this condition being imposed on the subsequent purchaser.

No part of this publication may be reproduced or transmitted in any form or by any means, electronic or mechanical, including photocopying, recording or any information or retrieval system, without the prior permission of the publisher in writing.

Contents

Introduction

Introduction

In this book I bring together creative and critical writing on motherhood in Ireland in an attempt to understand its complexity. I am conscious that motherhood has been used as a symbol in Ireland in political, cultural and social life. In the course of editing this book, I met many men and women who told me that they did not feel qualified to write about motherhood and some expressed a fear of speaking on the subject. This, they all agreed, was because they had not experienced physiological motherhood. I found this very disturbing, as it seemed to imply that a whole section of the population had been silenced. I thought again and again of Rich's words:

> All human life on the planet is born of woman. The one unifying, uncontrollable experience shared by all women and men, is that months-long period we spent unfolding inside a woman's body.[1]

We are all born of women. We have all had mothers even though we may have had very different experiences of motherhood. This alone qualifies us all to speak on the subject. It is necessary to see motherhood in much broader terms than physiological reproduction. We need to look at social reproduction, which does not have to be the work of the physiological mother only. We need to look also at the institution of motherhood. Rich, writing in *Of Woman Born*, distinguishes between biological motherhood and motherhood as an institution. The latter she claims is subject to male control and 'has been a keystone of the most diverse social and political systems'.

In Ireland, the institution of motherhood needs close examination. The different powers which have constructed and controlled the institution of motherhood also need attention. Unfortunately, what emerges is not a very pleasant picture. While motherhood undoubtedly brings women much pleasure and happiness, what we see in this book are the struggles of many women, in a society which claims to value motherhood. While women are often confined and constrained by their reproductive role by a patriarchal State and Church, they are often unsupported in that role.

The role of mother was even institutionalised in the 1937 Constitution.[2] The status of the family hinged largely on 'woman' or 'mother' who was also endowed with a particularly 'favoured' status, which she was expected to live out within the home.

Article 41.2

1. In particular, the State recognises that by her life within the home, woman gives to the State a support without which the common good cannot be achieved.

2. The State shall, therefore, endeavour to ensure that mothers shall not be obliged by economic necessity to engage in labour to the neglect of their duties in the home.

These articles find resonance in Rich (1977), who states that there:

> ... has been a basic contradiction throughout patriarchy; between the laws and sanctions designed to keep women essentially powerless and the attribution to mothers of almost superhuman power (of control, of influence, of life-support).

Women have been seen primarily as mothers. There are good mothers and bad mothers. There are physiological birth mothers. There are adoptive mothers. Mothers who leave and mothers who stay. Mothers who breastfeed and mothers who don't. There are mothers who work outside the home and mothers who don't. Mothers who live, die and nurture, mothers who commit crimes. There are mothers of different ability, race and culture.

The contributors who coincidentally are, in most cases, mothers, base the chapters in this book primarily on original research. However, they were selected because of their writing and not because of their 'maternal status'. I was anxious to include men's voices in the book and the voices of women who may not have reproduced in the traditional sense. Often these voices were best heard through poetry. There is a huge wealth of poetry and song on the subject, which evokes very strong emotions. In chapter one, I have chosen a poem or a song to complement each succeeding chapter, as I feel that both forms of addressing a subject, one creative, the other critical, evoke strong images and emotions and together give a more complete picture. The body of work presented here presents the essence of, and elucidates the symbolism of motherhood in Ireland.

1 Rich, A. (1977) *Of Women Born, Motherhood as Experience and Institution*, Virago. London

2 *Bunreacht na hÉireann* (*Constitution of Ireland*), (1937) Govt Pub., Dublin.

CREATION I

St Kevin's Hand
© *Caroline Canning*

CHAPTER ONE
Creation and Context

Patricia Kennedy

The body of work presented in the subsequent chapters gives a holistic view of what motherhood in Ireland means in relation to both the experience and the institution. The following poems each reflect the central theme of the corresponding chapter and, in a different written form, relay a similar or related message.

I begin by presenting Seamus Heaney's poem 'St Kevin and the Blackbird' as it reinforces my belief that everyone has a right to speak on motherhood, as we are all born of woman. I feel that this poem captures the essence of nurturing, which both men and women can do, yet it also captures the discomfort and pain of birth, which on this occasion is felt by St Kevin rather than by a mother. St Kevin is presented in a midwifery role and the blackbird is the fruit of his labour. It reminds me that motherhood has a variety of meanings tied up with creativity and nurturing and not solely the physiological labour of woman as mother.

St Kevin and the Blackbird
Seamus Heaney

And then there was St Kevin and the blackbird.
The saint is kneeling, arms outstretched, inside
His cell, but the cell is narrow, so

One turned-up palm is out the window, stiff
As a crossbeam, when a blackbird lands
And lays in it and settles down to nest.

Kevin feels the warm eggs, the small breast, the tucked
Neat head and claws and, finding himself linked
Into the network of eternal life,

Is moved to pity: now he must hold his hand
Like a branch out in the sun and rain for weeks
Until the young are hatched and fledged and flown.

*

And since the whole thing's imagined anyhow,
Imagine being Kevin. Which is he?
Self-forgetful or in agony all the time

From the neck on out down through his hurting forearms?
Are his fingers sleeping? Does he still feel his knees?
Or has the shut-eyed blank of underearth

Crept up through him? Is there distance in his head?
Alone and mirrored clear in love's deep river,
'To labour and not to seek reward,' he prays,

A prayer his body makes entirely
For he has forgotten self, forgotten bird
And on the riverbank forgotten the river's name.

Opened Ground Poems 1966–1996,
Faber and Faber (1998)

The first section of this book concentrates on creation in the physiological sense. Mothers live their lives where the public and private meet. Pauline Dillon Hurney in her chapter on infant-feeding gives us a sense of how the extensive female emotional and instinctual knowledge, passed on through women, has been lost, as expertise has become more highly valued than mothers' own experience. Eavan Boland's poem 'Night Feed' reminds us of the intimacy of infant-feeding and portrays a sense of peacefulness, solitude and intimacy in the pre-dawn darkness.

Night Feed
Eavan Boland

This is dawn.
Believe me
This is your season, little daughter.
The moment daisies open,
The hour mercurial rainwater
Makes a mirror for sparrows.
It's time we drowned our sorrows.

I tiptoe in.
I lift you up
Wriggling
In your rosy, zipped sleeper.
Yes, this is the hour
For the early bird and me
When finder is keeper.

I crook the bottle.
How you suckle!
This is the best I can be,
Housewife
To this nursery
Where you hold on
Dear life.

A slit of milk.
The last suck.
And now your eyes are open,
Birth-coloured and offended.
Earth wakes.
You go back to sleep.
The feed is ended.

Worms turn.
Stars go in.
Even the moon is losing face.
Poplars stilt for dawn
And we begin
The long fall from grace.
I tuck you in.

Night Feed
Carcanet Press (1994)

Mary Moynihan's personal account of her mother's death following childbirth gives us a sense of a life being snuffed out prematurely. The silence following death is palpable as is echoed in Theo Dorgan's poem 'Rosa Mundi'. He writes of 'the silence after'. Referring to the 'human flow of talk', we are very much aware that it has stopped. This also comes across in Mary Moynihan's writing. Both give a glimpse of the face behind the statistics, even describing the geography of these women's lives and their sense of being interwoven into families and communities which are touched by silence and emptiness left behind in the vacuum which follows death.

Rosa Mundi
Theo Dorgan

April, a day off school. Indulged, bored, hungry for something new.
The road bends below Driscoll's and I see her coming clear,
Laden with shopping bags, eyes bright in the full flow of talk.

I've been signalling Collins Barracks on the hill across Blackpool,
Morse book open on the window-sill, weighted with a cup.
Nobody answering no matter how I flash 'Help, I am being held prisoner ...'

It sets in early, disillusion with the State, its idle soldiers.
The flash of her eyes as she greets Peg Twomey now. I scamper upstairs,
Hook the bevelled mirror back in place. From the bedroom window

I see her reach the gate.

*

How he'd tumble downstairs, crash through the front door, taking the
Garden steps two, three at a time. Up close, the strain on her face.
Tufnell Park years later, the fireflash of news in my face. The silence after.

Grooves in her fingers, released from the heavy bags, the rings –
Wedding, engagement, eternity – clicking against his nails.
Remembering suddenly when she smiles that he is meant to be sick.

Slowly, backwards, up the steps, her scraps of thought and talk as she fought
For breath. Who she'd met and who had died, who was sick and who had
A new child, news from a world she waded in, hip-deep in currents of talk.

A spoon for each of us and a spoon for the pot, not forgetting to scald the pot.
What a span of such days unreeling now, my eye on them both, reaching
Down through the haze to bring them back, herself and her son,

My mother and me.

*

Dust everywhere when they broke the news, my friends, these sudden
        strangers.
Dust of the Underground on my lips, dust on their newpainted window, dust
On the leaves outside, in the heavy air banked high over the city.

I stared down at the gate, a vacuum in my chest, hands clenching and
        unclenching.
*So easy the words, so treacherous the comfort. Old enough to know I had
        failed her,*
Too young to know what in, too greedy for life, really, to have cared enough.

*

This is the ring I conjure for them, the stage for their dance.
For a child to live, his mother must die. For a man to die, his mother must live.
Here on the brink of forty, close to midnight, I conjure them all –

My brothers and sisters, my mother and father, my neighbours and friends,
The most absolute strangers of my life, my heart's companions. Nothing
Is ever lost that has shone light on simple things.

*No child is without a mother, no father can lose his son,
No mother is unregarded, no sister can fail to learn,
No brother escapes unwounded, no friend can salve the burn.*

The road bends out into the drunken heft of space and nothing can be lost.
Not her life's sacrifice, not our unquenched and stubborn love,
Not that child's faith in light flashing from mirrors, or her faith in

The human flow of talk. The human flow of talk is all we have. Who we've met
And who is sick, who's had a child, who's lost a job. Her eyes flash,
He scampers upstairs, rushes downstairs, taking the steps two at a time,

Feeding his heart's hunger for life and life only. The mask of strain on her face,
The ritual of the teapot, hesitant access of heartbreak and knowledge. I
would these words could soothe the pain from her fingers, conjure her
patient grace.

Rosa Mundi
Salmon Publishing (1995)

In her chapter on infertility, Flo Delaney captures the emptiness of
infertility, the loss, grief and coldness. Mary O'Donnell in her poem
'Antarctica' also captures the silence, the aloneness, the sense of
being apart from other women; mothers. Reading 'Antarctica' one
can feel the softness of the baby clothes that will never be worn and
the breasts that will never be suckled. Similarly, Delaney writes of
the women she interviewed who talked of 'having no voice or no
words, being silent or isolated'. Both writers succeed in voicing the
pain of infertility, of 'the silent tragedy'.

Antarctica
Mary O'Donnell

I do not know what other women know
I covet their children; wardrobes
Stocked with blue or pink, froth-lace
Bootees for the animal-child
That bleeds them.

Their calmness settles like the
Ebb-tide on island shores –
Nursing pearl-conch, secret fronds
Of wisdom, certitude.
Their bellies taunt.

I do not know what other women know.
Breasts await the animal child.
I want – maddened by
Lunar crumblings, the false prophecy
Of tingling breasts, turgid abdomen.

Antarctica: the storm petrel hovers;
Waters petrified by spittled winds:
Little fish will not swim here.
Folds of bed-sheet take my face.
Blood seeps again.

'But you are free,' they cry,
'You have no child!' – bitterness
From women grafted like young willows
Forced before time. In Antarctica,
Who will share this freedom?

Reading the Sunflowers in September
Salmon Publishing (1990)

Chapter five challenges some of the myths which exist in relation to childbirth in Ireland today. It presents statistical data on the women who do give birth and looks at the increase in medical interventions. De Paor's poem 'Ceas Naíon', or 'The Pangs of Ulster' portrays the physiological experience of childbirth and reminds us of the hard labour involved.

Ceas Naíon
Louis de Paor

Scoite amach
ar imeall an tinnis
a riastraigh do chabhail
le pianta Uladh,
a thimpeallaigh an tocht
mar a rabhais i luí
nár luí in aon chor
ach únfairt ainmhí
i gcró, chonac
mo bhean ghaoil
ag cur straein ar a croí
chun mullán nárbh fhéidir
le trí chéad fear a bhogadh,
leac a mheilfeadh
cnámha bodaigh,
a theilgean dá gualainn oscartha.
Nuair a bheir an bhean
chabhartha deimheas
leis an ngad
a cheangail
don saol eile í
tháining aois Fhionnuala
ar a snua cailín
leathláimh chomh min
le cliathán eala
ar an ngin a rug sí
ón tsíoraíocht abhaile,

The Pangs of Ulster
Louis de Paor

Outside
the circle of pain
that racked your body
with the pangs of Ulster,
surrounding your bed
as you lay
not lying
but writhing like
an animal in a crush
I watched my kinswoman
strain to lift a stone
three hundred men
couldn't lift,
to catapult a marble slab that would
crush the spine of a stickman,
from her arched back.
When the midwife
sheared
the cord
that bound her
to the other world
I saw her age in an instant like
Fionnuala and her blessed sisters
one hand smooth
as a swan's wing
on the gift
she brought back from nothing,

leathláimh chomh seargtha
leis an mbráilín smeartha.

the other wasted
as crumpled sheets.

Corcach agus Dánta Eile
Coiscéim (1999)

The second part of this book focuses on creativity of another kind. It explores the symbolism and treatment of motherhood in Irish literature, both in the Irish language and the English language as well as in the visual arts.

Máire Mhac an tSaoi reminds us that Irish mothers' relationships with their infant children are preserved in the oral tradition and that 'mother-love exists in the present; it does not feel the need to survive in printed books'. Nevertheless, Nuala Ní Dhomhnaill in 'Ag Cothú Linbh', 'Feeding a Child' offers us a glimpse of mothering, of the special relationship between the mother and child. We can sense the soft skin of both the baby's 'small hand' and the mother's breast from which the child drinks its fill. We can sense the intimacy and love, which bonds both together.

Ag Cothú Linbh
Nuala Ní Dhomhnaill

Feeding a Child
Nuala Ní Dhomhnaill

As ceo meala an bhainne
as brothall scamallach maothail
éiríonn an ghrian de dhroim
na maolchnoc
mar ghiní óir
le cur i do ghlaic,
a stór.

From honey-dew of milking
from cloudy heat of beestings
the sun rises up the back
of bare hills,
a guinea gold
to put in your hand,
my own.

Ólann tú do shá ó mo chíoch
is titeann siar i do shuan
isteach i dtaibhreamh buan,
tá gáire ar do ghnúis.
Cad tá ag gabháil trí do cheann,
tusa ná fuil,
ach le coicíos ann?

You drink your fill from my breast
and fall back asleep
into a lasting dream
laughter in your face.
What is going through your head
you who are but
a fortnight on earth?

An eol duit an lá ón oíche
go bhfuil mochthráigh mhór
ag fógairt rabharta,
go bhfuil na báid
go doimhin sa bhfarraige
mar a bhfuil éisc is rónta
is míolta móra
ag teacht ar bhois is ar bhais
is ar sheacht maidí rámha orthu,

Do you know day from night
that the great early ebb
announces spring tide
that the boats
are on deep ocean,
where live the seals and fishes
and the great whales
and are coming hand over hand
each by seven oars manned,

go bhfuil do bháidin ag snámh
óró sa chuan
leis na lupadáin lapadáin
muranáin maranáin,
í go slim sleamhain
ó thóin go ceann
ag cur grean na farraige
in uachtar
is cúr na farraige
in íochtar?

that your small boat swims
óró in the bay
with the flippered peoples
and the small sea-creatures
she slippery-sleek
from stem to bow
stirring sea-sand up
sinking sea-foam down?

Orthu seo uile an bhfuilir
faoi neamhshuim?
is do dhoirne beaga
ag gabháilt ar mo chíoch.
Tánn tú ag gnúsacht le taitneamh,
ag meangadh le míchiall.

Of all these things are you
ignorant?
As my breast is explored
by your small hand.
You grunt with pleasure,
smiling and senseless.

Féachaim san aghaidh ort, a linbh,
is n'fheadar an bhfeadaraís
go bhfuil do bhólacht
ag iníor I dtalamh na bhfathach,
ag slad is ag bradaíocht,
is nach fada go gcloisfir
an 'fi-faidh-fó-fum'
ag teacht thar do ghuaille aniar.

I look into your face child
not knowing if you know
your herd of cattle
graze in the land of giants,
trespassing and thieving,
and that soon you will hear
the 'fee-fie-fo-fum'
sounding in your ear.

Tusa mo mhuicín a chuaigh
ar an margadh,
a d'fhan age baile
a fuair arán agus im
is ná fuair dada.
Is mór liom de ghreim tú
agus is beag liom de dhá ghreim,
is maith liom do chuid feola
ach ní maith liom do chuid anraith.

You are my piggy
who went to market
who stayed at home
who got bread and butter
who got none.
There's one good bite in you
but hardly two,
I like your flesh
but not the broth thereof.

Is cé hiad pátrúin bhunaidh
na laoch is na bhfathach
munar thusa is mise?

And who are the original patterns
of the heros and giants
if not me and you?

Rogha Dánta (Selected Poems)
Translated by Michael Hartnett
New Island Books (1988)

Mary Dorcey captures the essence of time passing, seasons, years moving on. With it comes a sense of loss, but also a sense of transformation as she herself is reborn as mother, the one who gave her life. She describes her own experiences of one who was mothered well and for who that mother/child relationship is now changing. This transformation is echoed in Áine McCarthy's chapter when she draws our attention to the daughter/mother perspectives in the writings of Irish women writers. She reminds us that being a mother can be a barrier to writing because of the way that the institution of motherhood is structured.

Each Day Our First Night
Mary Dorcey

What a beautiful mother
I had –
Forty years ago,
When I was young
And in need of a mother,
Tall and graceful,

Dark haired,
Laughing,
What a fine mother, I had
When I was young.
Now I climb the steps
To a cold house

And call out a word
That used to summon her.
An old woman
Comes to the door:
Gaunt eyed, grey haired,
Feeble. An old woman

Who might be
Anybody's mother. She
Fumbles with the locks,
And smiles a greeting
As if the name spoken
Belonged to her.

We go inside
And I make tea.
The routine questions
Used to prompt her
Fall idle.
She cannot remember
The day of the week,
The hour, nor
The time of year.
Look at the grass,
I say,
Look at the leaves –

You tell me!
Autumn, she answers
At last. Her hands
Wind in her lap,
Her eyes like a child's,
Full of shame.

Each day,
A little more
Is lost of her.
Captured for an instant,
Then gone.
Everything that

Made her particular,
Withering like leaf
From the tree.
Her love of stories
And song, her wit,
The flesh on her bones.

What a beautiful mother
I had, forty years ago
When I was young
And in need of a mother.
Proud, dark haired
Laughing.

Now I descend the path
From a cold house,
An old woman
Follows to the window,
An old woman
Who might be

Anybody's mother.
She stands patiently
To wave me off –
Remembering
The stage directions,
Of lifted hand

And longing gaze.
In this Experimental piece –
Each day,
Our first night –
She plays her part

With such command –
Watching her
Take a last bow
From the curtain –

You could swear she
Was born for it!

Like Joy in Season, Like Sorrow
Salmon Publishing (2001)

The creatrix in Michael Hartnett's poem seems to share the same need with Róisin de Buitléar and Maree Hensey: 'the need to create is compelling'. All three women immerse us in images of glass, textiles, paper, painting, origami, Indian inks and watercolours. Hartnett's paper babies are as alive as Ella, Somhairle, Cuan, Conor and Tuathla all mentioned in the writing of Róisín de Buitléar and Maree Hensey. The constant anxiety that consumed their minds before giving birth parallels the unoiled swing in Hartnett's poem.

Creatrix
Michael Hartnett

She cuts out paper children
and festoons
her ghetto-blasted room
with bunting lines.
She writes out paper children,
folds them into boats
to float on the canal.
Essence of baby
is distilled
in her bitter tears.
She doubted seed for years:
all rampant men were lairs
strutting their inches –
yet she is full of love,
her paper children
nestle at her breasts.
Each has a name,
each prammed in her handbag
through the playground
full of swings and slides,
complaints and cries.
She sits and rocks and folds
new creatures
in her origami room.
An empty swing, unoiled,
grates in the playground of her womb.

Collected Poems
Gallery Press (2002)

The third section of this book presents the context in which the institution of motherhood unfolds. Bresnihan reminds us of the universal symbolism of motherhood. She links the symbolism of motherhood as understood by those who claim to represent the pro-life movement in Ireland to classical thinkers. Similarly, the images presented in Paula Meehan's poem remind us of the importance of symbolism in Irish culture.

Ard Fheis
Paula Meehan

Down through the cigarette smoke
the high windows cast
ecstatic light to the floorboards
stiletto pocked and butt scorched

but now such golden pools of sun to bask in there.
I am fish
Water my demesne.
The room pulses in, then out, of focus

and all this talk of the people, of who we are,
of what we need, is robbed of meaning,
becomes sub-melody, sonic undertow,
a room of children chanting off

by heart a verse. I'm nine or ten,
the Central Model School,
Miss Shannon beats out the metre
with her stick.

I wind up in the ghost place
the language rocks me to,
a cobwebby state, chilled vault
littered with our totems;

a tattered Starry Plough,
a bloodstained Proclamation,
Connolly strapped wounded to a chair,
May blossom in Kilmainham.

I am following my father's steps
on a rainy Sunday in the National Museum,
by talisman of torc, carved spiral,
sile na gig's yoni made luscious in stone.

And somewhere there is vestige
of my mother nursing me to sleep,
when all my world was touch,
and possibly was peace.

I float down to a September evening,
the Pro-Cathedral, girls in rows at prayer,
gaze at the monstrance, lulled to adoration,
mesmeric in frankincense and candlelight:

Hail our life our sweetness and our hope
to thee do we cry poor banished children of Eve
to thee do we send up our sighs
mourning and weeping in this valley of tears.

I push back to the surface, break clear,
the light has come on fluorescent
and banishes my dreaming self.
It is, after all, an ordinary room

and we are ordinary people.
We pull our collars up and head
for the new moon sky of our city
fondling each whorled bead in our macabre rosary.

Don't even speak to me of Stephen the Martyr,
the host snug in his palm,
slipping through the wounded streets
to keep his secret safe.

The Man Who Was Marked by Winter
Gallery Press (1991)

Paul Durcan's poem reflects the complexity of the discourse around reproductive rights in Ireland. He captures the contradictions between the public and private and one becomes aware of how the personal is political. He refers to a shambles of a society, 'where women are hard put to get away with life, but men get away with murder day by day'. Pauline Conroy, in her exploration of reproductive rights, explains the way in which Irish society becomes this shambles, referring to the first referendum campaign as 'bizarre'. She reveals to us why the mother 'is a potentially criminal or threatening figure'.

A Catholic Father Prays For His Daughter's Abortion
Paul Durcan

Should that bank manager down in Connemara
Make my daughter pregnant and ditch her,
And should she dread
The prospect of being an unmarried mother,
I pray that she may find a nursing home
Tended with compassion by nursing nuns
In which she will be given the abortion that is her due.

When my other daughter told her boyfriend she was pregnant
He was scared stiff, not that she was pregnant –
He felt chuffed at being verified a virile, feckless fellow –
What he was scared of was what he might have to do
Something about the consequences of being a virile, feckless fellow.
Society has a duty to the individual
As has the individual to society;
Long before my daughters graced this earth
Society, such as it is, had come into being,
Organised itself into the shambles that it is,
Where women are hard put to get away with life
But men get away with murder day by day.
I stare into the church candles flickering
Consolatorily in the dark, while outside
The snow piles upon the icy, gritted street.
I pray for my daughter's abortion and well-being
In the caring hands of a merciful God.
As I take my leave the parish priest with the heart of gold
Throws me a stealthily murderous scowl –
He knows that I pray to God and not to him –
And across the street an old woman is selling newspapers from a pram
And the snow is driving on not leaping to greet me.

The Berlin Wall Café
Harvill Press (1995)

Paula Meehan uses images of grottos, 'Communion frocks', midsummer weddings, the bright and cheerful images fed to Catholic schoolgirls, but she also conjures images of darkness, crucifixion, death, 'ghetto lanes', 'garrison towns', dark secrets, fear, helplessness, pain and death. Similar images are evoked by the words of the women who shared their stories with Betty Hilliard. Hilliard refers to the women as painting a picture of 'domination, ignorance and fear'. Secrecy is a strong theme of Hilliard's chapter and echoes Meehan's description of the fifteen-year-old girl who 'pushed her secret out'.

The Statue of the Virgin at Granard Speaks
Paula Meehan

It can be bitter here at time like this,
November wind sweeping across the border.
Its seeds of ice would cut you to the quick.
The whole town tucked up safe and dreaming,
even wild things gone to earth, and I
stuck up here in this grotto, without as much as
star or planet to ease my vigil.
The howling won't let up. Trees

cavort in agony as if they would be free
and take off – ghost voyagers
on the wind that carries intimations
of garrison towns, walled cities, ghetto lanes
where men hunt each other and invoke
the various names of God as blessing
on their death tactics, their night manoeuvres.
Closer to home the wind sails over
Dying lakes. I hear fish drowning.
I taste the stagnant water mingled
with turf smoke from outlying farms.

They call me Mary – Blessed, Holy, Virgin.
They fit me to a myth of a man crucified:
the scourging and the falling, and the falling again,
the thorny crown, the hammer blow of iron
into wrist and ankle, the sacred bleeding heart.
They name me Mother of all this grief
though martyred to no mortal man.
They kneel before me and their prayers
fly up like sparks from a bonfire
that blaze a moment, then wink out.

It can be lovely here at times. Springtime,
early summer. Girls in Communion frocks
pale rivals to the riot in the hedgerows
of cow parsley and haw blossom, the perfume
from every rushy acre that's left for hay
when the light swings longer with the sun's push north.

Or the grace of a midsummer wedding
when the earth herself calls out for coupling
and I would break loose of my stony robes,
pure blue, pure white, as if they had robbed
a child's sky for their colour. My being
cries out to be incarnate, incarnate
maculate and tousled in a honeyed bed.

Even an autumn burial can work its own pageantry.
The hedges heavy with the burden of fruiting
crab, sloe, berry, hip: clouds scud east
pear scented, windfalls secret in long
orchard grasses, and some old soul is lowered
to his kin.
death is just another harvest
scripted to the season's play.
But on this All Souls' Night there is
no respite from the keening of the wind.
I would not be amazed if every corpse came risen
from the graveyard to join in exaltation with the gale,

a cacophony of bone imploring sky for judgement
and release from being the conscience of the town.

On a night like this I remember the child
who came with fifteen summers to her name,
and she lay down alone at my feet
without midwife or doctor or friend to hold her hand
and she pushed her secret out into the night,
far from the town tucked up in little scandals,
bargains struck, words broken, prayers, promises,
and though she cried out to me in extremis
I did not move
I didn't lift a finger to help her,
I didn't intercede with heaven,
nor whisper the charmed word in God's ear.

On a night like this I number the days to the solstice
and the turn back to the light.
                    O sun,
centre of our foolish dance,
burning heart of stone,
molten mother of us all,
hear me and have pity.

The Man Who Was Marked by Winter
Gallery Press (1991)

The beautiful image evoked by the title of Pearse Hutchinson's poem 'She Fell Asleep in the Sun' is in stark contrast to Patricia Burke Brogan's writing from her own experiences of working as a nun for a short period in a Magdalene laundry. She describes herself as a 'white veiled jailer'. She uses poetry and drama to bring us with her inside the walls of the institution where thousands of Irish girls suffered at the hands of other women, sisters and mothers of the religious kind. Patricia Burke Brogan evokes images of dampness and 'no-colour air'.

She Fell Asleep in the Sun
Pearse Hutchinson

'She fell asleep in the sun'.

That's what they used to say
in South Fermanagh
of a girl who gave birth
unwed.
A woman from Kerry told me
what she'd always heard growing up was
leanbh ó ngréin;
a child from the sun.

And when a friend of mine from Tiernahilla
admired in North Tipperary
a little lad running around a farmyard
the boy's granda smiled:
'garsúinin beag mhistake'.

A lyrical ancient kindliness
that could with Christ accord.
Can it outlive technoaltry?
or churches?

Not to mention that long, leadránach,
latinate, legal, ugly
twelve-letter name not
worthy to be called a name,
that murderous obscenity – to call

any child ever born
that excuse for a name
could quench the sun forever.

Collected Poems
Gallery Press (2002)

Don O'Sullivan, poet and songwriter, challenges us with rich and vivid images of the sea and treasure being washed ashore and derides us for the breakdown of civilisation which corners a pregnant woman into concealment, secrecy and shame. He captures the loneliness and despair of a woman with an unwanted pregnancy, silenced. It is an expression of the low value we put on life when a baby can be a 'brief nameless treasure'. Alexis Guilbride, through her analysis of court reports, brings the mothers behind them alive. It is evident that they are pushed beyond unimaginable limits by fear, shame, exhaustion and most of all patriarchy. The stories of women like Mollie Byrne, Frances Smith and Eily Murphy prove Alexis Guilbride's thesis that while women 'may be compelled to endure unwanted pregnancies' they cannot be forced into motherhood.

Brief Nameless Treasure
Don O'Sullivan

The bounty washed ashore
To smear our conscience on a quiet beach
Carried on an unforgiving ocean to our door
What strange depths have we reached?

Our civilised veneer
shows a crack

For a bitter little indictment to appear
In a plastic sack
Life is surely meant to be
Less pointless than this would make it seem
This strange fish out of water
Somebody's son.
Somebody's daughter
A silent scream.

Chance now finds a twin
Buried in the farmyard
Is this an abyss we're sinking in?
Secrets to God.

For nine long spinster months no one to tell
Speak of it never.
Speak of it never.
Unwanted even by the cold Atlantic swell.
Brief nameless treasure.

Brief nameless treasure.
Speak of it never
Our shame beyond measure
Speak of it never
Change us forever.
Brief nameless treasure.
Brief nameless treasure.

My Country
Little Don Records/Lowstrand Media (1999)

John Montague's poem 'The Locket' portrays the ambiguity of adoption. This most complex of subjects is addressed by Eileen Conway who helps us appreciate that there can be loss and gain for all concerned in what she poignantly refers to as 'this emotional transaction'. As the mother in Montague's poem says to her son: 'Don't come again, you say, roughly, I start to get fond of you John, and then you are up and gone'. He captures the child's longing and his satisfaction in knowing that his mother, who had given him away, had always worn his picture in a locket around her neck.

The Locket
John Montague

Sing a last song
for the lady who has gone,
fertile source of guilt and pain.
The worst birth in the annals of Brooklyn,

that was my cue to come on,
my first claim to fame.

Naturally, she longed for a girl,
and all my infant curls of brown
couldn't excuse my double blunder
coming out, both the wrong sex,
and the wrong way around.
Not readily forgiven.

So you never nursed me
and when all my father's songs
couldn't sweeten the lack of money,
When poverty comes out the door
Love flies up the chimney,
your favourite saying.

Then you gave me away,
might never have known me,
if I had not cycled down
to court you like a young man,
teasingly untying your apron,
drinking by the fire, yarning

Of your wild, young days
which didn't last long, for you,
lovely Molly, the belle of your small town,
landed up mournful and chill
as the constant rain that lashes it,
wound into your cocoon of pain.

Standing in that same hallway,
Don't come again, you say, roughly,
I start to get fond of you John,
and then you are up and gone;
the harsh logic of a forlorn woman
resigned to being alone.
And still, mysterious blessing,
I never knew, until you were gone,
that, always around your neck,
you wore an oval locket
with an old picture in it,
of a child in Brooklyn.

Collected Poems
Gallery Press (1995)

Goretti Horgan explores mothering in a disabling society. Looking at
the experiences of mothers with disabilities as well as mothers of
children with disabilities, she impresses on us feelings of confinement

and limitations imposed, not by the disabilities themselves, but by society's structures and attitudes. Tony Davis, in his 'Song for Christy' inspired by reading the work of Christopher Nolan, echoes this imprisonment with his opening line 'Locked behind his eyes'. Davis recognises that hard work and dedication reap rewards in his line, 'It took a mother's love to reach inside that mind so wild, and helped the man emerge from the body of a child'. This idea emerges powerfully from the mothers in Horgan's writing. The theme of 'constant struggle' is central to her writing.

Song for Christy
Tony Davis

Locked behind his eyes, the mirror of the soul
A million jumbled words his tongue cannot control
Trapped inside his heart, full to overflow
A love of life so pure, he'll find a way to let you know
Spurred on by a constant need to let his voice be heard
In language straight and true and not in sound absurd

Chorus:
Touched by the hand of God, crippled by the ignorance of man
Taunted by schoolboy jibe, it's just another case of head in the sand
Why do they look away, why don't they understand
That behind the twisted mask, an extraordinary man

Under the eyes of the world, they watch his every move
And as his dreams realise, there's always more to prove
Now they come from everywhere, some to praise, some to doubt
Or simply stare
At that shell that's opened to reveal a pearl beyond compare

Chorus

It took a mother's love to reach inside that mind so wild
And helped the man emerge from the body of a child.

Anne Coakley reminds us that mothers have a central role in the dynamics of poverty in low-income households. She explains to us why some women live in poverty while others do not. She outlines possible exit routes from poverty. The women who speak from Anne Coakley's chapter remind us of how they find themselves 'spending hours shopping for bargains, saving pennies here and there on over-ripe vegetables and sell by date groceries'. Their hardship and marginalisation is echoed in 'How do you sleep?' by Chris McCarthy, who reminds us of the hopelessness felt by women living in poverty.

How do you sleep?
Chris McCarthy

How do you sleep?
How do you sleep my wealthy friend?
When your purpose filled day draws to an end
Are you tormented with a guilty conscience?
Of the poor and the 'have nots' and all the nonsense.
When your head hits the pillow do you think with pleasure
Tomorrow will bring even more of the treasure?.
Have you any idea what its like to be
Caged like a bird that should be free
Living in flats, bogged down by oppression.
The need for space a real obsession.

Can you imagine that hopeless feeling
To look from your window to see pushers dealing
Young children playing in dirt and squalor
While you share an empathy from your cosy parlour.
No you could never in your wildest imagination
Know what its like to have no education,
To have been abused, to feel confused,
To put up a fight, only to lose.
Of that Celtic Tiger I know you've met him,
With all your skills you can vet him.
Justlike the ring master you take control
One lash of the whip, on his belly, he'll roll.
If from your path that tiger should stray
Show some guts and guide it our way.
So tonight my dear friend when you take to your bed
Please spare a thought of all I have said.

Celesta McCann James exposes us to the harsh reality of life for mothers in prison. She gives us a glimpse of the coping strategies adopted by women in an effort to survive their time in custody. She introduces us to Suzanne, Darina, Brenda and other mothers who spend weeks, sometimes months without seeing their children. James argues that mothers are 'systematically undermined by imprisonment, being reduced to one hour of interaction with their children per week'. Bolger brings alive the loneliness and longing of these mothers behind bars.

Dublin Girl, Mountjoy Jail, 1984
Dermot Bolger

I dreamt it all, from end to end, the carriageway,
The rivulet behind the dairy streaked with crystal,

A steel moon glinting in a guttered stream of rain,
And the steep hill that I would crest to find her,
My child asleep in my old bedroom beside my sister.

I dreamt it all, and when I woke, furtive girls,
Were clambering onto the bars of the windows,
White shapes waving against the dark skyline,
Praying for hands to reply from the men's cells,
Before screws broke up the vigil of handkerchiefs.

I dreamt it all, the times I swore never again
To walk that carriageway, a rivulet of heroin glowing
In my veins until I shivered in its aftertaste,
And hid with my child in the closed-down factory
Where my brain snapped like a brittle fingernail.

I dreamt it all, the longing to touch her, the séance
In the cell when we screamed at the picture falling,
The warmth of circled hands after the frozen glass
Between my child and me, a warder following her words
To be rationed out and lived off for days afterwards.

I dreamt of you, who means all to me, my daughter,
How we might run to that carriageway rivulet,
And, when I woke, a blue pupil was patrolling my sleep,
Jailing my dreams in the vacant orbit of its world,
Narrowed down to a spyhole, a globed eyelid closing.

Taking My Letters Back, New and Selected Poems,
New Island Books (1998)

Dennis O'Driscoll's words hammer home the feeling of powerlessness felt by mothers as they lie awake at night 'on standby', waiting 'to find out whether you are still with child'. These words resonate with the feelings of constant fear and anxiety conveyed in Margaret Ward's chapter on the subject of mothers living in Northern Ireland. She conjures up images of Union Jack bibs; plastic bullets; women wrapped in blankets and through it all the resilience of mothers raising their children in a hostile environment 'that has been anything but "normal"'.

Out of Control
Dennis O'Driscoll

Worry on, mothers: you have
good reason to sleep,
to let imaginations run riot
as you lie in bed, not counting sheep

but seeing sons and daughters
like lambs led to slaughter
in the road kill of Friday nights.

Remain on standby, mothers –
you never know your luck –
for the knock that would break
the silence like the shock
of a metallic impact against brick.
Keep imagining a police beacon,
a blue moon shattering the darkness.

Lie warily, mothers, where,
eighteen years before, conception
took place in the black of night,
a secret plot; wait restlessly,
as if for a doctor's test,
to find out whether
you are still with child.

Exemplary Damages,
Anvil Press Poetry (2002)

In popular conversation, young mothers are referred to as if theirs is
a constant state, that, like those lost in Tir na nÓg, they will never
grow old. Angela Greene in her poem 'A Young Woman with a Child
on each Hand' shatters this illusion when she refers to the everyday
routine of women in this stage of life. She reflects that 'she walks into
the life I am leaving', a reminder that time passes, roles change and
life moves on. Valerie Richardson also focuses on the dynamism of
young mothers or as she refers to it 'children having children'. In her
research she has found that, despite what we are often led to believe,
that these child mothers 'were concerned and caring about their children, and did the best they could, using the limited resources at their
disposal'.

A Young Woman with a Child on each Hand
Angela Greene

A young woman with a child on each hand
turns at the zebra crossing
to join two more young women
one pregnant, one tilting a pram.
she is vital, almost beautiful.
her sons are sturdy and neat.
she walks into the life I am leaving.

When she greets her friends, I am aware
mothercraft has blinded her, till anxiety
thins her voice. I want to call out,
that for her, now is filled

with simple certainties – a spilled cup,
a rowdy room, a bed-time story. But
as she moves down the street, I can
only guess the weight
of her sacrifice, her tenderness
as her hands keep emptying, emptying …

Silence and the Blue Night
Salmon Publishing (1993)

In chapter twenty, Traveller women: daughters, mothers, grandmothers and great-grandmothers recount their experiences of mothering and of being mothered as members of Ireland's indigenous ethnic minority. The richness of their culture is glimpsed against a backdrop of discrimination and disadvantage. McColl's 'The Moving On Song' focuses on the sentiment 'not in my back yard' which is often expressed by the settled community in relation to the provision of services and in particular adequate accommodation for Travellers.

The Moving On Song
Ewan McColl

Born in the middle of the afternoon
In a horsedrawn carriage on the old A5
The big twelve wheeler shook my bed,
'You can't stay here,' the policeman said.

Chorus:
You'd better get born in someplace else.
Move along, get along,
Move along, get along
Go! Move! Shift!

Born on the common by a building site
Where the ground was rutted by the trail of wheels
The local Christian said to me
'You'll lower the price of property.'

Chorus

Born at potato picking time
In a tent in a tatie field
The farmer said, 'The work's all done,
It's time that you were moving on.'

Chorus

Born at the back of a hawthorn hedge
Where the frost lay on the ground
No eastern kings came bearing gifts
Instead the order came to shift.

Chorus

The eastern sky was full of stars
And one shone brighter than the rest
The wise men came so stern and strict
And brought the orders to evict.

Chorus

Wagon, tent or trailer born
Last month, last year or in far off days
Born here or a thousand miles away
There's always men nearby who'll say.

Chorus

Harmony Music

Grace Neville brings to life the stories of people from marginal social groups who emigrated from rural Ireland to North America in the late nineteenth and early twentieth centuries. She focuses on mothers and emigration, particularly on the effect emigration had on mothers. Billy Kennedy, a songwriter, echoes the loss and pain of those left behind in 'Horizon', inspired by his own experience of emigration in the 1980s in pre-Celtic Tiger Ireland. It expresses the pain and longing of ageing parents left behind.

Horizon
Billy Kennedy

I know you had to go
it wasn't your fault things didn't work out
Boats and trains
take you to foreign places
but don't worry
they always come back.

Chorus:
When I get up in the morning
I'll look out to the sea
wait for the tide
and hope your ship will be
on the Horizon

I know you'll be ok
you were always able to look after yourself
when I think of you
awake in the lonely night
I will feel your letters
and kiss your photograph

Chorus

I watched you grow
helped you and you didn't know it
now boats and trains
take you to foreign places
but I won't worry
they always come back

Chorus

CHAPTER TWO

Infant-Feeding

Pauline Dillon Hurney

While the activity of infant-feeding is a central one in the experience of every mother, it is one about which little is known from her perspective and with which there has been little engagement in Ireland, outside of the medical field. The shift away from breastfeeding, along with the development of homogenised milk for babies, represents, 'important, if frequently over-looked, elements of change in the family sphere' (Kennedy, 2001). The primary emphasis here is on breastfeeding as a process in which a mother actively engages, rather than on breast-milk as a product (Van Esterik, 1989). Too often, in concentrating exclusively on the needs of the infant, the welfare of the mother is eclipsed in the discourse on infant-feeding.

From Breast to Bottle

A dramatic change in infant-feeding patterns has occurred in industrialised countries throughout the developed world since the beginning of the twentieth century: a culture where breastfeeding was almost universally practised has gradually been replaced by one where bottle-feeding is now the choice of the majority of mothers. Ireland is no exception: the breastfeeding initiation rate (the number of women who start out breastfeeding) here has been estimated to be in the region of 30% (Wiley and Merriman, 1996) and in one recent study carried out in twenty-two European countries, the Irish rate was the lowest recorded (Freeman, 1996). Currently no national data is collected on the duration of breastfeeding, but there is evidence that only about 15% of mothers continue for the four-month period recommended by the Department of Health and Children (Ryan, 1996).

It is generally recognised that the mothers who are least likely to breastfeed are those in the lower socio-economic groups (Murphy, Parker and Phipps, 1999). Again, this is the case in Ireland (Wiley and Merriman, 1996) and a recent study has recommended that mothers in this sector be targeted for priority intervention (Centre for Health Promotion Studies, 1999). However, at the beginning of the twentieth century, it was among working-class Irish mothers that the practice of breastfeeding was most widespread, while it was the mother in the higher socio-economic group who was more likely to feed her infant artificially (Cameron, 1904, 1910, 1911; Coey Bigger, 1917).

My consideration of this change in infant-feeding practices is informed by recent feminist work in this area and the emergence of a discourse that challenges the positivist, medical one that has dominated for so long (Maher, 1992; Carter, 1995; Blum, 1999). Breastfeeding is not simply a female biological function – it is an activity that has always raised a myriad of complex issues for mothers – regarding access to and availability of economic resources and social supports, bodily and maternal autonomy, negotiation of public and private space. The pertinence of these issues varies at different historical periods, in different societies, among different classes, but they are invariably complex and important in determining maternal behaviour in this area.

This discourse has prompted questions regarding the possible factors that contributed to the decline of breastfeeding in Ireland. Was it the result of the 'new', scientific model of infant-feeding that emerged in the early years of the twentieth century and the increasing hospitalisation of birth? Was it the result of official policies and philanthropic initiatives that, in problematising mothers, failed to address their underlying basic needs? Or was it an inevitable outcome of what Foucault (1991) has termed 'the great enterprise of medical acculturation' at that period and its subsequent displacement of traditional sources of female knowledge with the expertise of the professional?

The Problem of Infant Mortality
For the majority of Irish mothers today, the experience of maternity is no longer inextricably bound up with loss: our infant mortality rate has fallen from 99 to 6 per 1,000 live births during the period from 1900 to 1995 (Kennedy, 2001). However, in the early 1900s, when poverty was widespread, many mothers' lives were a constant struggle dominated by economic insecurity; one outcome was that infant death was commonplace. The public health authorities were seriously concerned about the high infant mortality rates, which were worse in the cities than in the country, and were particularly problematic in Dublin (O'Brien, 1982; Barrington, 1987; Prunty 1998). These rates remained persistently high in the first half of the century, not showing a marked decline until the 1950s (Clear, 2000). The role of the medi-

cal profession was seen as crucial in effecting a reduction in this death toll.

While today, the benefits of breastfeeding in countries in the developed world can be said to be relative rather than absolute (Blum, 1999), at the turn of the last century this was not the case. In the conditions of poverty that prevailed in many homes, the benefits of breastfeeding for the infant were clearly undeniable and artificial-feeding presented major hazards. However, the knowledge of the Irish medical profession at that period regarding how the process worked on a physiological level was very limited, as was their understanding of the importance of cultural, societal and economic supports in sustaining the activity. In effect, their attempt to promote and encourage the practice of breastfeeding may have done more to hinder than to help mothers having trouble in this area.

The Medical Model of Breastfeeding

In 1901, amidst growing public and professional concern about the high rate of infant mortality, particularly in the Dublin area, a committee of doctors was formed specifically to draw up instructions on the subject of infant-feeding. The committee, which was established by the Section of State Medicine of the Royal Academy of Medicine in Ireland, met in Dublin and comprised members of both the Royal College of Physicians of Ireland as well as members of the Royal Academy of Medicine in Ireland. The following year, it published its 'plain suggestions as to the care and feeding of infants', stating that 'the mother's milk is the most natural and therefore the proper and most wholesome food for the infant'. Very precise directions were given as to the number of feeds an infant required and exclusive breastfeeding was advocated for the first nine months. Night-feeding was disapproved of, as was the extension of breastfeeding beyond this period (*Dublin Journal of Medical Science*, 1902). While instructions regarding hand-feeding were also given, there was unanimous agreement that breastfeeding was the best method of infant-feeding.

Physicians William Langford Symes (1899) and John Lumsden (1897, 1906 and 1909) both produced pamphlets on infant-feeding at this period, advocating breastfeeding as the best practice and laying down directions in keeping with those of the committee. Both disapproved strongly of feeding on demand, Lumsden cautioning that 'The custom of giving it the breast, whenever it cries, is a bad one, and if given-into, is harmful to both mother and child' (1906). Both were adamant about the importance of regularity, irrespective of whether the infant was being bottle-fed or breastfed. Langford Symes stated that 'the number of feeds required in either method of rearing is the same, and they should be given at the same intervals' (1899).

This medical model of breastfeeding became an integral part of maternity hospital practices and, as the slow but steady trend towards hospital confinement began (Robins, 1995, 2000; O'Dwyer and Mulhall, 2000), so its influence on this aspect of Irish women's maternity became more pervasive. Dr Brian Crichton, the first paediatrician to be appointed to the Rotunda in 1927, recommended in his book, *The Infant* (n/d c.1930) that breastfeeding begin four hours after the birth and that, while the schedule could be either three- or four-hourly, it was important to adhere to it rigidly. If the breast-milk was insufficient, test-feeds should be carried out. Where these revealed that the supply was deficient, supplementary bottle-feeds should be given to replace some of the breastfeeds, thus, in his opinion, enabling the mother to continue breastfeeding for many months. Dr Robert Collis, his successor in 1932, advised that breastfeeding begin eight hours after the birth. Three-hourly feeding was recommended but, until the breast-milk appeared, he advised that the infant be given boiled water and sugar in ample quantities in order to supply enough fluid. In cases where the supply of breast-milk was insufficient, he felt that complementary bottle-feeds given at the end of the breastfeed were preferable to supplementary feeds, which led, in his opinion, to the drying up of the milk (Collis, 1938). These practices remained in place for many years. Although Dr P. C. D. Mac Clancy, a later paediatrician at the hospital, stated in 1958 that they were 'aware of the recent work on demand feeding', breastfeeding at fixed times and for fixed periods was still 'justified by experience'.

The Morality of Breastfeeding
Also incorporated into this medical model of breastfeeding however, was the concept of maternal nursing as a moral responsibility, in the light of the high mortality rate among artificially-fed infants. Lumsden was very forthright on this point, stating unequivocally that it was 'the bounden duty of every mother who has any sense of her responsibilities or desire for her child's well-being to breastfeed it, unless ordered by the doctor not to do so' (1906). In fact, the exhortation to women to fulfil their duty in this regard contained the implicit assumption that to do otherwise was to act irresponsibly and to be less than

a good mother. Edward Coey Bigger (1917) summarised this position when he stated that 'it should be impressed upon every mother that she is capable of rendering her child less liable to disease by breast-feeding than by artificial-feeding'.

This view that breastfeeding was a 'duty' of motherhood also informed the practices of some hospitals for many years. There is evidence that mothers were subjected not only to a model of breastfeeding now known to be detrimental to the successful establishment of lactation, but that an enforced breastfeeding regime existed in both the Rotunda and Holles Street. In 1938, Dr Collis of the Rotunda warned against becoming 'fanatical' on this subject:

> I have seen nurses take up an almost moral attitude upon the matter and subject unfortunate mothers, who cannot feed their babies for perfectly legitimate reasons, to long tirades, thereby upsetting the home and making any possibility of even partial breastfeeding impossible.

The correct attitude, he advised, should be 'scientific, humane and objective'. In 1951, the Master of Holles Street, Dr Arthur Barry stated that it was 'a regulation of this hospital that every mother feed her infant unless such conditions as phthisis, absence of nipples, etc., render this impossible' (Farmar, 1994). Change was slow to come. In 1958, Dr Mac Clancy of the Rotunda stated that to establish lactation successfully, the right approach was necessary. He complained that, all too often, doctors and nurses tried to force the mother to breastfeed rather than seek her co-operation.

While the view that mothers should not be coerced into breastfeeding gradually gained acceptance, there is evidence that harsh attitudes persisted in some of the other institutions where women gave birth. Midwife June Goulding (1998), in her memoir of the period she spent from 1951 to 1952 in a home for unmarried mothers in Bessboro, describes her shock when, on her first day, she witnessed a young girl in distress who was trying to breastfeed, while holding a swab of cotton wool to a suppurating abscess. The sister in charge of the ward ordered her not to let the pus into the baby's mouth and failed to reply to Goulding's question as to whether antibiotics were being administered. In the nursery, a group of mothers sat breastfeeding on milking stools. As one girl's newborn infant was handed to the mother of a three-month old baby, she realised that mothers were often expected to feed infants other than their own.

The Failure to Breastfeed

Doctors in the early years of the century all agreed that breastfeeding was best, but artificial-feeding with 'modified' milk was also beginning to acquire the seal of medical approval. It was seen both as an acceptable alternative to breastfeeding for mothers in the higher socio-economic groups and as a possible solution to the problem of the high infant death toll among the poorer classes. Langford Symes was totally in favour of 'the scientific regulation of artificial-feeding' and felt that 'it would diminish, if not abolish' this problem of infant mortality (*Dublin Journal of Medical Science*, 1901). His colleague Lumsden had used pasteurised milk to feed two of his own children and had ordered it for some of his private patients 'with admirable results' (*Fourth Annual Report of the Women's National Health Association*, 1911).

Furthermore, there was a growing recognition that factors that were socio-economic in origin, and as such outside the medical remit, were frequently involved in the mother's 'failure' to breastfeed, factors such as nutritional status, ill health and poverty. Thus, many mothers who initiated breastfeeding were unable to maintain an adequate supply and resorted to artificial-feeding, often with unsuitable foodstuffs. In 1917, Edward Coey Bigger, in his 'Report on the Physical Welfare of Mothers and Children', commissioned by the Carnegie United Kingdom Trust in an effort to ascertain the causes of the high infant mortality rates, highlighted the problem of maternal malnutrition and its consequences for breastfeeding mothers:

> It has been shown fairly clearly that the nourishment of the mother during pregnancy has a definite effect on her capacity to suckle her infant ... In the majority of cases she suckles her child herself, but her food being scanty, and the drain on her system having been severe, the milk is not always forthcoming, and she is frequently compelled to abandon the breast in favour of the bottle.

In 1925, Dr Brian Crichton stated that he frequently encountered mothers at the Rotunda who could not breastfeed 'due to lack of nutrition' or even sometimes because they were on 'the verge of starvation'. Mothers who attended the clinic run by Dr Colman Saunders at Holles Street during the 1920s experienced similar difficulties (Farmar, 1994). In fact, maternal malnutrition was prevalent in Dublin for many years. In 1939, a survey carried out into ante-natal nutrition among a group of mothers attending the Rotunda's ante-natal clinic revealed that only 6% of the mothers were consuming an adequate amount of protein and that all the women were anaemic (Dockeray and Fearon, 1939).

Increasingly, in the face of social problems about which they could do little, artificial-feeding was seen as a means of solving the high infant mortality rates. However, Coey Bigger (1917) was aware of the dilemma that this presented for mothers in the poorer classes:

> When the child is weaned ... the difficulties of infant foods arise. Milk is expensive, dried milk prohibitive, and so recourse is often made to skim-milk, an unsatisfactory diet for an infant, and one which is not improved by the addition of potatoes and other scraps from the parents' scanty table.

In his outline for a planned Maternal and Child Welfare Centre in Dublin, he advocated the distribution at cost price of dried, powdered milk in cases where infants were not breastfed. This, he felt, would offer 'a fairly pecuniary advantage' to mothers attending the centre and act 'as an inducement for them to come' (1917). In 1925, Dr Brian Crichton recommended that the maternity hospitals should have 'a Milk Kitchen, where foods already prepared would be given out to the mothers at as near cost as possible'.

The Carnegie Child Welfare Centre, which was envisaged as a prototype for future centres to be opened throughout the country, was opened in Dublin in 1927. The following year, it began to distribute pasteurised milk initially and then also dried, proprietary infant foods 'for the use of infants of the necessitous cases, free of charge'. There was also an effort to promote breastfeeding and a scheme was run, in conjunction with the St John's Ambulance Brigade, to provide free dinners to pregnant and nursing mothers for two months before the confinement and three months afterwards. However, the free milk scheme appears to have been by far the more popular choice of mothers, as the numbers attending the Maternity Dining-Rooms were always very small in comparison to those who availed of the free milk (Department of Local Government and Public Health Report, 1929–1937). In 1933, for example, an average of 6,766 pints of milk was distributed daily, while the number of mothers who received free dinners was approximately 240 daily (Reddin, 1934).

Doctors did try to promote the free dinners scheme in cases where they recognised that maternal nutrition was inadequate, but the eventual solution that was arrived at appears to have been a compromise: that of advocating breastfeeding but combining it, when difficulties arose, with artificial-feeding. In 1938, Dr Robert Collis of the Rotunda stated that if a mother was poor with a large family and if she was anaemic, undernourished and worn-out, it was wrong to 'rant at her' for not breastfeeding. Instead, an effort should be made to obtain extra nourishment for her through the social services, and complementary feeding advised, in the hope that her milk supply would later increase. This attempt to feed nursing mothers did not appear to make any significant impact. In 1943, the Master of the Rotunda, Dr Falkiner expressed his disappointment that, in spite of the work being done by the dining-rooms, many mothers were only breastfeeding for a few weeks (Clarke and Matthews, 1995).

The Power of the Professional
Another equally important, though less tangible, factor which must be considered in attempting to account for the demise of breastfeeding in Ireland, is the implicit notion throughout this period, of the superiority of the scientific authority of the professional over the emotional, instinctual knowledge of the mother (Apple, 1987). For years the attitude of the health professionals towards the mother's lay network was a highly critical one. In 1917, Coey Bigger stated that 'The great evil was lack of good mother-craft' which was something that had to be taught for it was not instinctive. He advocated that senior schoolgirls be instructed in the proper care and management of infant and young children in order that 'the present ignorance and the firmly-rooted evil traditions' which had survived for so long be overcome. In 1934, Dr Kerry Reddin, the medical officer in charge of the Carnegie Model Child Welfare Centre in Dublin, attributed the large number of infant deaths to maternal ignorance and to 'the young mother's aptitude to follow the advice of elder female relatives versed in the ancient lore of ignorance and superstition' which was seen to surround baby management.

In this promotion of the expertise of the physician, began the slow erosion of a culture where women had traditionally sought guidance and support from a network of female kin. In fact, the importance of this network was clearly articulated by the individuals who were the subject of a recent oral history of tenement life in Dublin in the 1920s and 1930s (Kearns, 1996). For mothers, it served as a valued source of informal mutual aid and support, particularly at the time of childbirth. Many mothers spoke highly of the 'handywomen', as the untrained midwives in the community were called, who not only delivered the baby but also fulfilled another important function, in that they cared for the mother in the post-natal period. One woman recalled how they would 'do everything for you ... look after that baby and do your washing for you and look after you for the whole nine days'. Another remembered how her grandmother, who held such a position, made mothers who were breastfeeding drink a glass of stout as so many of them were undernourished. This was a community where a strong culture of breastfeeding appeared to flourish without professional expertise. There *was* a high infant mortality rate, but statistics conceal as well as reveal, and there were many mothers who did successfully breastfeed, possibly enabled to do so by the practical support they got following childbirth, support now acknowledged to be crucial for the establishment of successful lactation. One wonders about the consequent loss to subsequent generations of Irish mothers that resulted from the rising power of the physicians whose authority, as Ehrenreich and English have stated 'rested on the denial or destruction of women's autonomous sources of knowledge: the old networks of skill-sharing, the accumulated lore of generations of mothers' (1979).

The Rise of Artificial-Feeding
During the 1940s and 1950s, there was some concern among the medical profession that the practice of breastfeeding was declining. The Master of the Rotunda, Dr Falkiner, noted in 1943 that many mothers changed to bottle-feeding a few weeks after their discharge (Clarke and Matthews, 1995). The Master of Holles Street, Dr Arthur Barry was concerned when, in 1951, a survey undertaken at the hospital revealed that, a few weeks after discharge, only 51% of mothers were still breastfeeding exclusively (Farmar, 1994). However, as the problem of infant mortality began to decline in the 1950s, so too did public and professional interest in infant-feeding practices. It was not until medical research in the 1960s revealed that breastfeeding had benefits hitherto unknown, that the topic began again to attract attention.

In a national survey of infant-feeding practices among Irish mothers (McSweeney and Kevany, 1982), 68% of the mothers were bottle-feeding, while 32% were breastfeeding. Of the breastfeeding mothers, 3% were using either complementary or supplementary feeds. The survey revealed that only 22% of breastfeeding mothers fed their babies immediately after the birth, while 25% did not commence breastfeeding until twelve hours or more later. Only 46% of breastfeeding mothers fed on demand. While most mothers had their babies with them during the day, only 17% of breastfeeding mothers and 24% of bottle-feeding mothers had their babies with them all the time. 30% of the breastfeeding mothers stated that their babies had been given artificial feeds during their hospital stay. However, there was also evidence of a knowledge-gap as mothers did not know to whom to turn when they experienced difficulties. On being asked about their awareness of sources of help available to them on discharge from the hospital, over half the mothers (60%) knew of no other source except the hospital, while almost a quarter (22%) knew of none at all. 13% viewed their GP and/or public health nurse or clinic as a source of help and only a tiny number (1%) were aware of La Leche League.

A further study carried out in 1986 (McSweeney) revealed little change: there was still evidence of breastfeeding having to suit the hospital schedule, of breastfed babies being given artificial feeds and of test-weighing before and after feeds. The survey failed to address the issues raised by the previous one. Many of the respondents expressed their dissatisfaction with hospital practices and the lack of support available. The questionnaire relied 'on self-reports of behaviour, not on observation of their actual behaviour' and there was no independent measure to assess their validity.

In 1984, the Perinatal Reporting System was set up and national data on this subject became available for the first time. During the period 1986–1992, the breastfeeding initiation rate never exceeded 33% (Department of Health, 1992). In 1994, the role of hospital practices in the decline of breastfeeding was eventually addressed by the Department of Health in its policy document 'A National Breastfeeding Policy for Ireland'. It recommended that the practices detailed in the 'Ten Steps to Successful Breastfeeding', as elaborated in the Baby-Friendly Hospital Initiative, a program launched by the World Health Organisation and the United Nations' Children's Fund in 1991, be implemented. Ward management was to 'be centred round the mother-infant dyad to facilitate breastfeeding' (Department of Health, 1994). Breastfeeding should commence in the first hour after birth; babies should be roomed-in with their mothers; and schedules relating to frequency and time on the breast should be avoided. It also recognised the role of the non-professional in promoting the practice of breastfeeding, acknowledging that voluntary mother-to-mother support groups, such as the La Leche League and the Irish Childbirth Trust, are 'an important community resource to assist health professionals in their task of supporting breastfeeding'. The Ten Steps have in general been welcomed but there has been some unease in Britain regarding the potentially coercive implementation of the Baby Friendly Hospitals Initiative in some hospitals there. Also, there has been disquiet about step number six (which states that newborn breastfed infants should be given no food or drink other than breast-milk 'unless medically indicated') in that a decision that should be the prerogative of the mother is offered as the mandate of the professional (Murphy, et al, 1999).

A recent study here (Centre for Health Promotion Studies, 1999) demonstrates clearly that today, again, it is for Irish mothers in the most under-resourced sector that breastfeeding presents the greatest challenge. Mothers who bottle-feed are no longer open to the charge that, as a result, their infants will fail to thrive. However, they are aware that, in choosing not to breastfeed and in resisting the advice of health professionals, they can be perceived as in some way deficient. It is also significant that the mothers in the study who had chosen to breastfeed expressed a much higher level of satisfaction with the level of support they had received in the maternity hospital than those who had chosen to bottle-feed. In fact, many of these mothers presented negative accounts of their contact with health professionals and felt they were being pressurised into breastfeeding. It would appear that current attempts to encourage breastfeeding as a health-promotion strategy run the risk of becoming counter-productive, unless there is a clear acknowledgement of the difficulties inherent in this for mothers among whose lay-network the practice is not now the norm.

While there is no doubt that the practices of Irish hospitals today are more likely to facilitate successful lactation, their previous practices in this area were clearly a contributing factor in the decline of breastfeeding during the last century. The recognition now that expertise does not reside solely with the professional is also encouraging, but one cannot but wonder at the legacy left by their former attitude. However, the demise of breastfeeding is also about the failure of the Irish state to address the underlying social problems that lay at the heart of the high infant mortality rates during the first half of the last century and to attempt to remedy, with a medical solution, a situation that required political commitment. The distribution of free milk was a short-term strategy, which, in effect, proved to have long-term consequences.

CHAPTER THREE
Death of a Mother

Mary Moynihan

While there has always been the element of risk and death associated with the life-giving act of pregnancy and childbirth, maternal mortality in Ireland today is a rare occurrence. But when it does happen it can have devastating consequences for those left behind. Over the years, the national figures for maternal mortality have declined from 17 in 1970 to 1 in 2002 (Kennedy, 2002). However, between 1970 and 2000, over 145 women have died and their deaths are referred to as maternal mortality deaths.

In Ireland, maternal mortality is defined as the death of a woman while pregnant or within forty-two days of the termination of the pregnancy (Kennedy, 2002). Maternal mortality is further divided into direct and indirect obstetric deaths. Direct obstetric deaths:

> ... are those which result from obstetric complications of the pregnant state (pregnancy, labour and puerperium), from interventions, omissions, incorrect treatment, or from a chain of events resulting from any of the above (Murphy-Lawless, 1998).

Indirect deaths are:

> ... those which come about as a result of previous or pre-existing diseases or from diseases which developed during pregnancy, but which is not related to the pregnancy as such, although it is aggravated by the pregnant state (Murphy-Lawless, 1998).

Who are these women? What were their names? And what of their families and friends left behind? And more importantly, how and why did these women die? I know nothing about any of these women except for my own mother, Helen Moynihan, who died in 1981, seven days after giving birth to a baby boy.

There is no official body in Ireland charged with investigating the causes of maternal deaths and neither is there a detailed record of what happened to these women. Such a report is published in England, for example, where many health professionals and doctors are willing to carry out clinical audits into all cases of maternal deaths.

'Why Mothers Die? Report on Confidential Enquiries into Maternal Deaths in the United Kingdom, 1994–1996' is the fourth such report published and it continues a series of confidential enquiries into maternal deaths which started in 1952 for England and Wales, in 1956 for Northern Ireland and in 1965 for Scotland. These reports into maternal mortality not only identify the causes that lead to each death but also put forward recommendations for improving future obstetric practice. The reports recommend ways for doctors and midwives to review their work and help bring about dramatic improvements in modern maternal care.

These recommendations are important because, as the above report states, 'while some maternal deaths are inevitable events, many are associated with a degree of substandard care'. These enquiries help to ensure that lessons can be learned to help avoid future unnecessary deaths and to ensure that all women receive optimal care. Because no such report exists in Ireland today, we do not know how many women have died here because of substandard care. How can we be sure that women in Ireland are receiving optimal care in pregnancy and childbirth? In the absence of such enquiries, there is a strong lack of accountability. Families are forced to go through difficult and unnecessary processes to find out what happened, particularly because of the apparent codes of secrecy that operate in hospitals when patient care is questioned. And how can we be sure that statistics on the number of maternal deaths are correct without proper procedures for reporting and investigating maternal deaths?

Independent enquiries cannot bring back a loved one but they may offer some comfort to the families of women who have died unexpectedly while pregnant, or in childbirth, by giving people information about what happened. Some form of accountability is important, particularly if substandard care has played a part in a woman's death.

My mother died in 1981 from a brain haemorrhage (an indirect obstetric death), seven days after giving birth. She was examined by a doctor in the maternity hospital and sent home, only to collapse minutes after leaving the hospital. This fact is omitted from a very brief, one-page, clinical report conducted by the hospital into my mother's death. Unfortunately, a full investigation into her death was never carried out so, while we have our own suspicions, we cannot know exactly what happened. The following is my father, Eddie's, account of what happened to my mother on the day of her death:

> She had headaches and her doctor came to the house, and he could do nothing for her. And he sent her back to the maternity hospital. She had only a bad headache at this stage, so I took her into the hospital. They gave her tablets and sent her home ... and on the way home, just around the corner from the hospital, she got sick, very suddenly ... she went semi-conscious. So I just turned around and went straight back up and the doctors came out and they were all flying around the place then at that stage ... and I thought they put her in the ambulance and brought her away down to the Richmond. They asked me did I want to go in the ambulance but I had to go home to get someone to mind the baby.

My father came home and told my brother Joe and me that our mother was ill and he arranged for someone to come in and mind us and he then went straight back to the hospital. My mother was transferred to the Richmond Hospital where she died about ten hours later, never regaining consciousness, and according to my father 'they were very helpful in the Richmond ... but by then it was too late, I suppose'. Obviously we are not medical people, but we do believe that whoever saw her in the maternity hospital should have treated her sooner. My father said:

> It should have been diagnosed. I mean if you have a threatened brain haemorrhage, these experts should have been able to diagnose it. Because if it was now, I'd make a fuss about it, I'd insist on having these things checked out but at that time I was young and I didn't know the difference.

After all these years I still don't know exactly how and why my mother died and why we were left with a small baby to rear. It seems my mother had no serious illness during her pregnancy although she did have a threatened miscarriage early on and later she had swollen hands and feet. My mother's symptoms on the day of her death were described as 'severe right-sided headache, breathlessness and upper abdominal discomfort'. I find it strange that the clinical report omits the fact that my mother was seen and then sent home only to be brought straight back, in a semi-conscious state. I can only speculate that the hospital did not listen to her properly or take her complaints seriously. Would her symptoms, along with raised blood pressure, not indicate something was wrong? Was the fact that she had just experienced a difficult and demanding labour taken into account? What about her age, giving birth at thirty-nine after a gap of sixteen years? Why was she sent home?

In the course of writing this chapter, I made a written request to the maternity hospital asking for the clinical records and nursing notes relating to the day of my mother's death. The request was refused because of patient confidentiality; even though my mother is dead more than twenty years now and all her immediate family supported the request. We were told that our only option was to contact a solicitor, which we are now doing. After all these years my family does not want to cause any trouble for the hospital, we only want information. Do all families face the same difficulties when trying to find out the truth? The maternity hospital did send me a very brief synopsis of my mother's death and stated that she had suffered a 'subarachnoid haemorrhage' whereas the internal hospital report for 1981 described it as an 'intracerebral haemorrhage'. For a laywoman like myself, this apparent confusion and/or contradiction only causes further upset and worry.

Without any proper report into my mother's death, our family can only speculate. Should the doctors have known what was wrong? As my father said: 'She had a bad headache, they were very slow about it'. After my mother's death my father did not ask the hospital about the cause of her death due to a mixture of grief, shock, a belief that it now made no difference because she was dead and the fact that he now needed to find a way to cope with a week-old baby to look after. Like many Irish families, we were encouraged to get on with life and not talk too deeply about our loss. But my family will always suspect that the situation was not handled as well as it should have been. Perhaps if the hospital had explained things better at the time, we wouldn't have been left with these lingering suspicions. Writing this chapter is like a journey for me as I go back and try to find out the answers to questions I've carried around for years but never dared ask. I may not get answers but it is like a personal healing journey for me, to try to bring some sort of closure to a very painful event. Writing about my mother's death is not intended to create fear around the joyful occasion of childbirth but rather to acknowledge those who have died, to remember them and to recognise the close links between birth and death.

*

This is the story of my mother, Helen Moynihan, who died in 1981 aged 39, seven days after giving birth to a healthy baby boy, and the story of how those of us left behind tried to survive. A husband and father, two teenage children, a new baby, parents, brothers and sisters and friends, all trying to come to terms with an act that seemed to have no justifiable explanation or meaning. The family had to deal with losing a mother who had just given birth, care for the new child and cope with the pain of death.

My mother was born Helen Brennan Roe on Saturday, 12 September 1942. She was from a tiny village in Kilkenny called Clogh, near Castlecomer and was named after her father's mother who came from Massford. Her official name was Helen but as she grew up her family shortened her name to Ellen. She was the eldest of eleven children, nine girls and two boys. Her father, James (Jimmy) Brennan Roe, worked as a miner in the Castlecomer mines and her mother, Mary (who I am named after), worked in the home, rearing her eleven children. She went to school in Clogh village and then, at the age of sixteen, emigrated to the United States of America where she first stayed with relatives. While my mother was in America she met my father, Eddie Moynihan, who had just come out of the American army and was now working as a plasterer on buildings while my mother worked for the Blue Cross (the equivalent of the Voluntary Health Insurance [VHI] in Ireland). My father was also Irish, from a place called Kilmacrane in Banteer, Co. Cork. He too had left home early to work in England for a year and then in America. My grandmother said she always prayed that my mother would meet an Irishman and not someone from another country because it was the only chance to bring her daughter home. My father knew my mother to see as they both belonged to the Irish community in New York and they met at a dance hall. My father asked my mother to dance and about eighteen months later they were married on Saturday, 3 November 1962 in Our Lady of Mercy Church, New York. My parents lived in the Bronx but both of them always wanted to come home and have their family in Ireland and a year later they did so.

My mother's parents hired a car and drove up to Dublin to meet them from the airport. This was the first opportunity for them to meet their new son-in-law and it was a big occasion for all my mother's younger brothers and sisters. From the airport, they drove straight back to Kilkenny and my parents lived there for a few months and with my father's parents in Cork, before they finally moved to Dublin. Through an advertisement in the papers, they found a beautiful place to rent. My father described it as 'a big place, three or four bedroomed', that was part of an old, very large house on its own grounds in Clontarf. Apart from my parents' apartment, the rest of the house was used as a secondary school for boys and was called Cosca College.

Mary Moynihan with her mother, Helen, taken in 1965

This was where my parents were living when I was born in 1965 and my brother Joe was born eleven months later. My earliest memories are of playing in the gardens and watching the children who lived next door who seemed to spend much of their time sitting on top of the high stone wall that separated the two houses. My father used to help the owner of the college look after the place and he was very disappointed when my parents decided to leave, but as my father said, 'we bought our own house in Coolock and we were delighted'. My parents then moved out to this new home in Coolock with two small children. My father started his own business as a building contractor and my mother looked after Joe and me. From my own memories and from talking to those who knew my mother, two things stand out about her. She was a very happy woman who was loved deeply by those who knew her and that she loved children. According to my mother's sister, Margaret:

> there were nine girls in our family but Helen was always my favourite, to me she was always happy, that's the way I remember her. She loved life, she seemed to love life so much, but most of all she loved children. She had just had her second child, Joe, and already had the name picked out for the next one but of course she never had another child, not until Edmund came along sixteen years later ... but the only thing she ever seemed to want in life was children.

My mother wanted more children but for no obvious reason was un-able to become pregnant. My grandmother would laugh as she remem-bered my mother saying 'the doctor said there is nothing wrong with me, all I need is a good man'. My mother would say this jokingly, while eyeing up my father to see his reaction.

Apart from not being able to get pregnant again, my mother was very happy. She did not work outside the home and enjoyed looking after my brother and me. My father started renovating old houses and while he did the external work, my mother was responsible for the in-terior decoration. She also became heavily involved in many cultural activities particularly with the local GAA club, Kilmore. My mother loved Gaelic games; she played camogie and became chairperson of the club, which was very unusual for a woman at that time. She was a set dancer herself and trained the club's juvenile set-dancing team. Joe and myself danced in the team and my mother was delighted when we became the Dublin set-dancing champions for two years running. My grandmother used to be full of pride speaking about my mother's involvement in the acting scenes for the Scor competitions in Du-blin. My mother also loved to sew and could make anything from full-length curtains to wedding dresses. When her sister Margaret was get-ting married, my mother said, 'If you pick me as your maid of honour, I'll make the bridesmaids' dresses'. She did become maid of honour and she made beautiful purple dresses with white beading for all the bridesmaids, including a small one for me as flower girl.

My mother travelled down to Kilkenny regularly to see her par-ents and as a child, I always felt I grew up half in Dublin and half in the country. We always had wonderful times in Clogh, walking through the fields and visiting friends and relatives. My mother used to spend hours talking with her father and would always take him out for a drink (my grandmother wouldn't go into a pub then) and my grand-father would be delighted. Like my grandfather, my mother loved to play cards and Margaret remembers that, as children, we would arrive down to Kilkenny, take out our pack of cards and badger my grand-father to play with us. My grandfather would be horrified saying 'Oh God, what is she thinking of (referring to my mother), letting them children play cards'. He believed it was a sin for children to play cards and that we would all turn out as gamblers, but we played anyway. My mother would always do what she believed in and was not afraid to stand up to anyone who thought differently. Throughout the years she also had a very equal and very happy relationship with my father.

My mother's sister, Margaret, would often go up to Dublin, along with her husband Danny and three children, to stay with my parents for the weekend. My mother always welcomed them and she loved people calling to see her. Margaret could never get over all the friends my mother had:

> She was always very popular. We used to love going up for weekends and there would always be people around. We always got out for a drink and even though we would always be in company, it was never just your mother and father, Danny and me, there were always friends of your parents with us.

As a child, our house always seemed to have callers and even my own friends who called up would spend more time with my mother than with me. Margaret remembers my mother during those years as always being:

> very, very happy, very jolly. She loved Coolock and her home. I'm sure if she was still alive today, she'd probably still be living there at number 39 Kilmore Crescent.

My parents were happy over the years, my father's building company was successful and life was good. When I was about eight years old, my parents decided to adopt because as my father says 'your mother wanted to, she liked having children, she wanted more children'. So, they adopted a baby girl when she was a month old and they called her Eileen. Eileen soon became a part of our family and was with us until she was a year and two months old when she was taken back from my parents. Her mother had, months earlier, refused to sign the final adoption papers because she was now uncertain about the adoption (she had signed the earlier adoption papers), but she changed her mind and wanted the child back. According to my father:

> We were stupid at the time because we should have insisted on the papers being signed earlier rather than letting things drag on. The adoption agency knew the mother wasn't signing but they let things drag on. And your mother got very attached to the child and it broke her heart when she had to give the child up. It was wrong for the child to have been left so long with Helen and then have her taken away. When we realised the mother wasn't signing we eventually did put pressure on the adoption agency to find out what was happening and then things ended very quickly. They made us bring the child back and hand her over. It was very cruel. Your mother was very upset and I was too, we loved that baby, but there was nothing we could do.

My parents did try to keep Eileen, they contacted a solicitor, and my mother held onto the child longer than she should have and she even spoke about running away, but there was nothing they could do. In the weeks before Eileen was taken, my mother said it was as if the child knew something was wrong. Every evening my mother would put Eileen to bed and she would lie on the bed with the baby who would put her little arms around my mother's neck and hold onto her tightly. She probably felt my mother's anguish and pain. After Eileen was taken, my parents did try to find out how she was doing. Officially, the adoption agency could give them no information but one person in the agency would talk to my mother and told her that the baby was fretting and crying all the time for her. According to Margaret, my mother's sister, my mother would pray that Eileen would fret so much that they would bring her back but that was never going to happen. My mother told Margaret about receiving a call from the adoption agency saying they wanted to see her:

> she got straight into the car and drove like a lunatic, but when she arrived at the agency they had a little boy, another child for her to see. The agency told her this child would be hers from the moment she walked away with him, but your mother said no, she wanted her own child back, that was how she saw it.

The adoption agency asked my mother to see other children with a view to adopting but my mother refused because, as my father said:

> it's just not the same, she didn't want other children, she only wanted Eileen, she only wanted her own child back, she was very cut up about the whole thing.

I remember late at night hearing my mother crying in her room, with the door closed because she did not want Joe and me to hear. Both my parents were devastated over losing Eileen and Margaret said:

> all your mother would do was cry and cry and cry. For a long time, your father didn't even work after Eileen was taken, they were all upset. It was like a child dying, only worse, because with a death you can grieve. It was like a child going missing and you spend all your life looking and wondering.

But life goes on. My mother never really got over Eileen but learned to live with it and carry on, as we all do. For my family it was the biggest disappointment of our lives. Shortly after my parents lost Eileen, the adoption laws changed – making it virtually impossible for such a situation to happen again to other families. Even today my father often wonders how Eileen is doing and where she is but we know there is probably no way to ever find out. Wherever she is we hope she is well and happy. At the time, everyone was concerned that my mother would pull through and she did. But she never spoke again about having children until about eight years later when she suddenly discovered she was pregnant. I was now sixteen and Joe was fifteen.

I was with my mother when she found out she was pregnant. She came out of the doctor's surgery and got into the car where I was waiting. She sat still, staring straight ahead, in absolute silence. She then said in total disbelief and shock that she was pregnant and she started to laugh. My brother Joe remembers when she told him that she was pregnant how 'she was so excited that you couldn't help be happy and during the pregnancy she looked so well and was so happy'. Margaret also remembers being told about the pregnancy:

> I knew she had been to the doctor so when we went up to visit, I asked her 'what's wrong with you, are you sick?' And she started to laugh and she said 'Do you not know?' And I said, 'Know what?' I mean, being pregnant was the last thing on my mind, and she said 'I'm pregnant' and the laughs of her and the laughs of us.

A few months into the pregnancy, my mother started bleeding and had to stay in bed. It broke my grandmother's heart to see her lying day after day in bed because my mother was always so active and my grandmother would say to her 'Would you not get up and leave it in God's hands' and my mother replied 'Mammy, I'll hold onto this child if it kills me'. (Afterwards my grandmother would say 'O God, little did Helen think'. And my grandmother would be full of regret saying: 'I should have insisted more, to make her get out of that bed, if she had lost the child maybe she'd be alive today'.) My mother looked after herself during the pregnancy especially when she thought she was losing the baby and on 28 November 1981, she gave birth to a beautiful baby boy whom she called Edmund, after my father.

Seven days after giving birth, she died suddenly from a brain haemorrhage. Her death so soon after the birth was a terrible shock to everyone. Along with his own grief and pain, my father was left with two teenage children and a small baby to care for. He says that:

> Everyone was giving me their opinion about what to do, to foster the baby, give him up, but I decided to rear him myself and I got someone to mind

him during the day while I was working and you and Joe were at school and that's what we did.

My father's brother, Denis and his wife Doreen, who also lived in Dublin, took us into their home in the week after my mother's death. According to my father:

> Doreen was a very good woman, a very smart woman and she showed me how to mind the child, how to feed and bathe him and change him. And then after a time, I said right, I could manage it myself and we brought the baby home and that was it. You and me and Joe, we spoilt him rotten.

It seemed like death and loss were everywhere in our lives at this time, because six months after my mother's death, Doreen died from breast cancer. She had two small children and although she was ill when my mother died, she still found time to look after and help us through.

In the years after my mother's death, I found life very hard and even now, over twenty years later, I still find it hard to remember those times. I learned to live without my mother and get on with life, we all do, but I have always missed her. I would like to see her again some day, and for someone who is not religious, it is this thought that makes me hope, perhaps selfishly, that there is some form of afterlife. After my mother's death, I think that having to mind the baby kept us going in some way. My father was very good to all of us, keeping our home going, cleaning, putting food on the table and minding his new son. At that time, there was probably a reluctance to talk openly about death and my father especially found it difficult to talk. For him:

> at the time, we didn't talk about it because we couldn't ... I couldn't be seen to be talking about it, you had to ... I had to put on a brave face on things, for you and Joe and everything had to continue on, but ...

My father felt that he had to be seen to be strong in order to cope and to help us cope and this meant not talking openly about my mother's death. I found not talking about the death a difficult thing to do.

My father believed that we still had a good life after my mother died, as we had each other and no other major problems, except for the fact that we didn't have a mother. I'm not so sure. I feel I lost a certain number of years out of my life as I tried to get back on track. My brother Joe feels that 'it split up the family'. He moved into a flat about two years after my mother died and so did I. While there was no falling out amongst us, he feels that we all drifted apart. My brother feels that a mother keeps a family together and perhaps, if my mother had lived, we would have stayed at home longer. When someone dies, part of your life disappears with that person. Friends of my mother would have drifted away from the family and no matter what way you look at it; my mother's death changed all our lives completely.

My grandmother often spoke about my mother, remembering the days before she died. My grandmother remembered that she would catch my mother just staring at the new baby and saying: 'I don't believe it, I don't believe it'. On the day before her death, my mother was ill and lay on the couch resting while my grandmother looked after her and the baby. After the doctor arrived, he examined my mother and arranged for her to go back into the National Maternity Hospital to be checked. My father was at work but came home soon after to take my mother in. My mother went up the stairs to get dressed and as she was walking back down my grandmother asked her: 'What way is your head now?' My mother replied that her headache had just gone and my grandmother said: 'Now Helen, if they want to keep you in that hospital you will stay' and my mother put on her shoes and her last words to my grandmother were 'I'm coming home. I'm not going to stay no matter what they say'.

My mother died in the early hours of Saturday morning, 5 December 1981. She was waked for two days and buried on the following Monday. The rain was torrential the day we buried my mother. I remember being driven away from the graveyard in the black funeral car, my father in the middle and holding me on one side and Joe on the other. The day was black and as we stared in silence at the heavy rain, my father spoke: 'It rained the day I married your mother and it is raining the day I bury her'. To this day, I always think of my mother when I look out a window at heavy rain falling.

Even though my grandparents had eleven children, it seems that Helen was always their favourite. Her death had a terrible effect on them. I will always hear my grandfather's voice as he came to our house for the funeral. He arrived at the house and was crying and he called out: 'Why couldn't God have taken me instead of Ellen?' He was willing to die for her because he loved her. According to Margaret:

> Ellen was always mammy and daddy's favourite and I remember saying to granddaddy after Ellen died, 'If you had the choice daddy, and if God said to you, I'm going to take one of them, could you choose?' And he said 'I

would have told him, he can take the whole lot of you, and give Ellen back'.
And we said to him 'Do you mean that?' and he said 'Yes, I mean it, he can
have all of you, if he'd give her back'.

My mother always kept in touch with her parents and while my
grandmother would travel up to Dublin regularly, my grandfather always preferred to stay in Kilkenny, he hated to travel. There was always a strong excuse needed to get him to travel to Dublin. My mother was pregnant with Edmund and the baby was due any day. It was
a Friday evening and my grandmother was going up to Dublin on the
bus the next day to see her. Margaret remembers calling to see her
parents on the Friday evening, and granddaddy suddenly said, 'Myself and mammy (he always called his wife mammy) are going to
Dublin in the morning to see Helen'. Margaret was amazed that her
father was travelling up to Dublin for no reason as he could easily
have said he would wait until the baby was born and then go up.

So my grandparents got the bus up to Dublin the next day and
when they arrived out to our house in Coolock my father told them
my mother had only gone into the hospital that morning. And they
were in the house an hour when the phone rang to say she had given
birth to a baby boy. My grandparents went in to see her that evening
and, as my grandfather was going home on the bus the next day, Sunday, he went in to see her again on Sunday before he left. And he
said 'She was standing there at the window in the hospital looking
out and there was a pub across the road and she said: 'See that pub
over there Daddy, I'd love to be going in there with you now'. They
both laughed and then my grandfather got the bus back to Kilkenny.
As it was so unusual for my grandfather to travel to Dublin that time,
in the years after, he would often speak about how he could never
understand why he went up when he could easily have waited. But
he often said: 'If I had waited, I would never have seen her that one
last time'.

My brother Joe only has a few memories of my mother's death
and doesn't think it is good to talk about it too much although it does
not upset him to do so. He tries to get on with life and remember in
other ways. My brother remembers as a teenager, priests trying to tell
him that God needed my mother and that's why he took her, but for
him and us, her baby needed her just as much. My brother remembers my mother as someone who was very outgoing and who enjoyed
life:

She was well-liked, especially in Kilmore, even today I'd meet fellas from Coolock who remember her and always ask about her and talk about her, saying she was a great woman, a lovely woman, so people obviously liked her. She had a good personality.

Joe now has two beautiful children himself and his only regret is that he would like our mother to have seen them:

I would love them to have met her, for her to have met my children. My children are a pleasure and my mother would have loved it, that's the one thing I feel cheated on.

He says that:

I think deep down, you do hope there is a heaven where she is happy. That's not saying I believe in God and maybe it is selfish, it's just that I hope she is happy somewhere. I don't believe in saying that if I die I'll see her because I don't want to die, I want to spend time with my kids, but I do hope she's happy somewhere, maybe in heaven ... but I'd still like to have a mother and do feel that I've been robbed of something.

Like Joe, my biggest wish is to see my own three children grow up and be happy and I regret too that my mother never knew them, or they her. Like me, Joe would also have a fear of childbirth, for his wife Siobhán, and he was very nervous when she gave birth to their two children, afraid that something might happen.

My father reared Edmund himself, until he got married a few years later to Bridget Kelly. Bridget became a mother to Edmund and both Joe and myself were very happy for my father and Edmund to find someone new and special in their lives. It could not have been easy for Bridget but she was a great help to my father and they have been very happy together. When Edmund was older, he gradually became aware of the fact that his birth mother had died when he was born and both my father and Bridget have always been very open about this. While Edmund is aware that Bridget is not his biological mother, he calls her mother and she is in every sense because she raised him and loves him as her own son, just as my mother loved Eileen as her own child. As Edmund says: 'even though she didn't give birth to me, she is my mother in every other way'. Edmund was too young to be affected by my mother's death and it has not really affected his life, as he says:

Except for the fact that I have three grandmothers and three grandfathers and a load of relations down in Limerick, where Bridget is from, that you and Joe probably don't know very well.

All these years, Edmund has believed that he was the cause of our mother dying:

> In a way, I am responsible, I was born and as a result she died, but I wouldn't necessarily feel guilty about it, it's not something you can blame yourself for.

Edmund was surprised to learn that none of us ever blamed his birth for my mother's death. We all knew how much my mother wanted a child and how much the pregnancy contributed to her death is something we will never know but we certainly never blamed Edmund for her dying. In the last few years, all my family have become very close again, maybe because Joe and I now have children of our own. Their grandparents are very important to them and so is 'Uncle Ed' and children do help bring people closer.

Margaret remembers that when my mother lost Eileen:

> She never spoke, it really broke her heart, all she did was cry and cry and cry. That's why I thought it was so cruel that when she did have another baby she died a week later. I thought that was the cruellest thing to happen, even if she had been given a year or six months with the child.

My father too says:

> It's the one thing I feel so sorry about, that she didn't have the pleasure of rearing Edmund. She was delighted when she got pregnant, delighted. It was worth more than a million pounds to her.

Margaret says:

> I always took her to be a happy person, you know, she had a great personality. I can still hear your mother laughing, can you believe that! I can still hear her talking and laughing; I can still hear her laugh. I have my own memories of her that will stay with me for all time.

Someone once described death to me as 'turning off the light, because the dawn is coming'. Death is sometimes associated with darkness but death in the Celtic tradition is seen as an eternal world close to the natural world of nature and you are 'going back to where no shadow, pain or darkness can ever touch you again' (O'Donoghue, 1997). When we are born, we come from the darkness of the womb into the light, 'at birth you appear out of nowhere, at death you disappear to nowhere' (O'Donoghue, 1997). I am afraid of death, but know that in order to find peace, I must accept this part of my life. I have always felt that the dead are gone from us, yet are always near in ways that we cannot understand. None of us will ever know where this place of death is, but hopefully it is a place of peace. Death is a subject we can find hard to talk about but, for me, it is important that I talk about my mother and keep her memory alive. I want to remember her without being morbid and without pain and I want my children to know about her. I think she, Helen, would have liked that.

Chapter Four

Infertility: The Silent Period

Flo Delaney

Introduction

This chapter deals with infertility/involuntary childlessness, focusing on interviews undertaken with six Irish women who courageously shared their infertility/involuntary childlessness stories and broke their silence. The women talked in terms of 'having no voice or no words, being silent or isolated'. In such a book as this, it is fitting that women deeply desiring but unable to become mothers are given that voice. Infertility has no symptoms, causes no disability and is invisible to the naked eye. It is defined medically as the inability to conceive after one year of unprotected sexual intercourse. In fact, the onset of infertility is when a couple begins to fear or suspect that something is wrong. The effect of this worsening fear and growing apprehension is the real 'disease' of infertility. The process of infertility, that is the duration of the feelings of anger, guilt, sadness, isolation, loneliness and remorse vary amongst individuals but the reality of their existence is universal (Harkness, 1992; Morell, 1994; Ireland, 1993; Monarch, 1993):

> Although the physical ordeal was certainly stressful, and at times debilitating, it was the emotional and psychological trauma of being infertile that terrified and often overwhelmed me. We spent years on the emotional roller coaster of infertility ... Infertility seemed to eclipse every positive aspect of our lives, and we found it difficult to separate the fallout from this chronic crisis from the challenges and stresses of everyday living (Harkness, 1992).

A preferred term for infertility is Involuntary Childlessness (IC). It is a more recent term than infertility, which has a stigma attached to it, as do older words such as 'barren'. Other terms within feminism for childless women include: non-mother and not-mother (Poovey, 1988). These terms are more rooted in a sense of 'lack' or 'absence' and their definitions are secondary or are from a negative derivation, or from the term mother, which is seen as positive and primary (Morell, 1994):

> I don't know if I like the word infertile. Involuntary childlessness is probably better. I never liked the word infertility and I never liked saying it.

That to me sounds like you have a disease. I think to say that you are involuntarily childless, that is nicer. Softer. It doesn't sound like you have this
horrible contagious disease (Mary).

Medical treatments for infertility are costly, stressful and invasive
and have varying success rates. Opinion is that after treatments, the
infertility rate can remain at 70% (Pfeffer, 1987; Cooper-Hilbert,
1998; Harkness, 1992; Ireland, 1993; Monarch, 1993).

The Realities of the Infertility/Involuntary Childlessness Experience
Infertility is a silent tragedy. How do you explain to someone that
you had a rough night because there was no baby to keep you awake,
that your house is too clean and there are no toys cluttering up the
floor? Would anyone understand that you have cried over Pampers
commercials? (Harkness, 1992).

Although millions worldwide face this problem (thousands in
Ireland), each individual with infertility issues usually feels isolated
and alone. This is largely because infertility is an invisible and silent
problem. The isolation is largely self-imposed because of the stigma
that is attached to the issue. There is a huge reluctance on behalf of
the infertile/IC community to discuss their infertility and subsequent
childlessness (Monarch, 1993). This isolation and silence adds to the
difficulties in voicing the realities that surround the issue and in ana-
lysing their causes. It also hinders any efforts to improve the circumstances and experiences of those undergoing the trauma of infer-
tility/IC.

Rare and recent coverage of infertility in the *Sunday Tribune* (11
July 1999) quoted the Irish statistics for infertility as affecting one in
six people, one in ten couples. Over 2,000 people are believed to be
receiving treatment for infertility. These figures are very conserva-
tive and in fact it is impossible to estimate just how many people have
infertility issues as not everybody seeks treatment, and not everybody
chooses the mainstream medical road (Pfeffer, 1987):

I would only have one friend that went through it that I know of. Because
you see people don't tell you, people don't share it. So, you keep it to yourself ... I think it must come back to people being embarrassed or it is just a
social stigma, it is just like leprosy or something. You don't want to be seen
as having that sort of problem, I mean give me anything else, give me bu-
bonic plaque, but don't give me infertility. And I think it is just unaccepted
that people come out. I think that if there were more of a trend of people
saying yea, this is me, this is my problem, more people would come out and

> say, yea, that is me too. But because you don't know anybody or nobody openly talks about it, you are not going to be the first person to jump up there and openly say it is me (Fiona).

> I have often said that I think what we are going through should be highlighted. Because it is all ignorance, I mean they don't understand here. I get asked so many times by people I don't know, that I've only just met for the first time, how many children have you? That question just guts me because I never know what to say. And I just don't think it should be asked. I know people say 'sure they are only saying it like, for the sake of saying something'. But I think in a more aware society you just wouldn't ask just in case you were treading on something that was very delicate (Ellen).

The childless woman is repeatedly asked why she does not have children (Ireland, 1993) and is subjected to overt or subtle pressures. The media and literature seem to categorise them as either sad spinster types or career bitches (*Fatal Attraction*, 1987; *The Hand that Rocks the Cradle*, 1992). During the infertility process, much can be perceived as insensitive and felt as hurtful and some of it can be excused as ignorance and explained by the silence surrounding the subject.

There are many sensitive areas for individuals and couples facing infertility/IC issues. They include coping with the festive seasons and holidays, coping with the pregnancies of friends and family, the inquiries and social pressures of friends and families, altered self images, feelings of guilt, loss and resentment, loss of control over one's life and relationship struggles (Carter & Carter, 1989; Harkness, 1992; Monarch, 1993; Morell, 1994; Doyal, 1987; Cooper-Hilbert, 1998):

> I felt guilty, I felt guilty for a long time ... until I did the first IVF ... even though it didn't work (Susan).

> It was like, imagine your life was a canvas and you start off and you paint as you go along. And we had stopped and everybody else had painted in Christmases, communions, confirmations, theirs was all ahead of them. And ours was blank; what were we going to do? ... so there was that sort of lack of belonging ... and that lasted a while. It took you a while to get over that. You got over the initial grief and everything for the children. It was more the social fitting in that was the problem (Fiona).

As difficult as women find it to discuss their infertility/IC issues, men appear to both experience it differently and discuss it less. This may be because it is less socially acceptable for men to express feelings of hurt or anxiety, or discuss their emotions than it is for women. (Monarch, 1992; Harkness, 1992):

Despairing Couple © Caroline Canning

I don't know if you have ever read that book: *Men Are From Mars, Women Are From Venus*? It is so true. When I had my second failed IVF ... I was really in a bad state. Paul came home, I think it was three or four days afterwards, I couldn't get out of my dressing-gown ... I was just moping around the house, the fridge was empty ... I just had no interest ... and I remember Paul coming home this lunchtime and I remember saying to him, you know, why aren't you suffering the way I am suffering? And he said to me, 'I have dealt with it and I have shelved it.' I just resented him so much that he could do that. But now I realise that he has equally suffered as much as me. But it stays with women much longer that it does with men. Men are very fix it – this is it – it hasn't worked – now let's get on (Anna).

This polarity of experiences coupled with a monitoring and scheduling of their sex lives, humorously referred to as 'command performances', can cause severe stress and strain on the couple's relationship. Couples speak honestly of the stress of 'fertile nights'; many preserve their sanity through humour:

I don't even feel so strange anymore for having made love once when I had a strep throat and poison oak and he had a broken leg, simply because it was 'that time of the month!' (Harkness, 1992)

I think it is as well to inject some humour into it. You have to laugh don't you? I remember one day going up [to Dublin] for this insemination and trying to get the train home the same day so that nobody would miss you for two days. You are supposed to stay lying down for a while you know, about half an hour or something. And sometimes if it was running late, I wouldn't have time. And I would be like [I can lay here for] ten minutes that will give them enough time. And I'd literally be running down the road and I'd

> be killing myself laughing because I'd have visions of all these little sperms going, wow she's in a hurry hang on there! (Fiona)

Infertility couples also speak of feeling distanced from their peers, the majority of whom are parents. Some infertile/IC women refer to 'wedges' in friendships with women who are mothers, because of the contrasts in their lives. It is not that these women are without friends – just friends who can understand. At best, a lack of understanding evolves from an inability on both sides to share or to understand:

> I told all of my friends I was going through IVF and all of that ... and in a way they were there ... and they were terrified to ring because they don't want to cause you pain. And whereas there is nothing they can do for you, you know they have your absolute best will at heart. They are like rooting for you and if there was anything they could do, they would do it. So I suppose it is a very silent, background sort of positive energy. One of my closest friends who has three little girls, she doesn't know whether to bring it up or not (Kathy).

At worst, problems can stem from a perceived power imbalance (Morell, 1994; Ireland, 1992; Monarch, 1993):

> Women, who adhere more or less to traditional expectations, may assume an air of superiority towards their childless friends. If a woman is not a woman until she becomes a mother, in the eyes of the latter the childless woman has not proven her right to equal feminine status ... these women draw their superiority from an image of femininity reinforced by an army of supportive prescriptions and values. Childlessness is a form of aberration (Campbell, 1985).

A further challenge women with infertility/IC issues face is the misinterpretation of their lifestyles. Unfortunately, every aspect of a childless woman's life may be interpreted through the lens of deficiency. Whatever a childless woman does or has, may be viewed as merely compensation for the missing 'real' experience of motherhood. Motivations to achieve socially, career aspirations or successes (Morell, 1994) or relationships with pets (Monarch, 1992; Bartlett, 1994) are very often interpreted as efforts to fill the inevitable void left by the failure to mother (Doyal, 1987; Cooper and Hilbert, 1998).

Expectations about motherhood start early and are clearly expressed. According to Nielson Market Research, the best-selling boy's toy in 1992 was the Matchbox car range and for girls it was the Barbie doll (Bartlett, 1994). The message comes very early then, that a woman's role must necessarily involve maternity. For every woman there is a waiting pram, that immense weight of tradition that forces her into motherhood (Bartlett, 1994). Marriage, though decreasingly seen as the prerequisite for starting a family (more than one in three births in Ireland are now outside marriage) continues to assert its first function as the procreation of children. The Irish folk customs which accompany the wedding (itself perceived as the most important day in a couple's life and the 'best' day in a woman's life) make it plain. You keep the top layer of the cake for the first christening and your flowers include gypsophila, a symbol of fertility. You then have a possible two years (officially) before you get what the involuntary childless call 'the questions'. 'Anything stirring? Any news?' (Carter & Carter, 1989; Harkness, 1992; Cooper-Hilbert, 1998). The pressure on women in particular to settle down and have children often comes from anxious-to-be-grandparents, themselves under pressure from their peers, proving the pronatalist point that children (and subsequent grandchildren) are the passport to a 'normal' mainstream lifestyle, the way of demonstrating ordinariness (Payne, 1978 cited in Monarch, 1993).

Understanding the Infertility/IC Experience
There is an implicit assumption that motherhood is intrinsic to adult female identity (Ireland, 1993). This necessarily implies an 'absence' then for any woman who is not a mother. Women with infertility/IC issues, often discuss this feeling of absence or emptiness. Mardy Ireland (1993) divides childless women into three groups. These are traditional women, or women who chose to have a child and for health or medical reasons cannot; transitional women, or women who wish at some stage in their lives to have a child but delay their decision for career or relationship reasons and it becomes too late; and transformative women, those who make a conscious decision not to have children. They consciously make other lifestyle choices. Women with infertility issues generally fall into the first group of traditional women. The traditional woman has chosen to say 'yes' to motherhood but her body, or her partner's body, or both, have said 'no'. This group then, have thought about, desired, sought, but been biologically denied the identity of mother, an identity which they have sought to fulfil. This personal loss, coupled with the non-mirroring of them by society (except as objects of pity) creates their very real feelings of defectiveness, 'otherness', failure and banishment to the borderlands of deviancy (Harkness, 1992; Monarch, 1993; Morell, 1994).

The central issue amongst women with infertility/IC issues is one of mourning, or grieving one's loss. That process is often postponed until all hope, the currency of infertility, has been spent. (Cooper-Hilbert, 1998; Byrne, 1992). Mourning is a lengthy process and the longer a woman has been involved in treatments and procedures to resolve her or her partner's infertility issues, the longer the mourning process. The working through of this loss is a circling arc of lessening emotional intensity spiralling through their lives, never entirely fading, as it provides some structuring function or development of adult identity (Burch, 1989):

> No you see I don't think you will ever get there [emotionally] until you come to the end of the road. Do you know what I mean? You have to be at the end of the road ... the counsellor said to me, you have three embryos left. You will never get there until those embryos are gone and the outcome of those embryos [is known]. He said to me you won't mourn as bad if they do work ... because it will compensate ... whereas if it doesn't work, that is when you have to come to the coping side ... and I imagine it is a long process. And I would imagine that it is there all the time ... the pain [probably] gets less and it doesn't affect you as often (Anna).

Infertility requires a process of grieving. Analysis of the grieving processes following infertility/IC are based on Elisabeth Kubler Ross' five stages of grieving (denial and isolation, anger, bargaining, depression and acceptance) used in death and bereavement (Kubler Ross, 1969). Kubler Ross' model is often criticised for not including the equally experienced emotions of fear, terror or jealousy. Just as an individual fears their own death, a woman with infertility/IC issues fears life without a child. Jealousy is an emotion often discussed by women with infertility issues and something that creates great distress in their lives. However, infertility grieving is an 'unfocused grief'. The loss, particularly for the traditional woman, is that of her physical integrity, her anticipated dream child, her longed for identity as a mother (Carter and Carter, 1989). Unfocused grief is multi-focused grief. Every trip to the clinic, every failed procedure, every monthly period, every other pregnant woman, every cute baby on a nappy advertisement, every Christmas, every Mother's Day serves to remind the involuntarily childless woman of her loss. Infertility is a deathless death (Harkness, 1992):

> Initially, it is kind of weird but I actually grieved for these children that I never had. I mean to me, they had personalities; they had futures. I actually

grieved. I mean it was like a death. These children had died to me. That was the most impact (Fiona).

I feel that if you say that you had failed IVF, there is nothing there and people don't feel anything. I feel that I just want to identify with something ... I would like people to know that I have had miscarriages. Or to word it another way, that I have had little babies who have never made it into the world (Anna).

In very recent years voluntary childlessness has begun to receive the attention it deserves. Some feminist writers and sociologists have begun the important task of examining its realities (Veevers, 1980; Campbell, 1985; Ireland, 1993; Morell, 1994). There are some connecting circumstances and experiences between women who are childless, voluntarily and involuntarily. The issue that divides them is a huge one. It is the issue of choice. Veevers asserts that theoretically and pragmatically the consequences of a phenomenon must be assumed quite different depending on whether it involves the achievement of a major life goal or on the contrary the frustration of one. Choice may well be one of the most significant determinants of satisfaction with a particular lifestyle (Veevers, 1983; Byrne, 1992; Richardson, 1993):

I feel that if it was my choice not to have children this wouldn't bother me. That I could get on with my life and wouldn't have a family ... I could get on you know? It's funny; I just can't see myself growing old as a woman without having had a child. It's almost like I'd be missing out on a rung on the ladder going up, and how can you possibly do that and be sane and be totally fulfilled as a person. And yet people do it, people choose to be single; people choose not to have families. But this is not my choice (Ellen).

Unlike 'transitional' women or 'transformative' women who, if needed, to buoy their female identities can maintain the fantasy that they could have had a child if they had chosen to, 'traditional' women describe their empty wombs as a vast unfillable black hole (Harkness, 1992; Ireland, 1993):

It is still a big black hole you are heading into (Kathy).

Possibly when you are having children, you are looking for that to be a fulfilment in your life. And you have to say well what else am I going to put in and the only other thing you can put in is yourself. That is all you have to put into that gap isn't it (Fiona)?

It is ironic then that the work of detaching reproductive capacity from female identity should fall at the feet of the group which temporarily at least, is the most vulnerable, the most silent. Where are the voices of the feminist sisters? Are they to be heard shouting – 'there is more to life than motherhood'? Feminism boasts that it has provided a cultural context in which infertile women can begin to detach feminine identity from reproductive capacity and the institution of motherhood (Ireland, 1993). While this may have happened theoretically, the message does not seem to be filtering down into the experiences of infertile/IC women. Feminism espouses choice, going for it and getting it, saying 'yes' or saying 'no' to certain identities and certain ways of being (Morell, 1994). As women, we are all the richer for this diversity of choice if there is no hierarchy of value that accompanies our decisions. Infertile/IC women have very limited, and sometimes no, choices (Ireland, 1993; Morell, 1994; Wolf, 1993). The feminist argument that 'I' as an individual woman own my own body and have absolute control over it is a fallacy for the infertile woman. No amount of clearance in the patriarchal forest, provided (for the individual infertile woman) by feminism could produce the total control over reproductive freedom that eludes those with infertility issues. Within the Irish context, feminism's valiant battle against the Church/State's misogynist control of women's reproductive freedom (contraception, abortion, Assisted Reproductive Technologies) seems to have blinded it to the more silent realities of infertility/IC. In Ireland, the issues that face infertile women remain lost somewhere between patriarchal control and feminist choice.

The issue of choice is central to infertility/IC. Loss of choice is equal to loss of control. Infertility robs women of the control they thought they had over their bodies and their lives. During work-ups and treatments the infertile/IC are constantly reminded of this lack of control. When a woman's primary choice has been motherhood (and that option has been well endorsed and validated by pronatalist society and feminism), secondary choices, no matter how worthwhile objectively, can take on the form of consolation prizes. The deflation of feminism's heroic posture, the realisation that all women cannot 'have it all' falls heavily upon this group (Ireland, 1993). The pressure to choose and attain the role of parent, particularly within the institution of heterosexual marriage is tremendous.

Pronatalism

In order to comprehend the experiences of the involuntary childless it is important to understand the pressures they feel. It is accepted that there are persistent pressures to encourage people to have children and these are especially felt by people who themselves desire a child greatly but are unable to have one. Irish society is indeed pronatalist and this serves to increase the distress and sense of difference felt by the women concerned. The National Alliance of Optional Parenthood (NAOP) in the United States defines pronatalism as:

> the attitude that exalts motherhood and assumes or encourages parenthood for all. It is found in nearly all of the institutions in society; churches, schools, advertising, media, law and medicine and of course families. Pronatalism can be as direct as the question 'When are you going to start your family?' or as subtle as income tax exemptions for children (NAOP, 1979 pamphlet referred to in Monarch, 1993).

Perceptions of marriage are still inextricably interwoven with the expectations of child-bearing. Childless marriages are 'open house' in terms of conversation and speculation. Involuntarily childless marriages are the recipients of unsolicited pity, ignorance or probing and declared voluntarily childless marriages are allotted a deviant perspective. Both groups are left in no doubt of their non-membership of the 'freemasonry of the fertile' (Monarch, 1993):

> I think another thing that hurts an awful lot is the questions that are asked. 'How long are you married? You don't have any children?' I think because you are in the mould of falling in love, getting married and having children … I think [especially] in Irish society because it is a family oriented society … now people don't ask me anymore, unless I meet people I have not met before. I think you know you are missing out on christenings and holy communions and you know, confirmations and marriages and grandchildren. There is a huge section in life that you are missing out on completely (Anna).

Veevers (1980) confirms how synonymous heterosexual marriage is with children in the following four pronatalist, social beliefs: children strengthen marriage and are an indispensable statement of marital love; children are essential to the physical and mental well-being of men and women, particularly women; parenthood is an innately determined need; children confirm masculine and feminine sexual identity and competence.

The origins of pronatalism are ancient. Mythology and religion provide the earliest symbols of and reverence for fertility. The Madonna image is a pervasive and very ancient image in art and not confined to Christianity. The importance of the phallus as a religious image is also ancient and exemplified by the soaring spires of Chris-

tian Churches (Monarch, 1993). Organised religions in particular bear
testimony to the social value placed on fertility. The Judaeo-Christian tradition sees children as blessings and barrenness [their word]
as a curse or punishment. Like leprosy and other biblical plagues, infertility bears an ancient social stigma (Bartlett, 1994).

Pronatalism in Ireland finds a strong foundation within the Roman Catholic Church on which to base itself. The Catholic Church's
emphasis on procreation within heterosexual marriage only, is evidenced by its proscription of birth control, abortion, sterilisation,
homosexuality, donor insemination and in vitro fertilisation. Masturbation by a married partner in order to obtain a specimen for infertility investigations is viewed as an 'intrinsic evil':

> [our parents] just saw IVF as genetic engineering and didn't understand it
> whatsoever ... the Pope came out the very same time that we went for IVF
> and said that IVF was condemned by the Catholic Church (Susan).

> I remember saying to my mother – my parents were quite religious – 'you
> know IVF is against the Catholic Church'. She replied, 'don't mind them,
> they are man made rules' (Anna).

Despite the supposed separation of Church and State in Ireland, the
Church has had an enormous impact on the reproductive health care
of women, particularly women who have infertility issues (Coliver,
1995). Ethical committees, who are judge and jury when it comes to
assisted reproduction (the regulation of assisted human reproduction
bill is only being drafted) include heavy representation by the Catholic Church and no representation by the infertile/IC community
(National Infertility Support and Information Group – NISIG, personal communication).

The advertising industry itself subscribes to pronatalism. It uses
parenthood and the popular definition of the 'family' to sell anything
from detergents to fast cars with air bags. Watch daytime TV and count
how many advertisements either feature children or target children.

Despite the significant changes taking place within Irish society:
access to reliable contraception, the advent of divorce, increased dialogue on abortion, a major increase in the number of single parents
(mothers in particular) and altered perceptions of appropriate roles
for women; in none of these structural changes do women find support for childlessness. Whatever the reasons for, or causes of, her childlessness, the non-mother is still not seen as a proper person (Monarch, 1993).

The pressure of pronatalism is sometimes overt and sometimes so subtle that we would not even notice it. It is, as Jane Bartlett (1994) concludes, as constant as electricity, invisibly feeding into our lives. It is no surprise then why, when one considers the additional pressures experienced by the involuntary childless, the burden of infertility comes as such a painful and lengthy shock:

> It is terrible because it impacts on everything ... your life becomes dominated by it down to the level of, well, we can't go on holidays here ... or we had better not book anything because we don't know if we will be pregnant or not. Or ... do I buy a three-door car or a five-door car? All those stupid little things ... they are just so natural for other people to talk about ... or life events based around their kids sort of thing. Or if they know your kid is six, therefore you are probably married about eight years. But if you don't have any kids then you don't have any markers. They have no real perception about you (Kathy).

> I think it is different for everybody. Everybody has their own reasons. Some people decide not to have children, some people decide not to adopt. Some people can't and they want to get over that pain that they have from not being able to have them. But society should accept that and they shouldn't label them like they do. And they should be more understanding but that will probably take centuries (Mary).

The Absence of the Normative Female Identity for the Childless Woman
There is no normative female identity for the woman who is not a mother (Ireland, 1993). This absence of a 'normative identity' for childless women within psychology has influenced the way infertile/ IC women perceive themselves and are perceived by others. From Freud's theory of penis envy and women's subsequent absence of wholeness, female characteristics have become associated with negative value and absence. There is no sense of male and female as two different but equal forms, but a sense of one developmental line that is male development, with female development seen as based on a 'lack' (Ireland, 1993). The childless woman then, is seen to represent further absence and occupies a constant position of 'lack' or empty space. Ironically, it is from this empty space that new identities for 'non-mothers' can grow but that process requires much psychic solo flying by a group of pioneering women. Unfortunately with the universal social expectation that women should be mothers, the idea of absence is always present in the lives of infertile/IC women in the form of emptiness (Ireland, 1993).

It cannot be disputed that the depth of pain, isolation and loss women with infertility/IC issues experience, correlates with the negative value classic psychology ascribes to women. The 'black hole' the women speak of, is dug in part by absence within psychology of a normative identity for childless women. It comes as no surprise that psychology and psychological services, particularly in Ireland, have little to offer women struggling to find a way out of the black hole. At the time of writing, there were no qualified infertility counsellors in Ireland. Often specific supports offered are located in the Assisted Reproduction Units. NISIG (National Infertility Support and Information Group) a voluntary organisation and now a registered charity, was founded by three women in Cork in 1995. It is the only provider of support and information in Ireland. It does this with very little finances and support.

Infertility/IC is a process which is lengthy, painful, and lonely. In Ireland, it is surrounded by silence. Very little support is available. Ignorance and lack of awareness add to the isolation and lack of social inclusion that is experienced by women who wish to but cannot become mothers. These factors also contribute to the difficulty women struggling with these issues have in discussing infertility/ IC. Consciousness-raising (the original work of feminism) and increased education around these issues are necessary if an end is to be called to the silence. In testimony to the bravery, honesty, dignity and strength of the pioneering women who shared their infertility/IC stories, it is fitting to end both on a positive note and with a final statement of their experience:

> I don't want it [infertility/IC] to be portrayed always as a bad thing ... when I started I would have loved someone to say to me: 'look, if the worst happens and it doesn't happen for you, you are not always going to be forever in this sort of valley of depression or whatever it is' ... Now whenever you start you don't want to hear that and you don't think it is going to be you. But unfortunately, the reality is that a lot of it is going to be you, the chances are about seventy percent that it is going to be you ... but it could be a less painful experience if there was more awareness. And people say things that they don't realise are hurtful but if you make someone aware of it, maybe the next person along the road wouldn't have to listen to that. I think it is going to take time, I suppose we will get there eventually. But just small steps, just one person saying: 'look that is not the way it is' or something. Because everything starts with little steps. Doesn't it? (Fiona)

CHAPTER FIVE

Childbirth in Ireland

Patricia Kennedy

Many myths abound in relation to physiological motherhood. The most recent, reported in the media, is that Irish women are having more babies than ever before and that this is because of the new wealth experienced by many in Ireland in the last decade as a result of the economic boom. Female refugees and asylum-seekers are also blamed for this perceived 'baby boom'. Another myth is the belief that there is an abundance of teenage mothers giving birth outside wedlock.

In excess of 50,000 women give birth in Ireland each year. The majority of babies, over 90%, are born to women in the 15 to 49 year age group. In Ireland in 2000, there were 993,800 women in this age group (an increase of 366,800 since 1971). So the number of potential mothers has increased considerably in this period. There has been a steady increase in the number of births since 1994, when there was 47,928, up to 54,239 births in 2000. While this rise in the number of births has implications for the provision of maternity services, it is not a new phenomenon as there are, in fact, fewer births than occurred in the mid-1980s. Remarkably, in 1981, there were 72,158 births in Ireland, 17,919 more than in 2000. It is estimated that births to non-nationals in the three major maternity hospitals account for almost 20% of all births (personal communication, 2003).

Live birth is defined in the perinatal statistics as 'the complete expulsion or extraction from its mother of a product of conception, irrespective of the duration of pregnancy, which, after such separation, breathes or shows any other evidence of life, such as beating of the heart, pulsation of the umbilical cord, or definite movement of voluntary muscles, whether or not the umbilical cord has been cut or the placenta is attached' (Department of Health, 1991).

Fertility Trends
Age-specific fertility rates, that is, the number of live births to women in a particular age group per 1,000 females of the same age group, for the 1970–2000 period indicate a reduction for all age groups, from 3.89 in 1970, to 1.89 in 2000. The only exception is for the 15–19 age

group which shows an increase of 3.1 for the thirty-year period from 1970 to 2000 (Kennedy, 2002). The fertility rate for this age group is important in the context of risk for young mothers during childbirth. At the other end of the scale, the age-specific fertility rate for mothers aged 35–49, also classified as a high-risk group, has decreased from 60.3 in 1970 to 24.5 in 2000.

During the period 1970–2000, the total period fertility rate declined. The total period fertility rate, a theoretical concept, is the average number of children that would be born alive to a woman during her lifetime if she were to pass through her childbearing years (15–49) conforming to the age-specific fertility rates of a given year. While the birth rate (the number of births per 1,000 of population in Ireand) varied little before 1971, it has fallen steadily since that date. In 1971, there were 22.7 births per thousand population. In 1981, the birth rate had fallen to 21.0 births per thousand, while the actual number of births rose. But by 1994, the total number of live births had fallen to 47,928 when the birth rate reached a low of 13.4. However, looking at the birth rate in a European context, Ireland still has one of the highest national birth rates and at 13.5 is above the EU average of 10.9.

Since 1970, there has also been a huge decline in family size in Ireland. The number of women giving birth who already had four or more children decreased from 21.8% in 1971 to 4.5% in 2000.

Another important issue concerns those women whose pregnancies do not result in childbirth, that is the women who experience miscarriage and abortion and who are not included in the fertility data on which planning is based. It is impossible to estimate the exact number of women whose pregnancies end in miscarriage, as many women who miscarry are not aware that they are doing so. With regard to abortion, Irish women have generally availed of services in Britain because abortion in Ireland is unavailable (Smyth, 1993; Conroy, 1997; Mahon, et al, 1998). Figures again are inconclusive but 6,625 women who availed of abortion services in Britain gave Irish addresses in 2001 (OPCS, 2001).

First-Time Mothers
Between 1971 and 1998 the number of women giving birth for the first time in the under-25 and over-35 year age groups both decreased (by 7.1% and 0.5% respectively) changing the age profile of first-time mothers. In 1971, 52.8% of first births were to women aged between

25 and 35, while in 1998, the figure was 59.5%. It has tended to fluctuate around 60%, a trend that has developed since the late 1980s and is perhaps an indication of mothers attempting to reconcile childbearing and childcare with participation in the labour market.

This increase in first-time mothers has implications for support services for women. It is at first childbirth that women have to learn the skills of parentcraft, accomplish the difficult skill of breastfeeding and begin to reconcile employment with childcare responsibilities. In modern society, first-time motherhood has tended to take on major significance as a 'rite of passage' for women. Ann Oakley writes: 'First-time motherhood calls for massive changes ... becoming a mother is more than a change of job; it involves reorganising one's entire personality. For there is a chasm between mothers' needs and children's needs that mothers have to bridge' (1979).

Births Outside Marriage
Between 1971 and 2000, there was an increase in both the number and the percentage of births occurring outside marriage from 2.7% of live births in 1971 to 31.82% in 2000. This coincides with a period of rapid social change in Ireland, including a change in attitudes towards women who give birth outside marriage (McCarthy, 1995a; Kennedy, 2002), specific policy changes such as the Status of Children Act (1987) and the introduction of Unmarried Mothers Allowance in 1973 (Flangan and Richardson, 1992; Conroy, 1993, 1997).

Maternal Mortality
Childbirth throughout time and throughout the world has always been perceived as a dangerous event for both mothers and their babies. This danger was defined in terms of mortality. The debate has moved nowadays to issues of morbidity, as it is a very rare event in Ireland today for a woman to die in childbirth. Maternal mortality (defined as the death of a woman while pregnant or within 42 days of termination of pregnancy) has declined dramatically since the 1970s: maternal mortality patterns show a decline from 25 per 100,000 births in 1970, to 2 per 100,000 births in 2000 (Kennedy, 2002). These patterns are important as they are often interpreted as evidence that the increased hospitalisation of childbirth, as well as higher rates of intervention have been responsible for this improvement in outcome. This, however has been challenged (Kennedy, 2002). It is now known that factors contributing to this decline include: age of mother when giv-

ing birth, lower parity, improvements in women's general health and better socio-economic conditions (Tew, 1995).

Looking at the outcome of birth, i.e., perinatal, neonatal and infant mortality rates, one observes that these also have steadily declined between 1971–2000, from 22.8, 12.2 and 17.97 (per 1,000 live births) to 7.5, 3.9 and 5.9, respectively. *Perinatal* refers to liveborns surviving less than one week, plus late fetals born after 28 weeks of pregnancy). From 1995 in the Central Statistics Office (CSO), there is a new broader definition of stillbirths, as babies weighing over 500g or at a gestational age of 24 weeks or more. *Neonatal* refers to liveborns surviving less than four weeks and *infant* refers to liveborns surviving less than one year. Despite dramatic improvements in neonatal care, babies born before 26 weeks gestation still have only a 50% survival rate and neonatal death rates remain high up until 28–30 weeks gestation (Chamberlain, 1995). This is very important as risk of neonatal death is often suggested as a reason why all births should take place in a maternity hospital. Many of the risk factors associated with perinatal mortality relate to social conditions: social class, racial origin and smoking (Chamberlain, *et al*, 1995).

Young Mothers

In relation to babies born to young women, the number of births to women and girls aged 24 years and under as a proportion of all births has decreased from 26.2% (16,895) in 1970, to 20.3% (10,996) in 2000. The number of births to young women aged 20 to 24 has decreased. On the other hand, the numbers of births in the lower age groups, of 19 years and under have all increased, and for those aged 16 and under the numbers have more than doubled. In 1970, there were 28 babies born to girls aged 15 and under, 106 aged 16, 324 aged 17 and 613 aged 18, while in 2000 the respective figures were 65, 212, 511 and 995. While there has undoubtedly been an increase, it is hardly of the epidemic proportions often reported by the media. This has implications for maternity services, as the medical profession accept that teenage mothers are at particular risk in childbirth. It also has implications for support services for teenage mothers (Flanagan and Richardson, 1992; Richardson, 2001).

Place of Birth

The period from conception to childbirth is a period which reflects the public/private divisions of women's lives. Conception is a result of an intimate private act. However, the nine months following conception are a long journey for a woman as she travels in and out of the public world of hospital appointments, the public gaze, comments on her body blooming and growing, and the private, silent world of morning sickness, exhaustion, feelings of loneliness and isolation and at other times happiness, even ecstasy. For some, there is the private loss of miscarriage and for an increasing number of Irish women, pregnancy ends in termination. For others, the journey ends with a stillborn baby. The journey into the patriarchal world of medicine and eventually birth, takes place for the majority of women in a very public, male-controlled labour ward (Oakley, 1979, 1980, 1992; Tew, 1995). On the way to this ward women undergo a period of socialisation and education as they attend ante-natal appointments and classes.

Currently, there are two schools of thought underlying Irish maternal health care provision. The principal model dominant in maternity units is what is known as the 'active management of labour' and is best presented in the textbook of the same name for obstetric students in Ireland (O'Driscoll, et al, 1993). The book, first published in 1982, is in its third edition and the authors between them have served as masters to the National Maternity Hospital for almost twenty years. A fourth edition is due out but is not associated with the current personnel of the National Maternity Hospital. The third edition, published in 1993, serves as a historical document to show how this philosophy has become so dominant. The authors of the 1993 edition tell us that they:

> were directly responsible for 100,000 births and ... for the intervening years were closely involved with an additional 100,000 births – a total of some 200,000 births overall. The text encompasses a comprehensive approach to the conduct of labour as put into effect several times every day in one of the largest obstetric units in the British Isles.

Active management of labour (the mode of organisation whereby the consultant obstetrician became actively involved in the conduct of labour on an ongoing basis as never before, with the delivery unit of the hospital redesignated as an intensive care unit [Murphy-Lawless, 1998]) is currently a near blanket practice in Irish maternity units.

At the other end of the spectrum there exists what is referred to as 'active birth' and is best presented in the writings of Balaskas (1979), Kitzinger (1978, 1988, 1993), Odent (1984) and Leboyer (1975, 1991). It is identified in Ireland with those claiming the right to have a 'natural birth', that is, an 'active birth', supported by a mid-wife, either in a maternity unit or at home.

Wagner argues that behind the social and medical approaches to childbirth there lies 'a set of assumptions, ideas and thinking' (1994). He stresses that he is not concerned with labelling one model right and another wrong, but rather 'to explore how to combine them by iden-tifying the elements in each that might be effective in addressing specific health issues'. He explains how the conflict between the two models dates from ancient Greek philosophy, but has become deeply ingrained in western thought. The two models relate to the dichoto-mised world which views art and all that is subjective as feminine, based on intuition and quality, while on the other, there exists science, objectivity, masculinity, logic and quantity. He claims that before the modern era, health and birth were related to the artistic side, the so-cial model, whereas later on, pregnancy and birth were brought into the medical domain.

There has been a steady decline in home births in Ireland since the 1950s. In 1955, over a third of births in Ireland were domiciliary. The proportion of all births which were domiciliary in 1999 was less than 1% and amounted to only 246 births. Since the late 1970s, small-er maternity units have been closed down because of a government policy that all births should take place in obstetric-staffed maternity units. This has coincided with an increase in the number of births in larger maternity units.

Parallel to the increased hospitalisation of childbirth has come an increased medicalisation and a trend towards more obstetric inter-ventions, i.e., the active management of labour as opposed to active labour. Interventions include episiotomies, caesarean sections and epidurals. Statistics on these have been collated and analysed from the clinical reports of the Coombe Women's Hospital, the National Maternity Hospital and the Rotunda. More than 36% of births have taken place in these three hospitals, every year since 1988 (with the exception of 1990 when it was slightly below). The proportion has risen from 27.37% of all births in 1970 to 40% in 2000. In all three hospitals, there was a sizeable increase in the number of births in the late 1970s reflecting the higher number of births nationally during that period (Kennedy, 2002).

Caesarean Sections
Looking at national statistics for caesarean section – which, apart

from termination, is probably the most extreme obstetric intervention – there has been an increase in caesarean sections from 7.41% to 20.6% between 1984 and 1999 (the latest date for which statistics are available). In the context of the national rate of caesarean sections, the rates in 1992 for the Coombe, the National Maternity Hospital and the Rotunda were 12.0%, 8.5% and 13.7% respectively. So in 1992, the rate in the Rotunda was above the national average of 12.2%, while that in the Coombe was close to the national average and the National Maternity Hospital was below. Looking at statistics for 1999, the Rotunda Hospital had a rate of 25.1%, considerably more than either the Coombe (16.3%) or the National Maternity Hospital (12.9%). Furthermore, by 1999 the Rotunda's caesarean rate had more than doubled since 1978 when it was 8.9%. In the Coombe, the caesarean rate increased from 7.3% in 1978 to 16.3% in 1999 and in the National Maternity Hospital the rate again more than doubled from 4.7% in 1978 to 12.9% in 1999. This raises questions as to why such a serious intervention as caesarean should have such different rates in the three maternity units. Similar questions need to be raised regarding other obstetric interventions including episiotomies and epidurals, which have risen considerably.

Episiotomies
Looking at statistics for episiotomies for 1999, first-time mothers in the Coombe (41%) were less likely to be subjected to this intervention than in the National Maternity Hospital where the procedure was done to more than half of all first-time mothers (52%). The figures for the Rotunda are for both first-time mothers and mothers of one child or more combined, a rate of 35%. However, statistics show mothers of three or more children in the National Maternity Hospital were more likely to be subjected to episiotomies than in the Coombe. These figures should be read in conjunction with the rates for caesarean sections, as those women will not have given birth vaginally (Kennedy, 2002).

Epidurals
Statistics on the use of epidurals again show differences for all three hospitals. Overall, the epidural rate has risen dramatically. Again, the Rotunda comes top of the league table with 52.5% of mothers receiving epidurals in 2000, while the rates for the Coombe and the National Maternity Hospital are 51.4% and 48.6% respectively.

It is interesting to read these figures in the context of the increased hospitalisation of childbirth and the decline in domiciliary births. Women giving birth at home do not experience any of the above procedures (Kennedy, 2002).

Birth is part of a woman's biography. While she may appear to the health professions as a pregnant woman, she has a whole life to live and will find herself in many other roles:

Mothers in the Labour Market

It is difficult to statistically estimate women's participation in the labour market, as statistics available from both the live register and the labour force surveys do not give a true picture of women's participation, owing to the systems of reporting (Cousins, 1996). However, looking at labour force statistics on women of childbearing age gives some indication of women's under-representation (CSO, 1997). In the 25 years between 1971 and 1996, the number of women at work grew by 212,000, reaching 488,000 in 1996. There was a growth rate of 23,000 for males over the same period. These changes have particularly involved married women. In 1971, married women accounted for only 14% of the female workforce, whereas in 1996, about half the female workforce were married. In 1996, using ILO statistics, 41.1% of Irish women aged 15 or over were in the labour force, which compares with 58.7% for Denmark, the highest rate in the EU, and 34.6% for Italy, the lowest in the EU (CSO, 1997).

In 1991, a quarter of all mothers – a third of all mothers with one or two dependent children and over one-fifth of all mothers with three or more dependent children – were in the labour force. Overall, slightly more than 36.6% of mothers were in the labour force in 1996, including about 43% of mothers with one or two dependent children. Only 33.2% of mothers with three or more children were in the labour force (CSO, 1997). As family size increases, after two children, mothers' participation in the labour force decreases. In 1996, of the 507,700 women in the labour force, 111,000 were engaged in part-time work (CSO, 1997). Women's high representation among part-time workers is partly because women in Ireland have to balance their caring responsibilities with paid work with hardly any state support in accessing childcare services. Almost 50% of women living with a husband/partner in a family unit with children were in employment in June–August 2001 compared with 43.6% three years earlier. The most notable increase in employment participation was for mothers in family units where the youngest child was aged 5 to 14. In this category, the percentage in employment increased from 47.3% to 56.2% between mid-1998 and mid-2001 (CSO, 2001).

Mothers are faced with constantly having to reconcile work and family life with the roles and demands of physiological motherhood. The Chambers of Commerce of Ireland in a 2001 study examined the issue of childcare in a labour market context, from the employers' perspective. It highlighted ongoing labour shortages, despite recent changes in the employment environment. It noted the impact that the lack of affordable childcare is having on employers' ability to recruit staff. In half of the companies surveyed, women made up 50% or more of employees. In 21% of companies, staff with children aged 12 years or under comprised the majority of the workforce. Respondents in 57% of the companies surveyed were aware of a query or complaint being made by an employee regarding childcare provision in the previous twelve months. Requests for flexible hours (38%), or complaints about the cost of childcare services (33%) were the most common. 13% of the companies had experienced a situation in the previous twelve months where one or more of the employees resigned their post to care for children. Almost a third of companies (31%) believed that the lack of affordable or available childcare had a negative impact on their ability to recruit or retain staff. Cost (72%), unavailability (65%) and poor quality (13%) were the principal difficulties faced by employees when looking for childcare services. 72% of companies who had employees with children aged 12 or under had some form of family-friendly arrangements in place above those required by law. The most common were part-time (40%), flexi-time (34%), excess unpaid maternity leave (27%) and job-sharing (24%). 28% of all the respondents felt that employees had the main responsibility for childcare, while only 21% of the 503 employers interviewed felt that the responsibility should fall to the government. Only 2% believed that the main responsibility for childcare is that of the employer. 49% of those interviewed believed that responsibility should be split between a combination of employees, government and employers. Tax relief for employees' expenditure on childcare (62%) and employers' expenditure (39%) were the most common suggestions.

Conclusion
Major changes have occurred in Ireland in relation to childbirth since

the 1970s. Women are for the most part becoming mothers at a later age and are having fewer babies. Family size has decreased alongside the period during which women are likely to give birth. More women are travelling to Britain for abortion services while at the same time the number of women giving birth outside of marriage has escalated. There are more women in the labour market and maternity leave and maternity benefit have become more readily available. At the same time, women are more likely to give birth in larger maternity units and will experience more medical intervention than previously.

CREATION II

© Imogen Stuart

CHAPTER SIX

Motherhood in Gaelic Ireland

Máire Mhac an tSaoi

My knowledge of early Irish literature is limited and out of date, but it seems to me that, from the earliest times, right down to the eighteenth century, motherhood in secular writings, in the Irish language, figures mainly as the finite result of sexual intercourse rather than a continuing condition. It is a result whose primary importance is dynastic, political and economic. It seems that those affectionate and nurturing aspects of the state are displaced onto the foster-mother. Fosterage is a tenacious institution; we know that as late as 1775 Daniel O'Connell was fostered. When, well after he learned to speak, his natural mother came to visit him on Valencia Island, she enquired whether he often ate meat? 'Oh yes,' replied the child 'when my father killed one of Morgan O'Connell's beasts, we all ate our fill' (McCartney, 1980). 'My father' in this context denotes his foster-father. Morgan O'Connell was his natural father. I have speculated that it was his abrupt break with a loving, warm and of course, Irish-speaking foster-family, that formed the psychological basis for his conscious and well-attested self-severance from the Irish language, even while admitting that that language was 'connected with many recollections that twine round the hearts of Irishmen'. I remember, in the 1920s and 1930s, hearing the theory seriously advanced and defended, in the context of the Irish language revival movement, that *natural* parents, because of their *natural* partiality, were unfit to bring up their *natural* offspring, and that, as it were, Irish-speaking kibbutzim should take over the formation of the youth of the nation. There is no doubt in my mind today but that such theorising accurately mirrors the 'take' on child-rearing implied throughout Irish literature in Irish.

We can of course assume that the silent majority of unaristocratic and illiterate families continued to indulge and spoil their children, and pet them and afford them treats, and sing them lullabies, and tell them stories and invent games for them, but we have no literary records. Perhaps, the 'brehon' laws, now much more readily available to the public than they used to be, may reflect more humane usages. I know they are detailed on fosterage, to the degree that they can analyse the responsibility of a foster-father who accidentally causes the death of his fosterling by hitting the child's head against the lintel of a doorway through which he is carrying him/her on his shoulders. This brings me to an odd little observation: whenever, and it is rare, traces of tenderness towards children surface in a text, it is almost invariably expressed by the father, or in the case I am about to cite, concerning him.

When the poet-earl, Gerald Fitzgerald of Desmond was a little boy in the fourteenth century, the courtier poet, Gofraidh Fionn Ó Dálaigh, enlisted his help to mollify the old earl, his father, with whom the poet had had a falling-out (Osborn Bergin, 1918). He begs little Gerald not to hug or kiss his father until reconciliation is effected between the grown-ups.

There are a whole series of affecting poems by fathers who have lost children, so many indeed, that I am inclined to think that such a piece could have been a professional exercise, required of all student poets. In these compositions, the mother, if she figures at all, does so in a peculiarly mechanical fashion, as a necessary precursor to the existence of the dead child – usually a son. One is reminded of the famously terse reference to the mother of his children in Tomás Ó Criomhtháin's account of their deaths: 'The worry of all these things weighed on the poor mother, and she was taken from me'. But Tomás adds, 'I was not totally blind till then' (Ó Coileáin, 2002).

That note is exceedingly rare before his time, but was very much present in the life of rural Ireland from the nineteenth century on, and its expression flourished in the prevailing pietism. It must be remembered that the secular and the ecclesiastical were mutually independent in early Christian Ireland, and that the early Church was a humanising element in the society of the warring petty kingdoms. The motherhood of Our Lady and the childhood of Christ are, in religious verse, suffused with a tenderness wholly alien to the secular compositions (Greene and O'Connor, 1967): Saint Ita nurses the divine Child at her breast; a prestigious seventeenth-century cleric, who was also a poet, offers to launder His swaddling bands (Mac Aingil, 1971). We must assume that this wealth of feeling was always there, but surfaced only with the decay of the old, exclusivist, male hegemony. Mind you, the old, exclusivist hegemony was not unaware of the importance of mothers – even more reason to keep them in their place!

In the *Táin Bó Cuailnge*, the Ulster Cycle of hero-tales, Conor Mac Nessa, king of the Ulstermen, takes his surname from his mother.

It has been argued that the king whom he supplants, Fergus Mac Róich, does so as well, although his surname means explicitly 'son of great horse' – gender unspecified. Cú Chulainn is the son of the king's sister and his enemies are led by the formidable Maeve, Queen of Ulster, who prostitutes her daughter. To this day in Gaeltacht areas, in households where the housewife is the dominant partner, either financially or from the strength of her personality, the children take their name from her, a matronymic rather than a patronymic. Readers of my generation will remember Jimín Mháire Thaidhg and his masterful 'Mam' in the Seabhac's eponymous story for the young.

It is a truism that Ireland in Irish literature is always a female, but she is a spouse rather than a mother. She is the concept of sovereignty, whom the king, from the earliest claimants ever to the title, to the last of the Stuarts, must wed. She is pre-eminently a consort and, while good mothers are passed over in silence, wicked queens, wicked stepmothers, abound. The Phaedra motif is common and, of course, it implies the usurpation of the father's kingship by his son by his first wife. There are also wicked queens who hate their stepchildren, as every child who has been told the story of the Children of Lir knows. There the maternal virtues cluster in the little Fionnuala, who fosters her brothers at her breast and under her wings, after the evil stepmother Aoife has turned them into swans. Ireland, the virtuous spouse, remains chaste, beneficent and radiant, absorbed in the fortunes of her royal husband. The domestic duties of childrearing are taken for granted and passed over in silence. That is as long as all goes well. With the final collapse of the Gaelic polity, after Limerick, Joyce's 'old sow that eats her farrow' surfaces, most notably in the passionate resentment of Dáibhí Ó Bruadair:

> Vain is the trait of this cunning mother.
> Tricky and vexing, perverse and stubborn–
> She's forsaken her race, her fierce raider-children.
> Who first put a ring on the tip of her finger.
>
> (Ó Bruadair, trans. Hartnett, 1985)

'Mother Ireland' had always existed but she had yet to be sanitised. As an old man in the Gaeltacht put it: 'Bad luck to you, Ireland, and all the songs that they make for you'. The extraordinary understanding of by-gone literary conventions, which this remark exemplifies, was common among Irish-speakers at the beginning of the last century. Another striking instance of it is found in the saying: 'Priests and friars, and the poetic art disappeared between them' – a start-lingly exact definition of the ecclesiastical reforms of the nineteenth century. This cultural conservatism encourages us to look for traces of age-old custom in the daily life of rural Ireland in the early years of the last century.

Both Tómas Ó Criomhtháin and 'Máire' (Séamus Ó Grianna), the archetypal Ulster writer, describe idyllic childhoods. Tomás is the youngest, and his only brother is the eldest of a numerous family. In between come a long string of sisters. Tomás is everyone's pet. His father is a good provider and can set his hand to many trades. His mother is tall and white skinned – the preferred physical type, ever since physical characteristics began to be set down in writing. She is practical and hardworking, but above all humorous, patient and lov-ing. Tomás is not weaned until he is four years old; he goes with his mother everywhere, collecting shellfish from the shore, bringing home turf from the hill. The mother is an arbiter and a diplomat. It is a har-monious household and, in a good year, they are self-sufficient. Both 'Máire' and Tomás make a great story of their first britches, and of the accidents that can happen little boys of four or five on such occa-sions. In each case it is the father who sets all to right: Tomás' father is a tailor and has actually made the britches, so buttons are quickly made more manageable; 'Máire's' father takes his weeping son on his lap and lies down beside him on the bed when he puts him to sleep, to reassure him that he will not be sent to school in the old petticoat in the morning. Such are the households Gaeltacht mothers preside over. Grandmothers too are very child-friendly. In the famous incid-ent in Maire's novel, *Caisleáin Óir* (1938), where the hero, Séimidh Phádraig Dhuibh, goes to 'the Queen's school', in his petticoat at the age of five, he learns that his name is 'James Gallagher' and gets struck across the scalp and around the ears with a stick, lest he forget it. His mother and grandmother are upset by the blows and indignant at the master's insults, but are resigned to the cruelty of the outside world. The lessons Séimidh learns from them are contradictory but realistic and above all, loving.

Before moving on and in contrast to the familial scenes above, here is a comment on the downside of domesticity, by a male profes-sional poet in the days of the order's decline:

A small, unprofitable, rough-spoken wife
And a swarm of sullen demanding youngsters –
Alas! For him who has the crowd for company
In threadbare clothes and with nothing to eat.

(Ó Bruadair, trans. Hartnett, 1985)

A very different family life is reflected in the famous *Lament for Arthur O'Leary*, perhaps a hundred years later. This wonderful late flowering of an anonymous folk tradition, transmitted orally from generation to generation of women, almost certainly dates from pre-Christian times and is ascribed to Eibhlín Dubh Ní Chonaill (1750–1800) an aunt of the Liberator's. In the O'Connell family papers, in English, she figures as 'poor Nellie' a daughter of the house, who made an unfortunate marriage and is reduced to Victorian bourgeois dependence and obscurity. Yet she is connected on the one side with the courts of pre-revolutionary Europe (the Empress Maria Theresa stood godmother to her eldest) and on the other with the old, dangerous femininity of pagan Ireland (her mother came of the wild, poetic stock of O'Donohue of the Glen and was herself a poet and a 'wise woman'). So perhaps it is possible to imagine the widowed Nellie abandoning herself to a practice which, until the 1920s, the Church strove unsuccessfully to extirpate. Nellie was, after all, her mother's daughter. I am inclined to think, however, that the keening women both composed her part and declaimed it for her. It is clear, from the formulaic pattern of the lament and from the number of set phrases it shares with other surviving examples of the genre, that it draws in large part on the stock-in-trade of this redoubtable caste of woman 'weepers', some – though by no means all – of whom who were paid, quasi-professionals. It is remarkable that, in common with the rest of these pieces, O'Leary's lament employs no overt Christian concepts, except for a single exclamation 'Christ knows'. Indeed the traffic is all the other way; there are several dramatic laments for the crucified Christ, attributed to Our Lady and her accompanying holy women. It is not on the secular nature of the lament for Arthur O'Leary that I want to focus, but rather on the moving and beautiful account it gives of the lifestyle of prosperous, if proscribed, affluent Catholic families of Munster. Particularly significant is the startlingly individual reaction of the young widow to her bereavement, in which her children play an integral and unselfconscious part. As is the convention of the keen, each strophe is addressed directly to the dead person and there is dialogue among the mourners.

It could be any contemporary widow giving her story to the press. I incline strongly to the opinion that this immediacy and tenderness always characterised Irish mothers' relationships with their children, when not artificially repressed or soured by hardship, and that this is preserved in our oral literature, though for the most part unrecorded. Lullabies and dandling songs and, of course, Christmas carols convey the same message: mother-love exists in the present; it does not feel the need to survive in printed books.

CHAPTER SEVEN
'Oh Mother Where Art Thou?'
Irish Mothers and Irish Fiction
in the Twentieth Century

Áine McCarthy

Aside from feminist interest in the representation of the nation of Ireland as maternal – in particular, feminist scrutiny of the 'Mother Ireland' emblem – motherhood as a theme in Irish fiction has received markedly little *critical* attention. Exceptions are Weekes (1992, 2000) and Innes (1993). One reason for this is Irish criticism's fixated focus on 'the national question'. The belief that 'there is no fine nationality without literature and no fine literature without nationality' as expressed by W. B. Yeats (1888) in full revivalist flight, may once have stimulated Irish artists and critics, but as inspiration or interpretation, the notion of nation has been bled dry. Yeats himself came to repudiate nationalism as chauvinistic and political, in conflict with the artistic pursuit of 'higher things'. Yet a century later, Irish critics still insist on privileging nationhood over other aspects of identity and using it as the central tool of analysis.

Colm Tóibín gives the accepted view in his introduction to a recent anthology: 'The purpose of much Irish fiction, it seems, is to become involved in the Irish argument and the purpose of much Irish criticism has been to relate the fiction to the argument'. The argument? He goes on: 'Writers who have sought to evade the opportunities to interpret this, who have sought to deal [instead] with the individual mood ... seem oddly heroic and hard to place' (Tóibín, 1999). This statement, which purports to say something about Irish fiction, in fact reveals how *critical* frameworks have failed writers and readers. Irish novelists and short story writers – including Tóibín himself – have long used fiction to explore many other identifications besides nationality: class, religion, sexual orientation, marital status, gender and many others, including motherhood and fatherhood.

The concept of a singular, privileged strand of identity – the argument that subsumes or overshadows all others – is a fallacy, in Ireland as elsewhere, because identity is always plural. Always. Any literary, cultural or political theory that does not allow this is flawed. Yet still the national bandwagon rolls on, blaring its tedious monotone, lately set to new lyrics by post-colonialists in jazzy, up-tempo arrangements which fail to disguise that what's playing is still the same old tune.

The argument, the national argument, is a power struggle between men. It is a struggle that excludes women, especially mothers, from its analysis, except at the level of symbol. Mothers, more than any other group – both the living, breathing women and their fictional representations – expose the deficiency of such dichotomies as England/Ireland, Anglo/Hiberno, Protestant/Catholic, colonial/postcolonial as explanation. A fictional tradition that offers few fully realised portraits of mothers, and a critical framework that allocates no space to exploring literature by and about mothers, is not just incomplete; it is deformed. And deforming.

Irish Mothers Writing

In her 1972 book, *Silences*, the American scholar and writer, Tillie Olsen posited one to twelve as the ratio of female to male writers accorded recognition. Even more troubling is the proportion of that female one-in-twelve who have had children. Mothers are the women least likely to possess what Virginia Woolf (1923) deemed essential if writing is to be done: a room of their own and £500 a year (space in which to think and work and enough money to live on).

Money, of course, is a conundrum for all writers, who have, according to novelist and poet Margaret Atwood, only five financial options: 'You can have money of your own; you can marry money; you can attract a patron – whether a king, a duke or an arts board; you can have a day job; or you can sell to the market' (Atwood, 2002). Motherhood should be no worse than any other day job; in fact, it should be better than most, given that it encompasses elemental human dramas like pregnancy and birth and involves an intimate involvement with human development. And, on a more pragmatic front, the domestic work that goes with it provides just the right sort of mindless, mechanical tasks that best fill the hours away from the desk. No, the reason why motherhood is so incompatible with a writing life is all to do with the pay (none) and the conditions (none). As Olsen (1972) puts it:

> Motherhood, as it is structured [in our society] … means being constantly interruptible, responsive, responsible. Children need one *now* … [and] the very fact that … *there is no one else to be responsible for these needs* gives them

primacy. It is distraction, not meditation that becomes habitual; inter-
ruption, not continuity; spasmodic, not constant, toil. Work interrupted,
deferred, postponed makes blockage – at best, lesser accomplishment [my
italics].

Which is undoubtedly why so many women writers of accomplish-
ment have had no children: the roll call of such Irish novelists and
story writers would include Maeve Binchy, Elizabeth Bowen, Clare
Boylan, Maeve Brennan, Elizabeth Cullinan, Maria Edgeworth, Emily
Lawless, Mary McCarthy, Iris Murdoch, Eilis Ni Dhuibhne, Kate
O'Brien, Flannery O'Connor, Somerville and Ross.

Some mothers manage, through a combination of determination,
privilege and luck, to surmount the obstacles, but they are few in number. The result is that motherhood is generally written about from the
outside, by writers who have no first-hand knowledge of the experience and who often seem to believe that a mother's place is in the
wrong.

Writing the Irish Mother

The most cursory examination of the representation of mothers in
Irish fiction reveals three widely, almost obsessively, reproduced stereotypes: Good Mammy, an idealised mother figure (dutiful, self-sacri-
ficing paragon, devoted to God and family, provider of selfless love
and good dinners); Moaning Mammy, her negative counterpart (whin-
ing or silent martyr, drained by her feckless/alcoholic husband and
enormous brood of children); and the type that Irish-American novelist J. T. Farrell (1929) dubbed the 'Smother Mother', a dominant mat-
riarch who insists on her children's adherence to her principles.

In each of her three incarnations, Irish Mammy possesses an
unvarying set of characteristics: she is pious; she is pure (i.e. asexual);
she is devoted to her sons and demanding of her daughters; and she
is the repository of her society's ideals, being much concerned with
respectability and what the neighbours think. These stereotypes are
remarkably prevalent in Irish writing, not just in writing from the
Republic and North of Ireland (from Mrs Dedalus in *A Portrait of the
Artist* by James Joyce at the beginning or Mrs Brady and Mrs Nugent
in Patrick McCabe's *The Butcher Boy* at the end) but also in 'hyphe-
nated-Irish' writing from the UK. Some examples include Bill Naugh-
ton's *One Small Boy* (1957) and *Saintly Billy* (1988); *I Could Read the
Sky* by Timothy O'Grady and many of the works of Walter Macken)
and the US (Elizabeth and Mrs Rowan in *The Trouble of One House*

by Brendan Gill (1950); Julia Devlin in *House of Gold* by Elizabeth Cullinan; *Angela's Ashes* by Frank McCourt (1996) and Mrs Lonigan in J. T. Farrell's *Studs Lonigan* Trilogy). There are literally hundreds of other examples.

This stereotype, however, is not uniquely Irish. Irish Mammy's defining characteristics are shared with the Jewish-American mother (see Myrna Gold in *Fathers* by Herbert Gold (1967); Philip Roth's mother in *The Facts* for example and all those Jewish Momma jokes). Also British Indian mothers: the unnamed mother in Rajeev Balasubramanyam's *In Beautiful Disguise* for example and in numerous sketches from the BBC's comedy show, *Goodness Gracious Me!*

Mothers find themselves similarly portrayed across centuries, cultures and classes because their representation is the function of a trans-historical, trans-cultural social phenomenon: what Adrienne Rich has dubbed the institution of motherhood. In her influential and important work, *Of Woman Born*, Rich juxtaposes the 'experience' of motherhood, 'the *potential relationship* of any woman to her powers of reproduction and to children', with the '*institution* which aims at ensuring that the potential ... shall remain under male control' (Rich, 1976). This institution affects not just mothers but all women because under its ideology, 'all women are seen primarily as mother [and] all mothers are expected to experience motherhood unambivalently and in accordance with patriarchal values'. Within patriarchal societies – and these days, what society is not? – female possibility has been 'massacred on the site of motherhood' (Rich, 1976).

Reading the fiction of twentieth-century Ireland gives us an insight into some of the myriad ways in which patriarchy intersects with other identifiers (nationality, skin colour, sex preference and so on) in an individual life. It also illuminates the ways in which the institution of motherhood was structured in a certain place and a certain time and the ways in which the institution has shifted shape over the hundred years or so but remained steadfastly fixed and functioning throughout.

When the century opened, all Ireland was still under British rule and a literary revival was in full swing, with people of all classes and both creeds engaged in the project of restoring 'native' Irish culture and customs. This cultural nationalism underlay, perhaps even inspired, a resuscitation of political and military movements for Irish independence from Britain. 'Did that play of mine send out/certain men the English shot?' asked W. B. Yeats of the play *Cathleen Ní Houlihan*, pondering this link between culture and revolutionary politics, between the performance of the play and the 1916 Rising. (He should, incidentally, have written 'that play of ours', as much of Cathleen was written by Augusta Gregory, a writing mother whose reputation is beginning to be lifted from the ancillary role to which literary history consigned her).

Cathleen Ní Houlihan was one of Ireland's many female incarnations: Hibernia, Dark Rosaleen, the Sean Van Vocht, Erin. Through such female images, Irish cultural nationalists adopted and continued a correlation that had long been a feature of colonisation: the association of Ireland with weakness, irrationality, fervour, nature – all the feminine signifiers – while England (John Bull) epitomised sturdy, unprejudiced, progressive masculinity.

Through a campaign of violence and political pressure, Ireland won partial independence from Britain in 1921 and, despite a shaky start, the new twenty-six county state survived. From the beginning, it sought to limit the lives of women through legislation: laws limiting women's employment possibilities and their participation in juries; a censorship act, which prohibited the publication or purchase of any material about contraception or abortion as well as banning almost any book worth reading (to list all the books banned would be to list many of the major literary events of the twentieth century: Bellow, Faulkner, Gordimer, Hemingway, Koestler, Moravio, Nabokov, Proust, Sartre, Stead, Zola, all had works banned, as had the majority of Irish writers); and laws outlawing contraception, divorce and later, a constitutional amendment prohibiting the introduction of abortion.

The new, young, male leaders had the imagery of cultural nationalism emblazoned on their hearts and in their now largely Roman Catholic state, images of Mother Ireland, Mother Church and the Mother of Christ fused into a synthesis which few writers unpicked or even questioned. Variations on this theme were repeatedly, unthinkingly reproduced, particularly in poetry but also in the work of novelists. The effect of this fusion of the national and the feminine on the lives and work of Irish women writers has been eloquently voiced by poets such as Eavan Boland and Nuala Ní Dhomhnaill. Ní Dhomhnaill writes of how the 'diagrammatic and dehumanised image of woman' used by Irish male writers 'as a kind of literary shorthand long after it was either necessary or useful' means that 'the image of woman in the national tradition is a very real dragon that every Irish woman poet has to fight every time she opens her literary door' (1992).

For Boland, the false coupling was a violation of the 'necessary ethical relation between imagination and image' (1995).

Both writers address how 'the more the image of woman comes to stand for abstract concepts like justice, liberty or national sovereignty, the more real women are denigrated and consigned barefoot and pregnant to the kitchen' (Ní Dhomhnaill, 1992). Yet even the barefoot and pregnant had something: the status of wife and mother. Society's worst was reserved for those who breached the pitiless social law of the time: that a mother must be married. If she was not, her fate was literally unspeakable. A surface rhetoric about the ideal of motherhood (given constitutional expression in the 1937 Irish constitution, which uses the words 'mother' and 'woman' interchangeably and in a controversial article challenged by feminists of the time, that declares '... by her life within the home, woman gives to the state a support without which the common good cannot be achieved ...') co-existed with an underbelly of muted maternal reality – forced adoption, illegal abortions, infanticides, incarcerations in Magdalene Laundries or lunatic asylums.

The Irish Mammy presided in silence over fictional stereotypes. Writers of novels and short stories, whom one might expect to be drawn to profound human tragedies and compelled to break the socially imposed silence, in the main reneged.

Molly Keane

One writer whose black-comedic vision did allow mention of the unmentionable was Molly Keane. Keane, who in an interview with *The New Yorker* described herself as 'a great old breakerawayer', came from the privileged world of the ascendancy, the Anglo-Irish landed gentry and lived through their twilight: the years when their socioeconomic power dwindled. Underlying the beauty of the Big Houses which Keane depicts in loving detail are secrets which her characters find too noxious to discuss but which nevertheless make their way into the text: abortion, infanticide, homosexuality, adultery and domestic violence.

Like many a female writer before and since, Molly adopted a male-sounding pseudonym, M. J. Farrell, under which she wrote eleven novels and four plays over three decades (1928–1961). All except one (*Devoted Ladies*, 1934) caricatured the ascendancy world of meticulous manners, beautiful houses and gung-ho hunting in a way that anticipated its decline. In most of these novels, the moral atrophy, self-absorption and illegitimate claims of the 'Big House' class are depicted through amoral, self-absorbed and cruel mother characters.

A good example is *Two Days in Aragon*, her ninth novel, written in 1941. The book is uneven in tone and treatment, lacking the accomplishment of her later fiction, but it both tackles head-on what is avoided or implied in her other work – *the* Irish argument, specifically the Troubles of 1921 – and is also highly explicit in its treatment of motherhood. The privilege and beauty of gracious Aragon is built on a cruel, patriarchal foundation.

One plot strand centres on an 'illegitimate' pregnancy that crosses class boundaries as well as being conceived outside marriage and the text is riddled with references to 'babies, dead or dying, thrown to the river'. Anne Daly, Aragon servant and abortionist, 'tolerant, understanding, skilled and merciless', had a bedpost filled with pieces of gold given to her by young gentlemen.

Nan, the central character of the book, 'the beginning and end of Aragon', is constantly depicted in maternal terms. Mrs Fox, the mistress of the house, Grania and Sylvia, the daughters, Aunt Pigeon: each is her 'baby' or 'child'. The nursery is 'her kingdom'. Even the Aragon ghost that most repeatedly appears to her is 'The Child'. She indulges Mrs Fox with spoiling and petting and delicious trays of food and torments poor Aunt Pigie with perversions of maternal comforts: rationed food, inadequate bath water insufficiently warm. For her unthinking loyalty to amoral Aragon, Nan must die while the 'bad' girl Grania, survives: 'A house would be built here [on the site of burnt-out Aragon] for happy Grania's children.' Grania – who broke Aragon's rules by consorting with Nan's son – can remain once the Big House has gone; the others, who imbibed its values whole, must die or emigrate.

After her husband died in 1961, Keane, left with two small daughters to raise alone, stopped writing. It was twenty years before she published again, returning in 1981 with *Good Behaviour*, a book that distils all the wisdom, wit and ferocious clear-sightedness of the earlier novels into a dazzling, heartbreaking *tour de force*.

The crux of this novel is the relationship between the protagonist, Aroon, and 'Mummie', her cold-hearted, distant mother. The novel explores how Aroon's upbringing warped her: even in the nursery she knew 'how to ignore things … how to behave' but her best efforts could not dislodge her mother's disdain and mockery of her, so that in the end she kills her by giving her rabbit to eat when she knows, as Rose the servant says, that: 'rabbit chokes her, rabbit sickens her, and rabbit killed her ... if it was a smothering you couldn't have done it better.' It is a measure of Keane's skill that the reader equally fears, and fears for, Aroon. When she rebuffs Mr Kiely because *she* is Aroon St Charles of Temple Alice and *he* a mere solicitor, the snobbery and cruelty of her rejection show how truly she has become her mother's daughter: 'one of Mummie's phrases came to me and I spoke it in her voice: "... you must be out of your mind".'

'When I was a child I had no one else to love,' Keane once said of her own mother, Moira O'Neill, who also wrote, in her case sentimental rhymes about Ireland. 'I *adored* her, though I hardly ever saw her ... [but she] ... didn't really like me' and Keane developed a version of the 'grotesque, sentimental fixation' that she ascribes to Aroon (Devlin, 1982). It is noteworthy that Keane, to the end of her writing life and despite having two daughters of her own, never lost her 'daughterly' perspective of the mother/daughter relationship.

Mary Lavin

With Mary Lavin, it was different. Dubbed the Vermeer of the Irish Short Story (MacIntyre, 1977), though she also wrote two novels, Lavin's work depicted some of the social realities of life in Ireland in the 1940s, 1950s and 1960s: 'a mediocre, dishevelled, often neurotic and depressed petit-bourgeois society' (Brown, 1982). Her stories fall into two distinct phases with regard to motherhood. Early stories largely reproduce the stereotypes found in other Irish fiction: Good Mammys in *Mary O'Grady* (1950) and 'The Living' (1951) for example and Smother Mothers in 'The Will' (1956), 'The Patriot Son' (1956) and 'A Likely Story' (1957). These and other early work – 'Brother Boniface' (1942), 'Sarah' (1942), 'Magenta' (1947) – sometimes have a didactic tone; they use a reliable, omniscient narrator who may make intrusive interjections.

A breach occurs when she is widowed and has to raise her three daughters alone. As the girls grow, Lavin's strongly autobiographical (Leavenson, 1998) depictions of motherhood become more complex and multi-layered, often treating the tensions between generations, as mothers and daughters get caught in a web of similarities and differences, affection and irritation, deep familiarity and surface misunderstanding. Lavin offers no surprising twists or revelations in these stories, nothing more startling than a mother finding she has misinterpreted her daughter's long looks to her husband in 'A Walk on

The Cliff', (1985) or the fine balance between love and irritation in the title story of her final volume A *Family Likeness* (1985). Told in a muted authorial voice that takes the side of neither mother nor daughter, these stories appear to offer a conventional reading experience but are working at another level – through symbol or motif, through multiple viewpoints, through a skilful manipulation of time and memory – to complicate their effect.

These and other motherhood stories like 'Happiness' (1969), 'Trastevere' (1973) and 'Senility' (1977) leave what can only be called 'almost-questions' hovering in the mind, a suspicion that what you have been reading is deeper than it seems. Re-reading does not so much answer the questions as intensify their significance. These stories of motherhood, largely overlooked by anthologists, are among Lavin's most subtle and accomplished.

Edna O'Brien
Edna O'Brien's first book *The Country Girls* appeared in 1960 and was immediately banned for its frank depictions of female sexual longing and experiences. The priest in O'Brien's home village burned the novels in the churchyard and she was inundated with hate mail. While critics have always focused on O'Brien's depiction of sexuality, her interest in motherhood has received less attention, though she regards it as central to her work. In an interview in 1984 she said:

> If you want to know what I regard as the principal crux of female despair, it is this: in the Greek myth of Oedipus and in Freud's exploration of it, the son's desire for his mother is admitted; the infant daughter also desires its mother but it is unthinkable, either in myth, in fantasy or in fact, that that desire can be consummated (Roth, 1984).

This interest in motherhood as subject and theme grew as her career progressed. Like Lavin, O'Brien's work can fruitfully be divided into two periods: the first, launched by *The Country Girls*, lasted to the mid-1980s. These novels – particularly *A Pagan Place* (1970), *Night* (1972) and *Johnny I Hardly Knew You* (1971) – are characterised by an intense focus on *The Love Object* (1968), (the title of one of her short story collections). 'Love' in O'Brien's lexicon is a masochistic, sexual fixation on a dominant older man which is generally set in opposition to the sex aversion felt by her heroines' mothers (Mary Hooligan in *Night* is a lucky exception). The daughters reject their mothers at adolescence for this aversion to sexuality, and by inference, life.

By the time she wrote *Time and Tide* (1992), Edna O'Brien's standpoint, like Lavin's, shifted from a 'daughterly' to a 'motherly' perspective, a development that has been creatively enriching for her, leading to new depths in her fiction. Like earlier O'Brien heroines, the protagonist of *Time and Tide* fears being consumed by her mother, but also has a deep, important relationship with her own children (two sons, like the author) which makes the novel more complex and interesting. After this came *Down by the River* (1996), a novel loosely based on the notorious Irish X-case controversy, in which the parents of a 14-year-old girl were prevented from bringing their daughter to England for an abortion. In O'Brien's book, the impregnator is the father. 'What would your mother say' he laughs after the first time he rapes the girl 'Dirty little thing'. This book explores a dark side of motherhood in graphic, lyrical detail.

Her most recent novel, *In The Forest* (2001) treats motherhood through the lens of a real-life event: the shooting dead in an Irish wood of a young woman and her four-year-old son, and the priest who tried to minister to their demented killer. This murderous young man, Michen O'Kane, saw his father attack his mother with a poker and afterwards put his finger in the hole left by her knocked-out teeth 'and felt the damp of the blood and tasted it and it was warm. His mother and he were not two people, only one'. When she dies, he is soon in and out of detention centres, learning 'the cruel things ... taught ... in the places named after the saints': beatings, bullying and sex abuse. Although O'Brien thus explains O'Kane's alienation, she does not offer his lost mother, his lost childhood as justification. As one garda puts it: 'all this hand wringing ... his childhood, his loneliness, his mother ... lots of kids with no mothers don't steal cars and don't burn cars and don't take women at gunpoint ... little creep, little coward.'

The author does not shy from taking us right into his creepiness and cowardice, particularly in relation to his victim, Eily Ryan. Eily – who unwittingly moves herself and her young son into O'Kane's former forest den – exudes a maternal sexuality that fascinates him. He abducts her and her son at gunpoint. In O'Brien's rendition of this story, it is O'Kane's longing for mothering that leads to Eily's death: 'Herself and the child were one, indivisible and O'Kane, the outcast, had seen that and had wanted it and had had to destroy it in his hunger to belong.'

But male alienation from the bond of mother and child is not unique to O'Kane. At the funeral, Eily's ex-lover, Maddie's father, searches out O'Kane's father to shake his hand, 'two fathers, outside that boundary of mother and child, their hands briefly touching, touching on things that could never be said.'

In the 1970s and 1980s some 'things that could never be said' before in Ireland began to find voice, as an upsurge of feminist activity challenged, and in many cases reversed, the legal and economic repressions of women, introduced over the previous century-and-a-half. In line with these socio-political advances, a literary movement flourished. Attic Press and Arlen House began to publish books by, for and about women and British feminist presses like Virago also began to revive out-of-print women's writing, most importantly in the Irish context, the novels of Molly Keane and Kate O'Brien. Women's studies courses in the universities articulated a feminist understanding of literary politics. More women and mothers began to write and to use fiction to address subjects that were previously taboo: incest in Jennifer Johnston's *The Invisible Worm* (1991), leaving one's children for love in Julia O'Faoláin's *No Country for Young Men* (1980), lesbianism in the work of Mary Dorcey and Emma Donoghue, infertility and abortion in Mary Morrisey's *Mother of Pearl* (1996) and many, many others.

It is not necessary to be a mother to write convincingly about maternal experience. It is not necessary even to be female, as Roddy Doyle proved so successfully with *The Woman Who Walked Into Doors* (1996). But what does seem to be necessary is a minimal level of female autonomy in the society within which the writer works. It is impossible to imagine *The Woman Who Walked Into Doors* being written without the years of public feminist debate that preceded it and the changed social climate which that debate helped to bring about.

'Change' is the contemporary buzz-word in the Republic of Ireland, as a sustained financial boom brings money, jobs and immigrants to the state for the first time in its history, but it would be a mistake to believe that change is the same thing as progress. As the twenty-first century opens, the collective power-struggles of the 1970s have been replaced by a corporate-driven individualism in which everybody, male and female, is a marketing-department's target but women, through female sexuality, are disproportionately sold to (as consumers) and sold (in burgeoning glamour, pornography and prostitution businesses). If, at the beginning of the twentieth century, the female ideal through which women were regulated was Madonna, now it is Whore. Then, patriarchy operated through local laws and government, now through globalised consumerism and popular culture. What both ends of the century have in common is the silence of Irish novelists and critics on the contemporary maternal powerlessness.

Meanwhile, the institution of motherhood as defined by Adrienne Rich – the economic dominance of fathers in families; the guardianship of men over children in courts and educational systems; the male control of female reproduction, particularly abortion; the usurpation of birth process by male medical establishment and so on – may be dented, but remains troublingly intact in this time of alleged transformation. Some *women*, especially those willing and able to play by masculinist rules, have made social and economic progress, but life for *mothers* runs pretty much as it always has. More mothers can now work outside the home for money as well as inside it for nothing, but a decent childcare system remains as elusive as ever; single mothers may no longer be incarcerated in Big Houses but now they are confined to housing estates that are locationally and socially peripheral; and, while Irish society no longer denies the existence of issues like marital rape, domestic violence or sexual abuse, articulating such problems is not the same thing as solving them.

As for writing mothers, a computation of the mother/father ratio of writers included in literature courses at university, in critical surveys and anthologies, on the review pages of the newspapers or on literary prize lists, indicates that the ratio has barely shifted since Tillie Olsen computed her figures thirty years ago; and motherhood remains the great *terra incognita* of Irish literary criticism. A decade after the *Field Day Anthology* debacle (when twenty male editors of a collection trumpeted as an inclusive anthology of Irish work were widely criticised for their poor representation of writings by and about women, so much so that the work they overlooked had to be gathered into two separate additional volumes), male scholars continue to ignore, deny, erase and trivialise work by and about women, especially mothers. To take just one example, a book which says it has set out to articulate 'a range of voices which have been, or which continue to be, marginalised from the mainstream of life throughout the island', manages to have a section on family that omits mothers except at the level of the symbolic (Smyth, 1997).

A fundamental question is my central premise, a question of a different order to matters of aesthetics as posed by conventional literary criticism: how closely does the body of Irish fiction reflect life in Irish society? Such a question requires the critic to become attuned to the sound of absence, to recognise that censorship law is just one method by which the dominant muzzle what they don't want to hear. In the words of Edna O'Brien: 'Banning is only the tip of the iceberg. Keeping our psyches closed is the main bogey' (Carlson, 1990).

In another essay on motherhood, Adrienne Rich (1976) articulates some themes that must be addressed if motherhood is to be truly understood, a list of possibilities that might fruitfully be explored by novelists and critics:

> to speak of maternal ambivalence; to examine the passionate conflicts and ambiguities of the mother-daughter relationship, and the role of the mother in indoctrinating her daughters to subservience and her sons to dominance; to identify the guilt mothers are made to feel for societal failures beyond their control; to acknowledge that a lesbian can be a mother and a mother a lesbian, contrary to popular stereotypes; to question the dictating by powerful men as to how women, especially the poor and non-white, shall use their bodies (Rich 1976).

No group is so disregarded by our body politic, by our stories, by our criticism, as mothers, a fact that begs another question: if we don't know our own mothers, what do we know?

CHAPTER EIGHT

Motherhood and Creativity

Róisín de Buitléar
and Maree Hensey

It's 4 o'clock, we travel to Davies Hill and the journey to explore motherhood and creativity starts. We are not experts, but wish to share our experiences; we will be true and honest to you the reader.

In discussing pregnancy and motherhood and its relationship with our creativity, we have discovered common threads that run throughout. We wish to explore the physiological and psychological implications of pregnancy, childbirth and motherhood on our work as artists. In isolating these threads, it is necessary to look at aspects of creativity: why we are compelled to be creative, what spurs that motivation and why that is fundamental to our situation; how deciding to become mothers changed that dynamic; what effect that change has had on our work; what impact the need to create has had on our mothering, how our mothering has influenced our inspiration and direction. Interlaced with these issues are the recurring elements of time, physical implications and energy.

I first met Maree when she called to deliver an illustration to my husband on a Sunday afternoon. She worked from her home, which was back-to-back with ours. It was natural that she called around to hand-deliver the drawings instead of sending them by courier to his office in town. Everything is easy with Maree. She is gentle, listens and takes each moment as it comes. I wanted to know her more, and since then we've shared so many experiences. That was seven years ago when my Somhairle and her Ella were babies. Our friendship has evolved through the challenges and relationships of our families and the impact of those on our work. We have lived through each other's pregnancies, births and miscarriages. We have often discussed parenting and our reactions to mothering issues as they have arisen. Our work as artists has connected us from the beginning. Time is precious and we have had to seclude ourselves and isolate a limited time to explore our thoughts on this subject. What a privilege it is to document being an artist and a mother; it is a journey of discovery for us both. It is rare as working mothers to have these hours to exclusively discuss the implications of our pregnancies or parenting skills, overnight and in total submersion.

As an illustrator, Maree's work is immediate, she has a very intense relationship with the marks she makes on paper. These can either be for commissioned interior floor rugs or paintings. The significant difference between our work is that Maree's is flat and two-dimensional whereas mine is in the round and therefore three-dimensional. Both offer undeniable challenges in terms of creativity.

We don't have nine-to-five jobs; there is no pattern or regularity. The only consistent thing about my work is the material I work with. I was seduced by glass over twenty years ago. It can be hot, fluid, melting, cold, coloured, clear, shining, matt or smooth. There are as many different types as the methods I use in the creation of the work I make with it. I love the material and am constantly drawn to the challenges it offers me. It is a material full of paradoxes and it delights me as much as it frustrates me. This passion for glass led me to the National College of Art and Design (NCAD) where I now teach part-time, sharing with students aspects I continue to learn about this material.

Maree and I both work to commission, producing work for interiors and exhibitions. We deal with private clients, gallery personnel and architects. The scale, budgets and clients can vary greatly; we never know what to expect of an enquiry. We are both open to all kinds of commissions and have a confidence stemming from our passion for the medium with which we work. We have never worked together on a commission; this is our first joint project.

As a visual artist the need to create is compelling, it is in essence who you are. It motivates you to extend yourself beyond what you know you are capable of. Self-belief in your own creativity is essential to produce work that drives this motivation. This is not always consistent. On good days, you believe you can achieve anything, on bad days you are crippled by self-doubt. The manifestation of your creativity is evidence of that self-belief. In ordinary circumstances, the energy required to push a thought from an idea into a visual object is enormous. It takes huge mental and physical energy, co-ordination, rhythm, single-mindedness and a calm depth of focus. During pregnancy, your focus is diverted. You retreat into a private world of an intense relationship with the life that is growing within. This also means an acceptance of your changing body. As an artist, there is a need to find one's own identity. When producing creative work, one draws on internal thoughts to produce an individual response to the work in hand.

The responsibility of the existence of an artist's work lies with the individual. Even if a large team of people are involved in the execution of this work, you as the director are responsible for remaining true to the original concept. In pregnancy and subsequently as a mother you are no longer a single unit. The onset of pregnancy brings with it massive anxiety as to your durability as a creative person without this singular identity. As soon as you know you are pregnant, it consumes your mind. Like many other women, pregnant for the first time, the growth of the baby and impending motherhood brought its own anxieties. We each read obsessively, considering every unfamiliar tweak and watching our bodies change with awe. Maree, who had been a midwife for many years, drew little comfort in her medical knowledge, when it came to her turn to be the patient under scrutiny! The adjustment of focus drains and undoubtedly draws from the creative process. This adjustment brought on feelings of panic, a feeling of crisis, not in relation to the pregnancy and the growing baby, but more about our individualism as artists, which led to feelings of vulnerability. We each wondered if we would find the additional resources necessary to continue the quest for this kind of individual response. How could one separate this feeling of being no longer one, to finding that self again?

Our anxiety before the birth was that our existence as artists was in question. Creativity is essential for our existence and possibilities for creation after birth felt undefined and insecure. We felt our validity as artists was in question. The need to create as soon as possible after the birth as a form of reassurance was an emotion that Maree found compelling. Prior to Ella's birth she had promised to make a 'mark a day' meaning an emotive response on paper to her immediate surroundings, each day. This has always been an integral part of the thought processes behind her work. It is the most natural and honest of vehicles for her expression. She worked every day before Ella's birth and the pregnancy didn't affect her in this pursuit. From the crowning of Ella, an overwhelming change occurred. Later she likens this to a suspension. Such a life-changing event made her wonder how she could possibly immerse herself in mark-making again. More feelings of panic. Ella was only a few days old when a box of tools, Indian ink and watercolour paper were on the table once more and urgent drawings were made. She doesn't generally draw flowers but that day she drew lilies, which were in her immediate surroundings. She equates the relief with the first bowel movement after the birth!

Both our partners are also creative. Self-employment and self-motivation brings its own tensions. As artists, there is no mapping out of a year plan, no forecasts, no structure to follow. I lean on Terry, my husband, as a sounding board, a Richter scale of potential reaction. From that I measure my own feelings about a concept or form I am developing. Our situation differs somewhat from Maree and Mark's, in that I have some fixed income from my teaching hours. A regular income brings some security on a financial level and a further dilution of your creative energy on another. As artists, we have confidence in our own resourcefulness but meshing earning potential with pure creativity is something all artists struggle with at most times in their lives. Juggling practical issues is common to busy people, but redefining the shape and duration it takes to develop ideas, has taken time to evolve. It is essential for us both in attaining this confidence, that we have been able to interweave motherhood with our creative lives. This juggling of projects with child-rearing has been possible by learning how to realign life with creativity: adjusting the focus and re-shaping our individual approaches to work while managing the practical issues as a team with our partners.

Superwoman – What the Mind wants to do, the Body will Follow
Prior, during and after the birth of my first child, Cuan, I believed that I could do it all. I committed to my first solo show, and decided on working right up to the expected birth date. My plan was to blow all the required pieces in the middle period of the pregnancy and leave the last months to the time-consuming but more sedate occupation of engraving and painting the surfaces of the blown objects. The reality was that I was miserable in the middle phase of my pregnancy. I could not take a proper intake of breath as Cuan was sitting so high in my abdomen. My co-ordination was all over the place and I was constantly tired. The 'blooming' phase never happened for me. 'Blooming' was supposed to be the pay-off for the nausea and crippling tiredness of the early months. Blooming dreadful was how I remember it!

Everything I made looked clumsy and increased my sense of frustration. In a physically demanding job, I had to come to terms with a lumbering body which increasingly became less supple as my pregnancy developed.

Glass-blowing is a rhythmic activity that combines co-ordination, timing, strength and endurance in varying measures. I love it; to me it is like a dance in which I can immerse myself, a wonderful series of movements which result in an object that are a reflection of those movements. With time and repetition, these movements become fluid, and the objects reflect this. With a changing body shape and a disjointed mind, which seemed to be working at a different pace to my body, I had to learn a new rhythm.

All pregnant women have trouble in carrying out daily activities. I found the practical movement necessary to make glass was determined by the new pace I was learning to accept. The body's refusal to bend in normal places governed the shapes I could contemplate making. My need to continue to create and the absolute commitment to having a show at a time when my viability as an artist was under question, drove me to stand in front of a furnace belting out a heat of 1100c! Actions of a madwoman indeed, but I honestly didn't think it was extraordinary at the time.

I remember clearly a very strong sense of myself and my baby, working together to produce these pieces. I recall that this was indeed an unbelievable way of marking our time together, a moment in time – our internal-external dance. These pieces were ultimate statements of our dual creativity. My body shape had become round, soft and very full, my skin was stretched to bursting point, my baby was pushing on my ribs making it difficult to breathe. The work reflected those shapes, strong simple shapes, a series of vessels that by their form suggested what they could contain.

In the middle of working on a large-scale public commission, I had a miscarriage. Whenever I visit that site now, I feel a huge sense of sadness, of something incomplete, unaligned. That which gives me wonderful memories for one child, makes me ache for another.

Maree's experience was different. The actual making of her work is also physical and at times is of a very large scale. Many pieces evolve from a direct response to marks she makes on paper. This work is created through building a series of movements and actions, the results of which remain on the page. These movements can gather momentum through repetition and sometimes are the result of extended repetitive actions. This makes the movement fluid and intuitive, leaving marks that capture that very action. She describes her pregnancy as an ephemeral relationship, an intimate relationship building in intensity, an unspoken ongoing conversation. The dual creation experienced by her and her growing baby was pivotal in particular pieces of work she made at the time. However, it is in retrospect that she associates the imagery, now clearly visible, as intuitive responses to her pregnancy; fragmented spirals, rich full circles intersected by a strong horizontal line, large inky painterly strokes, soft and moving velvet prints. These are durable expressions of moments in time.

Learning from intensity of emotion is something we both describe as remarkable and ongoing. Our frantic pace, of thinking you need to be superwoman, trying to remain the same, has become a realisation that it isn't necessary to do everything. Releasing ourselves from those emotions has allowed us to slow down to a realistic pace. Redefining important things in our lives has allowed creative space to emerge.

A Realistic Pace – Time to See

Learning a new pace is about taking time. Watching and being part of the growth and development of a child can be a measure of time, which is easily quantifiable. You can find excitement and inspiration in discovering the world through your children's eyes. Visual responses to everyday activities: the hand slung across Conor's chest as he sleeps or the shape of a morning stretch. The tranquillity of Tuathla sleeping, or the reaction of Conor as Maree pretends she is a dog, caressing, licking, panting, to rouse him, can be starting points for a piece of work. The significance of our children's experiences make us reflect on our experience, and in turn become our inspiration. These experiences become part of your motivation to produce specific pieces of work. There can be a myriad of reasons for motivation. It can be the materials you use, the nature of these materials and the endless possibilities they offer. Motivation can be driven by your personal inspiration, for me it is a tapestry of culture and time, communication and rhythm, moments in time, these are all part of my identity. Storytelling, music, language, history, tradition and customs. In making these pieces in glass, I am telling my own story and leaving something in return. Motivation can also come from other sources, from other artists you meet, read about or whose work you see which is filled with passion. It re-ignites and fuels your own passion.

By drawing on new resources discovered through mothering, it is natural to find creative solutions to everyday problems. Normal activities become extraordinarily special with children, such as digging up the onions, making homemade pizza, building a cardboard box robot. It inspires and will filter through our work some day. These ideas are banked and held until a time when the children are not as needful of attention and this saturation of our time. Probably by that time our direction will find other influences. It is essential to have a full bank at all times for any artist and being a mother has not altered that fact. Motherhood is a positive experience for both of us, which has enriched and fuelled our creativity from the early days of pregnancy. What is most exciting is that motherhood and our lives as artists change daily for us as all our children grow and develop.

CONTEXT

© Helen S. Callary

CHAPTER NINE

Mind-Maps: Motherhood and Political Symbolism in the Irish Pro-Life Movement

Valerie Bresnihan

There is something universal and emotive about all our understandings of motherhood. Even modern understandings of 'mother' are derived from old and even ancient symbols of motherhood. In other words, the deep symbolism of motherhood or woman as mother is neither culturally specific nor new, even in these times of rapid change. Motherhood from the perspective of the pro-life movement is examined here, although it is beyond my remit to trace the deep or historical source of this understanding. The notion of mother presented in this chapter has been found to be fundamentally shaped by classical thinkers such as Aristotle, Agustine and Aquinas. The following analysis was part of a much larger project: *Irish Political Culture, a Symbolic Analysis* (Bresnihan, 1997).

The narrators represent three groups from the pro-life movement, whom I shall call James, Brian and Nora. Each representative was interviewed twice in 1996 and all interviews were open-ended. This chapter focuses on their notion of motherhood only, a notion that is deeply intertwined with their idea of women in the home.

To fully understand their notion of motherhood, it is necessary to highlight some aspects of the political context in which they exist and the political principles they espouse; concentrating on the discourse of this group relative to one of their central concerns: social stability, or as James calls it 'social nitro-glycerine'. My central argument is that although utterly sincere in the declaration of their own particular principles, their image of motherhood is ultimately a guise to justify their unconscious fear of women.

Transcendent Political Values
The original – and larger – project concerned symbols associated with democracy and equality, which were embedded in Irish political culture. Thus, the first topic considered was this group's principle terms of reference for democracy and equality. They were quite clear that all political and secular values should be derived from religious values.

Some of these values are absolute which means certain political ends ought to be beyond any discussion within the democratic process. James expresses this most eloquently:

> Religious life [should] sustain and generate secular values ... even though values can come from many other places, this just means that religious values are not closed, in the sense that religion will pick up on values that are generated elsewhere ... lifelong marriage is a secular value that is religiously both generated and sustained but also has an intelligibility as a secular value ... the older religious viewpoints were sanctioned divinely but secular values were only sanctioned by the authority of science ... the kind of liberal argument behind separation of Church & State suggests that you can have public life without values ... you can't ... the rhetoric of state neutrality vis-à-vis moral values is a rhetoric of transition used in order to dislodge Christian values so that they may substitute their own ... [since] religion is the *only* source of values in the private and in the political domain, to speak of a divide between Church and State is not political science, it's just rhetoric ... in other words, religion is *the* human reality which generates values.

In complete agreement Brian, also says:

> if you stop thinking that (meaning the supremacy of religious values) then your foundation of democracy is already shaken.

Thus, religion is the source of both absolute and political values. As James sees it:

> The politicians' job is to squabble and compromise over means to agreed ends ... the striking thing about the ADC [abortion, divorce and contraception] debates is the imperfection of the whole thing ... these kind of things are not debatable, these are fundamental values ... politics, here, is not about consensus. Political recognition of the ADC's will cause immense social disorder.

Thus, for this group, the limits or extent of political discussion is very different from any liberal notion of politics, where for instance, the ends are not necessarily agreed. For this group also, the 'right' cultural conditions encourage the flourishing of Natural Law; e.g. all three narrators firmly believe that Catholic children should be taught in separate Catholic schools, as only these schools put the correct emphasis on religious values and their connection with democracy.

In sum, transcendent principles, or values as guides for democracy, are paramount and absolute. Certain cultural conditions are essential for the encouragement of these principles, e.g., Catholic schools.

Politics of Containment

The primary function of politics is to contain a particular type of, as Brian has called it, 'social heat', that if not contained would cause immense social disruption. I look now at how this overall policy of containment needs to be practically exhibited with regard to women and motherhood.

Marriage: Marriage must be contained in the sense that it must be maintained as a political and public life-concept regardless of the inevitability of marital breakdown:

> divorce gives social sanction to the idea that marriage is not a lifelong commitment ... marriage is thus politically devalued (Nora).

Or as James says:

> The approach I use is based on a common sense observation of what the effect of divorce has been on society ... divorce shapes the way they go into marriage ... and anyway marriage as an [official] lifelong concept forces men to mature by attuning their shorter-term needs to women's longer-term ones.

All three narrators mention that the rearing of children takes twenty years. For Brain, marriage as a political and public life concept reflects 'the balance of advantage for the country'. All three believe that when divorce is introduced into society, social chaos results. Interestingly, they easily accept that marital breakdown is inevitable and they do not have a problem with the existence of second relationships, 'second liaisons', provided they do not receive social sanctioning. These are the ordinary 'complexities of human life' (Nora). 'Children of second liaisons cope, teachers cope, they digest the system ... they are taking it on board' (James).

These three narrators have in common very specific ideas on, above all, social stability. They believe that 'fundamental' or 'Natural Law' is superior to any political law. Political debate ought to be about politicians squabbling about means to agreed ends only. If Natural Law is not rendered dominant by the political system then social chaos will inevitably result. Practically speaking, the primary function of politics is *containment*, particularly for certain groups of people: family breakdown needs to be contained by a no-divorce policy, for example. There is, however, an explicit acceptance of what Nora termed, the 'complexities of human life', e.g., the unofficial recourse to 'second liaisons'.

The Social Nitro-Glycerine Problem
Here are their views on family and motherhood:

Gender Roles
It is clear from the narrators' comments on the political issues that society is to be ordered in specific and even stratified ways: not everyone deserves political (public) recognition, with what they call second liaisons, being a case in point. In order to understand the underlying theme of motherhood, it is important to first hear what the narrators say about men's place in society. This is James:

> Men are more naturally ambitious and aggressive than women ... men are more interested in status and power ... when women compete with men on the basis of those two qualities then women will [always] have to put in more effort to keep up with men ... the occasional [woman with a] Thatcher quality ... nothing would stop her, that's grand ... I believe she should have equal opportunity to pursue whatever course she wants ... equality of outcome [meaning reverse discrimination or gender quotas] is unjust because you will not get the quality there ... these quotas will pass over somebody of better quality on the grounds that they are the wrong sex, that's unjust ... [gender quotas] create a brain drain because the more intelligent men will leave because women are taking up their places.

Although Nora and Brian have much less to say regarding gender stratification, it is obvious that they see women as homemakers only. 'Mothers need their children and children need their mothers, something which is politically incorrect to say in today's society' (Nora). Her main practical reason for a no-divorce policy is that fathers will abscond leaving mothers financially vulnerable; the fathers are the providers. All narrators are quite clear that they wish to see 'traditional family values' (Brian) re-instated into the political system.

A gender picture is now clear: the qualities of male aggression and competition are the unquestioned terms of reference here for a worker and the average women cannot be expected to emulate these particular aspects of maleness or masculinity. The implication here is that only the male sex may work. The second, but equally important theme, is the notion that women are best equipped to nurture. Parenting, then, seems to be women's primary function – and it takes twenty years for each child to be properly parented. In short, relative to the family, men are to be providers and women are to do the actual parenting. Relative to society, men because of their particular characteristics are fit for the public sphere but women are not. I now examine their ideas on working women.

Working Women

Working women are roundly condemned by all three narrators and furthermore are strongly associated with poor mothering and social destruction. Nora is eloquent on this topic: women in the workplace cause society to:

> self-destruct [and] children run riot all over the place ... when women don't work in the home the consequences are enormous ... just like Britain and the murder of the Bolger child ... I mean they're blaming videos and things but what sort of rearing did they get? ... it's obvious that working mothers' children will need remedial care, remedial education, custodial care and so on.

Brian, referring to working women and the consequences, says:

> So many of the ills of society begin from the working [mother working] family.

There are several other associations connected to dysfunctional families, working mothers and social destruction. The most overriding one is phrased like this:

> On the face of it, this chaos would appear to be due, at least in part, to the 60s sexual revolution (Brian).

For James:

> The new ideology of sexual freedom, having a relationship apart from marriage [means that] the kids who involve themselves in sexual freedom outside marriage are not involved in liberation at all ... these are the people who have demolished self-esteem, they are non-achievers everywhere ... you get a concentration of single parent families in some of the worst areas along with unattached males who often have psychiatric problems, we are now part of an amoral society ... families like that [are] social atoms ... if a man is brought up in a family without a male role model ... they tend to become sort of floating Barbarians without culture ... you have all these guys floating around with short emotional fuses ... they are asserting their maleness by siring ... that's *social nitro-glycerine* ... we're all going to be torn to pieces by the social debris of violence that will follow. I don't know what

> women can do now that they have less housework to do ... she has so much spare time because of all the technical junk like washing machines ... I don't know what to do about the fact that a woman has raised her expectations ... what to do about that I don't know. (James, my italics).

There are several explicit connections here. Firstly, sex outside marriage is the precursor to social nitro-glycerine and working mothers take a fair share of blame, as it is ultimately they who produce un-socialised men. Even if credence is to be given to James' remark that fatherless males become 'floating Barbarians' who are also associated with social nitro-glycerine, this group's comments on the demographic fact of smaller families put a different perspective on James' remark.

There is another deeper logic to this group's solution to social destruction, which is nothing to do with the art of mothering despite their claims to the contrary. James comments on the inevitability of the demographic feature of smaller families:

> I don't know what women can do now that they have less housework to do ... if women work, that is perceived as a problem, for who is going to rear the children and who is going to do the housework? ... she has so much spare time because of all the technical junk like washing machines ... I don't know what to do about the fact that a woman has raised her expectations but has ended up doing a job and a half and the man is still toddling along and they haven't done half the housework ... what you do about that I don't know.

Nora was content with the notion that, post-child-rearing, voluntary work and caring for one's, by then, ageing parents were the only activities suitable for women. Importantly, at no stage in these lengthy interviews did any member of this group see that the demographic feature of smaller families might inevitably imply greater freedom and thus greater potential to work *outside* the home for mothers. It should also be remembered that this group accepted the unofficial existence of the complexities of human life (second liaisons). It is important to observe that the freedom to work due to smaller families was the one inevitability (or complexity of human life) that was not realistically acknowledged by this group. This omission is important. If they can be realistic, relative to the other complexities, why not be realistic relative to the consequences of smaller families? Or does the above discourse clearly imply that fewer children and labour-saving technology, e.g., washing machines or 'technical junk' is deeply problematic for their overall worldview. Other reasons must be looked at for why women have to stay at home.

To briefly re-cap: I noted the idea that although women are intellectually inferior, they are still fit to nurture boys who will become superior men. I have also observed that the realistic acceptance of 'unofficial' situations – or complexities – does *not* apply to women at home, despite the obvious demography of smaller families and increased domestic freedom. It would appear then that women must still remain in the home, in the private sphere – no matter what. It seems therefore that it is not the intellectual inferiority of women nor, in particular, the *art of actual mothering* – as they would claim – but the actual *transgression* into the public sphere by women that is really at issue here. I argue that the traditional type of mothering as expressed here may be a suitable guise to keep women out of the public sphere. Within the deep structure of this group's thought, then, the nitroglycerine problem really pertains *far more* to (working) women than to unsocialised men – and thus to the problem of transgression.

The problem here for this group is ultimately the transgression of private woman into the public sphere. This raises a paradox: why does this group need to see women as intellectually inferior, powerless and ill-equipped for public life, yet also capable of acting as primary nurturers of those who one day will be superior, e.g., boys who will become men? Why are nurturing or mothering women seen to be sufficiently powerful to be the root source of all political stability provided they remain in the private sphere, yet they are perceived as dangerous when they become working women in the public sphere?

Avenues of Enquiry
Several avenues of exploration have provided useful answers to these questions but I highlight two that may provide some explanation. The first avenue begins with Pitkin's (1987) hypothesis that the individual psyche always has its political counterpart. According to Pitkin and others, there is a possibility that a traditional society – where mothers undertake sole parenting and fathers are generally absent from this activity – may actually help fortify and perpetuate patriarchal behaviour. In a highly stratified/traditional society, men must have their separate psychological and subsequently, physical space. This all stems from the psychological development of an Oedipal 'alternative' strategy by both young males and, in a different way, by young females.

For the boy, since he is unable to identify with his absent father, there always exists the cultural tendency to identify with stereotypical images of masculinity only. The deployment of this alternative psychological developmental strategy is fundamentally shaped by fear of the all too dominant and all-present mother and the difficulty of identification with the distant father. The individual male psyche creates a much needed 'male' space for his own survival – which can legitimately exclude women – in the political or work sphere.

The stratification inherent in a traditional society has repercussions for the female too. She has to resign herself to inferiority and her only status now exists in producing male offspring of great superiority. Thus, she too may unconsciously perpetuate a patriarchal society. If Ireland as a society can be said to still have deep-seated traditional elements to it, then this hypothesis – that the individual psyche has its political counterpart – may be of particular relevance.

Linked to the notion of motherhood within the pro-life movement is an international academic and historical element. Literature from the history of philosophy reveals that as the early Christian Church opened up the transcendent good life for all (a morally right way of living) regardless of status or gender, so too, somewhat paradoxically, it radically transformed the political thought concerning gender. For the first time it made explicit its ideas on sexuality. The general theme from the feminist literature suggests that, although women were believed inferior, there was something about women which, despite their clearly stated inferior status, aroused in men sexual desires that were inappropriate and distracting to achieving the good life. Also, generally and historically speaking, women were chastised, not only because of their inferiority but also because of their power to destroy or distract men from the morally right way of life.

For instance, several feminist writers, including Lloyd (1993) and Coole (1993) have argued that political philosophical thought throughout the ages has intellectually constituted women as different. This difference renders them not only incapable of civic virtue of the type attributable to man, but more importantly, although inferior, they are considered a consistent threat to the well-ordered state. The image of woman includes the idea of wild elements to be controlled. Under-lying debates of womanhood, there is a deep unconscious consensus which presents the feminine, or anything that is coded as feminine, as antithetical to qualities of citizenship, humanity, reason, culture and civilisation itself. Importantly, motherhood is often the vehicle used to rationalise the inferiority of women, as Aristotle, among others said, women were 'misbegotten men'.

In short, universally and historically speaking, women are unconsciously and symbolically presented as gatekeepers of the emotions, which threaten, yet energise the polity. Therefore, it is worthy of note that historically-speaking, women have always been seen to be part of the paradox mentioned in this chapter. That is to say, a feminist critique of the history of philosophy reveals that as far back as Aristotle and Plato, the body had definite symbolic male-female connotations within political philosophy (the male symbolising power, the woman symbolising inferiority); political society was subsequently ordered around these connotations. The images of motherhood from the pro-life movement, as a political mind-map (the political, philosophical, underpinnings of the movement), turn out to be an interesting example of this intellectual tradition. It would be foolish, therefore, as is too often the case, to dismiss the discourse of the above narrators as trivial or even out of touch. They do have the weight of historical thought behind them.

This group argues for a transcendent form of political equality and democracy or social nitro-glycerine will result. A politics of containment, related to divorce (and abortion and homosexuality which are not discussed here), is a way of both adhering to the transcendent (the path to heaven) and of achieving social stability. There is, however, a realistic acceptance of certain complexities of human behaviour, e.g., 'second liaisons'. This group's particular focus is on women as the sole nurturers of the family. Although women were seen to be inferior – the mind map presented here is thus clearly patriarchal – some deeper logic became evident.

In summary, I observed two things. First, from the pro-life perspective, the fact of demographically smaller families and fewer domestic duties did not release the nurturing mother from a full-time stay at home in the private sphere. Secondly, there was an explicit reluctance to acknowledge or explain their unwillingness to believe that mothers might go to work once children had matured. A paradox became evident. Women were seen as both intellectually inferior yet ultimately functioning as the anchors of social stability with the sole capacity of nurturing boys who will become superior men. But when women as mothers transgressed into the workplace, they become the source of the social nitro-glycerine problem. I concluded, therefore, that the transgression of women as mother from private to public, and not the actual value or method of mothering, is a problem here for the pro-life movement.

Two avenues for further exploration led to some interesting insight. The first is Pitkin's (1987) hypothesis that the individual psyche always has its political counterpart. This provided at least a partial explanation as to why some male individuals need a particular political 'space' – hence the fear of feminine transgression. Finally, and to put things into a historical context, the history of philosophy suggests that the politics of the three spokespersons of the pro-life movement was not as unusual or culturally specific to Ireland as one might have thought. Hence, there is a need to treat a political mind map as described above as a serious issue of political inequality – and of patriarchy.

CHAPTER TEN

Maternity Confined –
the Struggle for Fertility Control

Pauline Conroy

Introduction

The struggle for reproductive rights has been intermittently sustained from 1935 into the twenty-first century, with the fifth referendum on abortion in spring 2002. Here we analyse and chart this journey, advancing a chronological account of this historical, and as yet incomplete, struggle against the suppression of fertility control.

From the 1930s to the 1960s, fertility control was driven underground, manifesting itself in the illegal importation of contraceptives, back street abortion and waves of legal prosecutions against those who broke the law. In a second period from the 1960s to the early 1980s, a vigorous women's movement and not-for-profit service-providers advanced the limited legalisation of contraception. The twenty-year period from 1982 to 2002 was marked by five successive referenda on the theme of abortion, dividing and redividing the country on the same topic of pregnancy termination. Emerging from this analysis, the 'mother' is a potentially criminal or threatening figure.

Fertility Studies

Ireland has never had a fertility survey, nor has a major survey of family patterns been published since the 1970s. For a country so preoccupied with its own demography, these observations – drawn by Nic Ghiolla Phádraig and Clancy (1995) and again by Fahey and Russell (2001) in their contemporary analysis of aspects of Irish fertility – are striking. Fertility in Ireland was consistently high by European standards from the 1950s to 2000. Even with a decline in total fertility rates during the 1970s and 1980s, Ireland's rates still remained significantly higher than other European countries.

The most significant factor in accounting for this fertility decline according to Fahey and Russell (2001) was the shrinking in size of the large family. In 1960s Ireland, one-third of all births were fifth births or higher. By the 1980s, births in the category of fifth births or higher fell to just 15% of all births, while by the 1990s, only a small minority of births – 5% – was the arrival of a fifth, sixth or seventh child. Putting it another way, the average number of children born live to a woman in Ireland in 1980 was 3.3 children; in 1999, it was 1.89 children (Eurostat, 2000).

By the second half of the 1990s, a 'boom' in new family formation was occurring among those children born in the 1960s. Emigration had reduced. A rise in first and second births in new households of varying and diverse compositions was compensating for the shrinkage of families of four and five children to families of one to three children Fahey and Russell (2001). This places Ireland among the few countries in the European Union where a natural increase in the population, as opposed to inward migration, continues to play an important role in population growth.

Fertility Control Goes Underground: 1935 to the 1960s
Contraception was effectively legal for the thirteen-year period between 1922 and 1935. The forms of contraception available were primarily those used by men. Knowledge about birth control was circulating widely in the English-speaking and literate world of the time. Margaret Sanger and her friends had founded the American Birth Control League in 1921. This remarkable event took place shortly before the first National Birth Control Conference in the Plaza Hotel, New York that year (Sanger, 1971). By 1935, when contraception was outlawed in Ireland, social reformer, Marie Stopes, had sold three-quarters of a million copies of her controversial 1918 book *Married Love*. She had already founded the first birth control clinic for mothers in Holloway in London in 1925, which was visited by many thousands of women (Eaton and Warnick, 1977).

In Ireland, contraception was first banned by Section 17 (1) of the 1935 Criminal Law Amendment Act. The Criminal Law Amendment Bill was introduced by Fianna Fáil in 1934 and was described as a:

> Bill ... for the protection and suppression of brothels and prostitution and for those and other purposes to amend the law relating to sexual offences (Saorstat Éireann, 1934).

Kennedy (2001) provides an insightful account of the disagreements which criss-crossed the government advisory committees, prior to the publication of the bill. Despite advice not to introduce a total ban on contraception, a proposal to outlaw contraception was put before the Dáil, with the following words:

> It shall not be lawful for any person to sell, or expose, offer, advertise, or keep for sale, or to import or attempt to import into Saorstat Éireann for sale, any contraceptive.

There would appear to have been little opposition in the Dáil. The single most coherent set of opposing arguments was that of Dr Rowlette, TD, an independent representative who presented a seven-point opposition, which included arguments that a ban on contraception would lead to an increase in criminal abortion and infanticide, would damage the health of women and would drive contraceptive sales underground (Saorstat Éireann, 1935). In the senate, Mrs Kathleen Clarke, widow of 1916 patriot, Tom Clarke, opposed Section 17. They had lived in the United States between 1898 and 1907 and the experience of living there influenced Kathleen's decision to oppose Section 17 of the bill (Kennedy, 2001).

The 1937 ban on contraception was part of a package of legislative instruments aimed at controlling women's intellectual and biological reproduction. The 1929 Censorship of Publications Act provided for the banning of books:

> … on the ground that they advocate the unnatural prevention of conception or the procurement of abortion or miscarriage or the use of any method, treatment or appliance for the purpose of such prevention or procurement.

In 1935, the Public Dance Halls Act was passed which controlled, licensed and supervised places used for dancing. The infamous Conditions of Employment Act, 1936 introduced sex-segregated employment (Conroy, 1987). Seán Lemass insisted in the face of strong opposition that the bans on women's employment should be used to:

> … check any tendency to employ women in occupations in which men are now employed exclusively or to prevent women being employed in work, which because of its nature is unsuitable for women (Saorstat Éireann, 1935).

By 1936, a well-fenced package of legislative barriers to the advancement of the status of women in production and reproduction had been put in place. This package was the prelude to the insertion into the 1937 constitution of clauses which prescribed the place of mothers as in the home and omitted any reference to equality between women and men. Far from the 1937 constitution being the onset of the formal exclusion of women from economic, cultural and social life, it was the culmination of a discriminatory process. Between 1929 and 1936, a series of planned legislative enactments had the effect of systematically stripping women and girls of the right to hold jobs in emerging occupations, prevent or space their pregnancies, protect themselves from venereal diseases or read informative books about their bodies.

Some of the gloomy predictions made by Dr Rowlette in 1935 happened in relation to fertility. However, many women and girls did not wait around and followed a nineteenth-century pattern of response: they left the country (Jackson, 1984). Between 1926 and 1936, 57% of emigrants were women and girls, the majority aged 16 to 24 years (Commission on Emigration, 1955). In the period 1946 to 1951, women made up 58% of all emigrants (Conroy, 1987). During the period between 1926 and 1961, some 0.4 million women and girls left Ireland. The representation of women among emigrants from Ireland is one of the few social, economic or political spaces where women achieved parity with men.

The departure of so many young women and its impact on fertility and population growth in the country was not officially regretted. The Commission on Emigration and other Population Problems was nevertheless alarmed at the fall in family size in Ireland and the drop in population. How this fall in family size was achieved in the face of a comprehensive ban on contraception remained a worrying mystery for the commission. They referred to:

> … words and such terms as 'family planning', family spacing', 'family-limitation' and 'family-control' are frequently and widely used to mean arranging to have a small family of one or two children, or indeed no family at all, either from selfish or purely materialistic motives which are morally indefensible, or by the use of contraceptives or artificial means, or by other methods which are contrary to natural law (Commission on Emigration, 1955).

As a newly founded state, Saorstat Éireann had to identify, plan, form and construct an armoury of bans, exclusions and prohibitions to the integration of women and girls into the economic, social, cultural and political life of the state. Control over women's fertility in all its aspects was an essential ingredient within this strategy, which was complemented by control over jobs, juries, property, social security, education and training. This socio-legal structure remained relatively intact until the late 1960s.

The ban on women's employment in any designated occupation was coupled with the marriage bar or legal permission for women to be fired from their jobs on marriage. These measures were mirrored in social protection by the exclusion of women from participation or benefit from the main social security schemes, other than as dependent spouses (Cousins, 1995). At work and at home, laws and regulations akin to fundamentalism circumscribed the lives of women and girls.

It was with considerable difficulty that women's views could be expressed. Not surprisingly, this expression often took a separatist path through trade unions such as the Irish Women Workers Union (IWWU), the Irish Countrywomen's Association (ICA) or the Irish Housewives Association (IHA) (Conroy, 1999).

Back Street Abortion
The prediction by Dr Rowlette that a total ban on contraception would lead to clandestine or 'back street abortion' in Ireland happened. Back street abortion was to be found in both rural and urban areas and among older and younger women. Between 1926 and 1974, some 58 cases of back street abortion were investigated or prosecuted by the gardaí. According to Bacik (1996), the law on abortion fell into disuse in Ireland around the 1940s and 1950s. This is not born out by the facts. The largest number of cases investigated and prosecuted was between 1938 and 1946 when travel restrictions were in place and pregnant Irish girls and women could not leave the country and obtain an abortion or give birth in the UK (Jackson, 1992). Cases were being investigated or prosecuted up to 1965, up to the eve of passage of the 1967 Abortion Act in England. Prosecutions took place under a range of sections of the 1861 Offences Against the Person Act. It proved to be a remarkably useful act for the purposes for which it was used. It did not however, appear to act as a deterrent to the supply and demand of back street abortion providers and users.

An examination of press reports of the day of many of the cases indicates that most of the investigations and prosecutions were of those who were accused of having carried out, or assisted in carrying out, back street abortions. Prosecutions and trials were reported in *The Irish Times* and were therefore widely known about among the educated and governing classes (Jackson, 1983).

Commercial networks and nursing homes and other centres for illegal abortions existed. At least one was located in Merrion Square in the heart of Dublin city. In some instances, individuals carried out abortions for a few shillings on these poor women. In other environments, it was more expensive. Often, those accused had no medical qualifications whatsoever to undertake a termination.

The practice of back street abortion in Ireland, as elsewhere, was lethal. Deaths occurred. It is not known how many women and girls died. As the 1967 UK Act came into force in England (but not in Northern Ireland) in 1969 and 1970, prosecutions for back street abortion seem to have reduced or disappeared. Irish women and girls with unwanted pregnancies re-started the trail by boat to England, an odyssey that continues to this day.

1960s to 1970s – the Struggle for Control of Contraception

The main landmarks in the struggle to repeal the ban on contraception were concentrated in the ten-year period from 1969 to 1979. The movement for women's liberation took off in the English-speaking world in the late 1960s. The demand for access to cheap and effective contraception was high on the list of many women's organisations. Dr Joan Wilson, co-founder of the first family clinic in Ireland in 1969, describes the changing mood of the time:

> Television is obviously very important, but more than that I think it's exposure to the outside world; through the exposure to the EEC, Ireland has discovered it is part of a bigger community. In ten years, people have taken a bound from the 1900s into the 1970s, particularly in their emotional and sexual attitudes, even though it may not have been very well digested yet (Sweetman, 1979).

Knowledge of how fertility and contraception work, was stimulated by the appearance of books in the English-speaking world such as *Our Bodies Ourselves* (Boston Women's Health Collective, 1971). These types of publications popularised complex scientific and medical knowledge – which had previously been confined to medical professionals – into an 'alternative' perspective.

The years 1969–1971 saw a convergence of feminist activists, lawyers and doctors taking action, each in their own field, to undermine the ban on contraception. The Irish Women's Liberation Movement went to Belfast in 1970 by train and bought condoms, waving them at customs officials on their return to Dublin in defiance of the ban on importation. This highly publicised event was to mark the beginning of a decade-long series of direct actions by women activists and women's organisations, such as Irish Women United. Actions included flouting the law on the distribution of condoms, the picketing of political events, the publication of information on contraception in leaflets and brochures, the holding of meetings and the formation of campaigns specifically on birth control. Their actions were not restricted to calls to be allowed 'plan families' but for access to contraception for all women.

Members of the medical profession in the 1960s took the (then) daring step of opening clinics, which offered advice and the means to obtain contraception, in open conflict with the legal ban on contraception and the censorship laws (IFPA, 2002). The Fertility Guidance Company Ltd clinics, situated symbolically north and south of the river Liffey, represented alternative institutional arrangements for the reproductive health of women, to those of the public authorities. The clinics were a visible reflection of the flouting of both the law and Catholic practice by the population at large. The oral contraceptive pill was being used by tens of thousands of women. Students were purchasing quantities of condoms in London and bringing them back to Ireland for their friends. While the birth rate was not falling, family size was beginning to fall – a decline, which established itself in the 1970s (Fahey and Russell, 2001).

Repeated attempts were made in the Dáil and Seanad between 1971 and 1979 to break the ban on contraception through the repeal of section 17 of the Criminal Law Amendment Act and the Censorship of Publications Acts of 1929 and 1946. These were led by lawyer and public representative, Mary Robinson, as well as by Labour Party TD, Barry Desmond (see Appendix 1).

Doctors and clinics were prosecuted for supplying condoms, for promoting unnatural methods of contraception and for printing booklets on family planning. Copies of the UK women's magazine *Spare Rib* and copies of the *Manchester Guardian* newspaper, which contained an advertisement for the Marie Stopes Clinic, were seized at Irish customs and prosecutions followed.

A legal landmark was the successful Supreme Court case in 1973 of Mrs McGee (McGee, 1974). Mrs McGee, a married woman with a medical condition, had attempted to import contraceptive materials by mail order from the UK. They were seized by customs on arrival in Ireland and she challenged the constitutionality of that seizure up to the level of the Supreme Court. Mrs McGee's status as a married woman played a part in the Supreme Court decision that the state could not intervene in the privacy of activities of the marital bed. The decision created an unenumerated right to (marital) privacy in the field of fertility and sexual activity. This may be viewed as a vindication of a human right or a form of judicial activism (O'Connell, 2001; Gwynn Morgan, 2001).

The first Commission on the Status of Women of 1972 was obliged to address the issue of contraception by the lobbying of non-profit organisations such as the Irish Family Planning Rights Association and the Fertility Guidance Company Ltd to make submissions to the commission. While its terms of reference included to 'examine and report on the status of women in Irish society' (Commission, 1972), this did not automatically include their reproductive status. Interestingly, the commission turned abroad for support for their arguments on contraception. Citing the programme of work of the United Nations Commission on the Status of Women, which was then preparing for a new UN decade for women in 1975, the members of the Irish Commission considered that they were justified in considering the issue of contraception (1972). The commission recommended that information and expert advice on family planning should be available to families and married couples. With a charming delicacy, the commission proposed that it was: 'desirable that husband and wife should have available to them adequate enlightenment as to their rights and responsibilities'.

The McGee case was highly significant in breaking the vice-grip of the legal ban on contraception and restricting fertility control. It was to be another five years before a very limited family planning act to legalise contraception in Ireland was allowed through the Oireachtas in 1979 (O'Leary and Burke, 1998). Under the 1979 Act, every type of 'artificial' contraception, including condoms and spermicides had to be bought on a prescription from a general practitioner, with a minimum age restriction and other conditions. Nevertheless, it was a victory. This victory had been wrenched by a convergent activism of intellectuals, such as doctors and lawyers, representative organisations, such as those represented on the Commission for the Status of Women, alternative institutions such as family planning clinics, and the militant activism of women's organisations. This unique combination of social forces combined to force a change in the laws on the use of contraception, but divided when it came to abortion. Many women's organisations and feminist-influenced groups demarcated between contraception and abortion.

Inglis (1987) cogently argues that the influence of the Catholic Church was exercised primarily through its dominance in defining the role of mothers in families. It had deeply impregnated society with beliefs as to what was morally good and bad, and with rigid outlooks and views of how individuals ought to behave sexually and socially. The Church hovered in the background as lay organisations entered the terrain of fertility control in the abortion referenda that were to divide the decades of the 1980s and 1990s, following the 1979 legalisation of contraception.

1980 to 2002 – The Five Referenda on Abortion
The ink was barely dry on the 1979 family planning legislation, when right-wing Catholic forces started mobilising in 1980 to insert a clause into the Irish constitution to give a 'right to life' to the 'unborn' (O'Reilly, 1988). This was surprising in that there was no widely based public campaign to legalise abortion in Ireland and the membership of feminist pro-choice groups was small (Murphy-Lawless, 1998). During the previous decade, the focus of legal and militant action had been on contraception rather than abortion. It was not that Irish women, both north and south of the border were not having abortions, they were, but not in Ireland. Since 1968, women in Ireland had been going to London, Birmingham and Liverpool or elsewhere, to terminate their pregnancies lawfully, at their own cost, in private clinics (Jackson, 1992; Conroy, 1993; Mahon, *et al*, 1998; NIALRO 1989).

The first referendum campaign, lasting almost two years, was bizarre. Abortion was already illegal under the 1861 Offences Against the Person Act. The campaigners who sought to insert a 'right-to-life' for the foetus into the constitution had to whip up a fear of women controlling their bodies. A huge national anti-amendment movement, led by a coalition of women's groups and progressive individuals and associations came together to embark on a public and political campaign to persuade voters to vote 'no' in the referendum. Unlike the experience of the battle for contraception, the Irish intelligentsia divided, with many doctors, lawyers and commentators on both sides of the campaign. Women's groups and organisations were often minority voices in the public arena and in the campaign. An eighth amendment was adopted in the first 1983 referendum on abortion giving a mother equal status to a foetus in law (see Appendix 2).

The very public casting of women, pregnant women and mothers in particular, as threatening killers of unborn life imprinted deep and sinister marks on Irish society. Less than a year later, a public tribunal was held to investigate the events surrounding the finding of dead infants in Co. Kerry. The tribunal turned into a public ridiculing and verbal assault on a local mother (McCafferty, 1985). A number of women who organised and had been active in the Anti-Amendment campaign went to live abroad and have never returned.

The events surrounding the 1992 case of the child, Miss X, who became pregnant having been a victim of rape, had been forecast a decade earlier. Miss X, a child aged fourteen years, had been abused from the age of twelve, molested and made pregnant without her consent, by a married man, the father of a friend (McDonagh, 1992). Taken to England by her parents for an abortion, a friendly garda sought advice from her superiors with a view to preparing a prosecution for her abuser. This triggered a chain of events in the High Court and Supreme Court under which Miss X was effectively interned in Ireland and her parents subjected to High Court injunctions invoking the eighth amendment to the constitution. Emergency debates in the European Parliament, large spontaneously organised street protests and alarm expressed by civil liberties organisations intervened, as a swell of public opinion identified with the plight of Miss X and her parents.

In the course of the X case furore, an extraordinary event became known. Journalists discovered that a secret, and as yet unpublished, protocol, had been inserted by government negotiators into a European treaty, the Treaty of Maastricht, only some weeks earlier in late 1991. The secret protocol, unknown to the public or even the Dáil, removed clauses on abortion in Ireland that were contained in Article 40.3.3 of the constitution, from the protection of European Community law (ICCL, 2002).

The case of Miss X was not unlike that of the 1938 Bourne Case in the UK (R.1939). Dr A. Bourne performed an abortion on a 14-year-old pregnant girl in 1938 in deliberate contravention of the 1861 Act. Ironically, her plight was the result of rape by three defenders of the state: three soldiers. She had been gang raped and had become pregnant. Her parents sought the help of Dr Bourne. He presented himself to the police, 'confessed' and was prosecuted. He was acquitted on the grounds that he was preventing the girl becoming 'a physical and mental wreck'.

In the case of Miss X, she and her parents were released from the legal injunctions of the state and allowed to travel to England for a termination of her pregnancy. Her case revealed a circumstance in which abortion could be legal in Ireland. Three further referenda on abortion, on the right to travel outside Ireland and on the right to information on abortion services outside Ireland, were proposed. The National Women's Council of Ireland (NWCI) campaigned to adopt the latter two proposals. The vote of the electorate to have travel outside Ireland for abortion and information on abortion services outside Ireland made legal, infuriated anti-abortion campaigners who embarked on further agitation to reverse these minuscule advances. Meanwhile, each year, an ever-greater number of Irish women availed of the 1967 Abortion Act and had pregnancy terminations in the UK (Mahon, *et al*, 1998).

A subsequent Green Paper on abortion in 1999, a Cabinet Committee and an All-Party Oireachtas Committee on the Constitution Report in 2000 formed the prelude to a Fianna Fáil-Progressive Democrat government bill in 2001 (ICCL, 2002). The twenty-fifth amendment of the constitution (Protection of Human Life in Pregnancy Bill), in 2001 was to be the fifth referendum on abortion. At the time, over 6,000 women a year were having abortions in the UK (IFPA, 2001). By now, the women who had opposed the first referendum in 1983 were accompanying their children, teenage and adult, to vote on women's bodies, twenty years later. By a narrow margin, the proposal was defeated in 2002.

The struggle in Ireland to assert the right to control fertility passed through three sharply demarcated periods. In the first period, from 1935 to the 1960s, fertility control was pervasively criminalised. The second period consisted of a ten-year legal, social and political battle to decriminalise the use of a variety of forms of contraception by women and men. The struggle brought together a wide range of organisations and social forces of otherwise differing outlooks. The singular and united focus on contraception camouflaged an absence of a shared outlook on women's control over their bodies and the status of pregnancy and motherhood. This was to become quickly apparent in the third period.

The limited legalisation of contraception in 1979 almost instantaneously opened a third divisive period of campaigns over abortion; a subject over which a veil of silence had rested for many decades. Discarding or ignoring the existing criminal law, proponents of a total ban on abortion embarked on a twenty-year uninterrupted national and international battle of five constitutional amendments. The population were battered and baffled by theological and philosophical positions on the origins of life and the contents of the uterus. As in England in 1938, it was the plight of a child, raped and pregnant, rather than women's rights, which eroded the absolutist position in law: that abortion is always wrong and criminal. The five referenda were successful in instilling a fear in the vast majority of women of ever admitting to having had a pregnancy termination or knowing anyone who had. Yet, by now, about 100,000 women in Ireland have had an abortion during the last three decades.

The division of intellectuals over abortion relegated the majority of the population to bystanders. Large proportions of the electorate declined to vote in the five referenda. It is an irony that those who favoured this strategic road of constitutional activism in the field of fertility, by relying on the 'silent majority', lost their support in 2002. The projections of the pregnant mother as post-virginal innocent or a threatening figure to her foetus began to recede. This opens the door for the first time for a more reflective and comprehensive view of motherhood and an end to her political confinement.

CHAPTER ELEVEN
Motherhood, Sexuality and the Catholic Church

Betty Hilliard

Introduction

This chapter addresses the experiences of a sample of mothers in Cork City who were interviewed as part of a project on family research in 2000. These women had first become mothers mainly in the 1950s and 1960s, decades before the impact of feminism and the availability of contraceptives in the Republic; the birth-rate was high among these women and motherhood was the central role of their lives.

In talking about their experiences of sexuality, motherhood and the Church, the respondents painted a picture of domination, ignorance and fear, which is documented here. It is rather a grim picture: perhaps it should be stressed that most of the following material emerged in response to a very general question about life when these women were rearing young children. They were not asked specifically about sex and the Church, but these themes emerged very quickly in the course of the long interviews conducted.

It was possible, later, to trace how these mothers had responded to the experiences they describe. One aspect of their response was a distancing from the Church in matters of sexuality. This in turn resulted in a much more far-reaching distancing, the implications of which can be discerned in Ireland today – an issue also discussed in this chapter.

It should be noted that these women had already participated, a quarter of a century earlier, in an on-going project on family life. For this reason, there is occasional mention of their 1975 interviews. Quotes used in this chapter are taken verbatim from the women interviewed, but names have been changed.

Church, State and the Role of Women

A powerful aspect of the domination which the respondents identified was the alignment of Church and State in ensuring enforced domesticity, especially for married women:

> At that time you couldn't go back to work, you had to give up your job and you had to stay at home and have as many kids as you could according to Church and State at the time.

With marriage and domesticity, this sense of being bound by forces outside of oneself extended to the area of sexual intimacy. This emerged in a conversation about the difficulty of controlling fertility. For the most part, respondents did not see this control – or indeed control over their sexual activity – as resting in themselves:

> It was a worrying time to be honest with you. We were reared in a time when you had to obey your husband, we couldn't refuse them.

The terminology used by respondents in speaking of their marital sexual relations frequently alluded to the 'rights' of a husband to the sexual availability of his wife. For the wife, sexual activity involving intercourse was closely bound up with the possibility of pregnancy, another aspect of sexuality over which she had little control. The emphasis on child-bearing as the main role of women was especially identified as coming from the Church, as the following excerpt indicates. It indicates also the extent to which such norms were internalised and informed individual systems of belief:

> I suppose with religion ... you had to have your family, that was true if you had 26 or you had none but you were still compelled to stay under that rule. It was expected of you and you never thought of anything else.

This acceptance of Church control over issues of individual sexuality was deeply rooted in a perception of the embodiment of power in the priest:

> We were brought up in this sort of time that we had to – you know – if a priest knocked on the door everyone dropped when he came into the room ... they were powerful people.

While these descriptions of prevailing norms do not represent the whole story of life at the time, there can be little doubt that in the experience of these women the two decades to which they referred were characterised by an ideology of control and submission.

Sexual Ignorance and Related Fear

Perhaps the most striking feature of the sexual dimensions of respondents' lives was the lack of any knowledge regarding sex and reproduction which they brought to their marriages. Not one reported having received any sex education in their homes or at school. This is not to say that no discourse of sexuality existed; on the contrary, the potential evils of sex were a common theme in Church teaching. However, Inglis (1997) has suggested that this was a discourse devised by the pope, theologians, canon lawyers and bishops; certainly it did not allow for the discussion of the lived reality of individual sexuality in the lives of the participants in this study: 'These things were not discussed at all in our time.' The possibility of learning anything about sex from adult conversation was limited:

> even when I was growing up and they would be talking about anything like that you would be hunted out.

Active attempts were made to stifle any such discussion. One respondent recounted her mother's pronouncement on the subject as follows:

> There were things you didn't want to know and when it comes it comes and you have to face it.

Another described her mother's attempts to keep such knowledge from younger siblings:

> I can remember that time my mother wouldn't bring my younger sisters of eight and ten to visit me in the hospital for fear I might tell them how I had the baby.

The resultant ignorance of sex, conception and childbirth was widespread and profound, not only among the women in the study but also among some partners:

> We had no idea (about sex, even when we got married). I think then some of the lads were telling (husband) what went on and that was it ... we were stunned when we were having the baby because we didn't know how.
> Interviewer: You didn't know there was a process, that you had this physical relationship?
> No, nothing like that. I hadn't a clue about anything.
> Interviewer: Didn't you know how babies were started or born?
> I hadn't a clue ... it was the other women in the hospital that told me what was going to happen. I hadn't a clue and (husband) hadn't a clue either where it was coming from. We didn't know how it was going to come out and we were like fools.

The most extreme misunderstanding of the process of conception came from a respondent who in 2000 was still only in her mid-fifties. She was the youngest mother in the original sample and had begun having children in 1966. She recalled her belief even after marriage, that, irrespective of sexual activity, one would only become pregnant if one willed the pregnancy:

> I thought that I would want to have one before I'd actually get pregnant. We were very innocent.

Ignorance of the process of birth was even more widespread than ignorance of the process of conception. For most respondents the actual process of birth was a mystery, even as they faced into it:

> It was never discussed ... you had the fear. I would have known about the lead-up to it but the actual birth – no ... what was at the back of my mind was how was the baby going to get out. What was going to expand to that extent?

> I remember when I was going to have my first child I didn't know where it was going to come from ... We didn't know anything.

> My mother said to my sister that we better go up to the hospital because Ann thinks it is out of her ears that child is coming from. I didn't know where it was coming from.

A very common misconception was that the stomach would open around the navel area, the baby would somehow appear and the stomach would close up again. Even after giving birth, such ignorance could persist:

> I remember when I had (name) ... I didn't know how he was born. I had to ask her (the nurse) ... I asked her where did he come out of?
> Interviewer: Even after he was born?
> That's true, I didn't know.

For several, even the signs of labour were unrecognised:

> I started getting these pains and I went out to my sister and told her. She had one child at the time and expecting another one and she said to me you'd want to go into hospital girl, your baby is going to be born.
> Interviewer: Even your sister didn't tell you before it happened?
> No, no, I never knew. Even now, I wouldn't talk about sex with my sister.

The outcome of this lack of knowledge about such issues went beyond the feeling of one respondent that 'we were like fools' to fear, humiliation and extreme distress. Even after many years, the experience was still fresh in the mind of a woman now over seventy:

> They said 'Mary what do you think we're going to do to you?' I didn't know, 'are you going to rip me?' I thought they were going to rip me down and take out the child. They said 'didn't anyone ever tell you about it' and I said 'no' ... I had three very bad births ... because I was a nervous wreck and that was written down in my notes.

This lack of knowledge and fear of the technology surrounding birth was echoed by others:

> I can always remember, forty years last February, and I had seen them come in with the big bars and I said oh my God, where are those bars going to go? I hadn't a clue where the baby was coming from.

Added to the fears which were rooted in ignorance of the processes of birth, conception and even intercourse, were fears of pregnancy itself and of relentless childbearing. In the absence of reliable methods of birth control, these latter fears affected respondents' relationships not only with their husbands but also with their religious institutions.

Sexual Relations and Attempts at Birth Control

The experience of childbearing overcame much of the initial ignorance reported. However, increased knowledge of sexual matters did not lead to any sense of sex having a recreational dimension. The association of sexual activity with pregnancy was a universal theme in these interviews. As a result, talk of sexual relations tended to be inextricably linked to an awareness of the likely consequences. Only one of the mothers interviewed had used the contraceptive pill as a means of birth control. She explained, unasked, that her GP was a 'Protestant'. It is also appropriate to mention that she was the youngest in the sample. Another 'Protestant' doctor introduced one other mother to the coil having had eight children. Her husband refused to sign the consent form. For many mothers, however, such an option did not exist. Some had heard of it and would have used it if available, but explicitly stated: 'I couldn't get it!' Others corroborated this. One respondent who even in the 1970s interview had expressed approval of contraception and had a particularly bad relationship with her husband, still had children every year 'Because I couldn't get it. No, you couldn't go and get the pill at that time. That wasn't there that time.' One woman who had had cancer was told to avoid having children but didn't know how to go about this. 'What did we know how to avoid it at that time?' They couldn't give me contraceptives. '"We're Catholic doctors", that's what I was told.'

For some women the idea of artificial contraception simply never arose. Its non-existence formed so much part of the everyday world that it was not questioned. It was simply accepted and even religious objections did not seem to be to the forefront:

> It never entered my head and I don't think it ever entered his head.
> Interviewer: And would there have been any religious objection to it?
> There might have been a little bit, yes. It was wrong in the eyes of the Church and wrong in the eyes of the people. *We never entertained the idea* (my italics).

A consequence of the perceived unacceptability, non-existence or non-availability of artificial contraception was that women relied on combinations of luck, natural methods and their partner's co-operation to curtail the number of their pregnancies.

For many women there was a conscious sense of risk and lack of control: 'It was hoping from month to month; you took the chance you wouldn't get caught.' Some used the rhythm method or *coitus interruptus* but as many pointed out, this in turn relied on the co-operation of one's husband: '(It was okay if) you had a good man behind you and he appreciated you had enough children and couldn't afford any more.' However, not all husbands were understanding in this way:

> They wouldn't wait until your time was right every month, they would want to be – you know – in between they would want their little bit of fun and you wouldn't want to in case you got pregnant.

Avoidance strategies were sometimes utilised in conjunction with natural methods: 'we used to work by that – the rhythm thing … that and saying you've a headache. I had to do it, otherwise I could have twenty children now.' A mother of eight children who tended to get pregnant very easily similarly resorted to claims of indisposition to avoid having sex:

> I could have had another eight … with all the backaches I had it definitely saved me having another eight, oh yes.
> Interviewer: Did you really have them or was that your way of avoiding sex?
> Respondent laughingly: Oh, I've a backache. No wonder I ended up with a bad back!

A 1950s Mother

The efficacy of claims to indisposition was uncertain and pointed up the lack of control which women had over their sexuality: 'You had backaches, you had this and you had that but then it depended on the man you were married to, one man might just call your bluff you know and that would be it.'

The uncertainty of these strategies was a central feature of these women's sexual lives. Intercourse, even when enjoyable in itself, was beset with fears:

> Anytime you did have sex you were afraid of your life next day, you have this dread ... the dread! ... ah, no it was like a disaster trying to cope again and you're not able when you were trying to look after all the small babies as well.

This was echoed by other respondents, who, when talking about the fear of pregnancy, were asked if this had an effect on the enjoyment of sex:

> It affected people's marriages – oh yes – I mean you had that fear over you all the time. Sometimes – now I'm talking for myself – you feel you can actually bring it on yourself more or less like a false pregnancy, you'd believe you're pregnant because you worry so much.

> Oh, it would of course. I'd be terrified of having another child before I could feed or look after the first one. I'm being honest about that. It would interfere with the way you would feel towards one another – definitely ... You were afraid of your life it would happen. The fear of having another child would nearly put you up in St Ann's ... it would put you off and I'd prefer to do without it ... and they say it's enjoyable, I tell you I never enjoyed it.

The lack of enjoyment of sex was allied not only to fear of pregnancy but also to the absence of any positive representation of sexuality in one's upbringing:

> I'll tell you something now and people say to me that I am very innocent but I have never enjoyed sex. I didn't know what it was, that was the way I grew up. If I was going out my mother would say to me 'don't open your coat for anyone now'. She never told me what I was opening my coat for!

Despite the risk of pregnancy and a lack of enjoyment, there was a strong sense of a husband being entitled to the sexual availability of his wife:

> There was a strain – definitely – you're holding back, you're afraid, you know, but then it was more or less, well, you satisfy your husband, once he was happy that was it, you didn't think of yourself ... well that's what it came down to.

> We were reared in a time when we had to obey our husbands, we couldn't refuse them.

> I felt it was a sin to refuse him his rights.

The combination of lack of enjoyment and lack of choice or control was summed up poignantly by a mother of eight who, speaking of sex, stated simply: 'I didn't like it ... I had a big family but I didn't have any choice. I didn't.'

Despite its frequency and normality, pregnancy seemed to occasion a certain amount of embarrassment among some respondents. While this emerged in only a few accounts, it is worth noting as a further example of the alienation from, and lack of ease with, their sexuality, which many experienced.

Church and Sacraments

A central issue in these women's lives was their belief that avoidance of pregnancy was viewed by the Catholic Church as sinful: sex was for procreation. This was the specific purpose of marriage:

> Long ago you had children and they didn't care whether you had money to rear the child or not, that's what you were getting married for and that was that.

A consequence of this was the expectation of large family size:

> They (priests) didn't consider ... every woman thought she had to have nine or ten children otherwise she would be damned.

The prohibition against avoiding pregnancy applied irrespective of how many children one already had:

> Back when we got married the Church wouldn't give absolution [if confessed to avoiding pregnancy], you might be a wreck but you still had to keep going (having children).

Foucault (1976) has identified the development of an internalised compulsion to confession in early modern western society as a means of policing sexual activity, among other things. Similarly, Inglis (1998) draws attention to the role of confession in regulating sexuality among Roman Catholics in the nineteenth century. The power of the confessional in this regard, at least up to the 1970s, was evidenced in the fact that the majority of respondents felt it incumbent on them to confess their attempts at limiting family size. 'You had to.' This experience was in the main a very unhappy one: 'I dreaded going to confession ... I did have to say it to them that I was avoiding having children.' 'I dreaded going.' 'We were scared to go to confession.'

The main reason for this dread was that the stark choice in many cases was either to resolve to stop avoiding further pregnancies or to be refused absolution. For many women in this predicament, they already had large families and found it extremely difficult to provide for them. In the case of the following respondent, this was exacerbated by her poor relationship with her husband:

> When I had Kate, I had eight. When I had her I went into the priest and told him I was avoiding having a family. Eight! I had nothing, I really had nothing, and I mean nothing. I'd do without my dinner to feed my children and many a day I did. He said come back when you're ready to have a family, he would not give me absolution and *I have never been to confession since* (my italics).

This refusal of absolution was widely reported even in cases of considerable difficulty and sizeable family: 'My sister-in-law had six children and six miscarriages and he wouldn't give her absolution.' It was also perceived as a sin to decline sexual activity against the wishes of one's husband: 'Women couldn't say no to their husbands no matter how bad they felt or anything. It was a sin.'

This view was supported by some clergy: 'The priest would kill you about it, telling me you should bow down to your husband and all that.' A distressing aspect of some respondents' experience of confessing avoidance of pregnancy was being forced to give intimate details of their sexual lives:

> If you had a young child and you were avoiding having a family for a while you would barely get absolution … You would have to go into every detail, it was dreadful … What way were you avoiding it? … They drag it out of you … There was no need for it.

There was considerable evidence of variation in priests' handling of the issue: not all priests took a censorious approach. In some cases, women found a sympathetic confessor:

> Some of the priests were forgiving, you hoped for the best when you went to confession and told them things and other priests didn't want to know how you were doing.

> Some priests probably said do the best you can or something like that.

However, priests who digressed from the general trend could pay a price:

> I know there were priests who were silenced for giving advice to women.
> Interviewer: What kind of advice?
> Like that now, the sexual relationship with their husbands … He (the priest) was sent out to Africa.

A priest who was consulted regarding the use of the coil and was reported as saying 'you had your number and do what you like about it yourself', i.e., you've had enough children, now what you do is up to you, subsequently left the priesthood.

Another area of Church practice alluded to in the data was the practice known as churching. This was the custom of a woman going to church for a blessing after the birth of a child. Whatever the intention behind this practice, it was perceived in negative terms as a form of purification:

> You couldn't go outside the door until you were churched. Your mother
> wouldn't let you. You were made to feel guilty. It was done at the small altar.
> They'd bless you for having been a bad person (for having the baby).

Having a child outside of marriage was particularly censured. Girls
who were pregnant were reportedly married behind the altar. A respondent recalled the baptism of a child born to her unmarried daughter and her partner, again manifesting the variation in the approach
of priests:

> When the baby was to be baptised they weren't married at all and the priest
> (in the local church) refused to baptise the baby so she went to (the church
> in a neighbouring parish). The priest there said they were trying to keep the
> young in the church, the baby is an innocent victim so there was no prob-
> lem, and he christened the baby.

An element of censure is perhaps still evident here, in the contrast
between the 'innocent victim' and the implicitly non-innocent party;
nonetheless, it represents a movement towards liberality.

Although harder to categorise, there were other accounts of incidents regarding clergy, which had left feelings of bullying and humiliation in the minds of respondents. These stories were notable in
the freshness with which the incidents were recalled, often prefaced
by 'I'll never forget ...' and also in the fact that they significantly
coloured and in cases changed respondents' relationships with the
Church. One story was told by a woman about a day, years earlier,
when she and her husband had been together at mass. She was almost nine months pregnant at the time and chose to sit near the door,
as she needed to be near the air. The priest told her to sit up near the
front of the church. She had some sense of embarrassment about doing
this due to her advanced pregnancy. She interpreted the priest's insistence that she move as a display of power and a conscious humiliation of her. She resisted, saying that due to her condition she wished
to be near the door: he responded by saying then you can go outside
the door. 'I stayed where I was for the rest of the mass *but I never went
again.*'

The stories presented in this section would seem to indicate that,
despite some variations in individual priests' handling of the issue of
sexuality, this was an issue which was fraught with problems for most
respondents in their relationship with the Church.

Acceptance and Accommodation

In the initial years of their marriages, respondents appeared to accept the situation in which they found themselves in relation to sexuality and Church teaching. As one woman put it: 'I'd say it was all God's will, then, whatever has to be.' They accommodated the demands of Church and family and didn't question the societal expectations, which they had internalised. Other women accommodated the situation by adopting a strategy of deliberate distancing, choosing not to comply with the requirement to confess aspects of their sex lives: 'I never told them.' With the passing of years, however, the experience of high fertility, sometimes combined with significant poverty, partnership difficulties and ill health, brought strain to many. As the previous section demonstrated, this gave rise to levels of tension between official Church discourse and the everyday reality of what had become for many a problematic sexuality. The initial response to this tension in many cases involved a certain amount of distress characterised by feelings of hurt, confusion and, eventually, anger.

Confusion, Hurt and Anger

A widespread reaction amongst participants in this study to their treatment by the Church in relation to marital sexuality was anger. In many cases, this took some time to develop. Very often, the initial response to the onset of the tensions alluded to above, was one of passive distress and confusion, and it was only in later life that feelings of anger were recognised and voiced. One woman described her feelings when refused absolution by a priest: 'You'd cry.' She was crying for more than the refusal of absolution, she related this refusal to a stereotyping of women which subjugated all dimensions of individuality to the reproductive role, diminishing any sense of acknowledgment of the individual. 'They believed that's what you got married for, to have children.' In subsequent years, the hurt thus suffered developed into a sense of alienation, as will be seen later. In other cases, the desperation of their lives and the perceived harshness of the Church elicited a more immediate sense of injustice and anger.

The process of moving from confusion and dismay to anger emerged in several accounts. A woman I will call Mrs Black gave one account; she had thirteen children at the time of the first interview in 1975. Several of these children in the house at the time of interview were observably malnourished, a fact reinforced by the respondent's report that the family's main food was white sliced bread, and the home circumstances were poor. Mrs Black recounted how, when she had seven children whom she felt she couldn't feed (and was still in her twenties), she confessed to a priest that she was trying to avoid another pregnancy. His apposite response was that there would be a bed for her in heaven and that she should continue having children. Four more children later, this Mrs Black brought her young daughter for her first day in primary school. She was met by a nun who enquired if the child had siblings. When the mother replied that she had ten, the nun responded by saying 'God never meant you to have all those children'. In recounting this in 1975, Mrs Black expressed her distress and confusion; in her world view of the time both of these people must be right in their pronouncements, but they were expressing contradictory opinions. This was a real dilemma for her. By 2000, however, her reflections on this and related experiences had led her to a different position. She recalled other examples of the Church's lack of support. Among these was an incident when one of her children had picked some flowers in the presbytery garden: ruinously poor as the family was, the priest called on her looking for financial compensation. ''Tis he should have been giving me the pound.' Looking back, Mrs Black stated, 'I was angry all that time about them (sic) things.' By 2000, the time of the follow-up interview, she was very angry, and would have nothing to do with Church or clergy.

Other respondents commented on how acquiescent they had been to the Church despite the stress they had been under in relation to childbearing. Looking back, one woman exclaimed: 'And then I'd say, was I a simpleton?' to have accepted what she now perceived to be domination by Church and State. In 2000, she reported: 'we're very cross about it. I think all the ones around my age (she was 66) are angry.'

Although expressions of anger were widespread, more passive but equally deeply-felt emotions were also identified by some, for example by the following respondent, one of those refused absolution having had eight children, who wept several times during the interview in 2000:

> I had really no life, I really hadn't. Sometimes I get very … I wouldn't say angry but I get very upset … I'm hurt. I am very, very hurt.

These feelings of confusion, hurt and anger were further exacerbated by scandals exposing unacceptable sexual behaviour on the part of certain religious figures.

Disillusion and Betrayal

The scandals emerged in the 1990s and involved the discovery of
sexual liaisons and paternity on the part of a popular bishop and several prominent priests, as well as many allegations of sexual abuse at
the hands of the clergy in previous decades. These occurrences were
brought up spontaneously by respondents, many of whom were angry
at what they perceived to be the hypocritical stance taken by priests:
'They were laying down the law to you and I and they were having
their own fun afterwards.' The respondent who had wept in response
to a refusal of absolution summed this up: 'That time you felt guilty,
then as you got older and hear what the priests were at – the cheek
of them!' Coupled with this was a sense of disillusionment with societal leaders in general as role models: 'I have preached to mine, start
at the top (seeking good example). Whose example are they going to
follow (now)?' A perceived consequence of this was a decline in the
status of the clergy. Speaking of the Bishop Casey saga specifically,
one ardent supporter of the Church concluded: 'He knocked all the
religion out of people … it lowered the priests down to nothing.' This
was corroborated by others 'they were a cut above everybody else. So
now, with what is happening with the priests over the years … it is a
complete let-down.'

For respondents who had propounded Church teachings and defended the Church to their children over many years, the perceived
betrayal was particularly acutely felt. One such woman described the
sense of betrayal and loss at length. The following excerpt describes
not only her reaction to the discovery of the behaviour of a well-
known bishop, but the undermining of her position with her daughter because of this. Although lengthy, it bears consideration:

> I will never forget until the day I die, the Bishop Casey saga. I was ironing
> out there and I thought I heard something on the radio. I came in and said
> to my husband, 'I'm sure Bishop Casey is resigning, he must not be well' and
> I continued with the ironing and lunch. Later on that night it came on again.
> The following day anyway, they talk about bereavement and things but
> shock was the initial thing. I can't describe to you what it did to me inside,
> it was like there was a hole there that could never be filled. The shock I got,
> personally, that day! The more I thought about it and the things that fol-
> lowed, I can say it damaged my whole life.
>
> This was a great opportunity for (daughter) to have a go at me so she
> came in to see me. 'Sit down there and we'll have a cup of coffee' and she
> draws a deep breath, 'well Mam,' she said 'what have you to say for yourself
> now?' 'About what, what did I do?' She puts this face on and said 'I don't

have to spell it out to you.' I said I had heard about Bishop Casey that morning telling her I thought he was ill. I sat there and *I hadn't the answers for her* but I said, 'to be honest it is a bigger shock to me than it will ever be to you' (my italics).

This passage is worth consideration for a number of reasons. Important among them is the identification of a moment when the authority of Church teaching is irreparably undermined, not only in the eyes of her daughter but more importantly in her own eyes – 'I hadn't the answers for her'. It captures the demise of the mother's role as the defender and transmitter of Church teaching suggested by Parsons' concept of the family function of latency (1956), a role to which Inglis (1998b) specifically attributes the implementation of the sexual discourse in Ireland. The sense of a crisis and a transition point is palpable: 'The more I thought about it and the things that followed I can say it damaged my whole life.' Further, it graphically illustrates the end of an era of certainty and affirmation: 'It was like there was a hole there that could never be filled.'

Discernible here too is her response as a form of bereavement, particularly the two early stages of shock and denial in that process. The anger stage was perhaps to be found in her 'grievance with our own clergy below' and her belief that 'he should have come out himself and made a statement.' The later stage of acceptance is also to be found in her account: 'I said Bishop Casey did wrong, he is human too ... the ten commandments are still there.'

This respondent went on to elaborate on related issues, which further undermined the Church in her eyes. Chief amongst these was the fact that the local clergy did not refer to an issue of such momentum:

> We were three solid weeks down there on a Saturday night and there wasn't one thing mentioned about it. I often felt like standing up and saying 'what do you propose to do or say to us?' To acknowledge it was all I wanted. Eventually a young clergyman, still only a deacon, was the one deputed to address the issue with the congregation. I don't know how he started anyway, something like 'I suppose you're all in a state of shock about what came out over the radio.'

The point she was making was the fact that the regular clergy, who should have been the ones to confront the issue, reneged on their responsibility:

He was the one saddled with the job, he wasn't even ordained [priested], to come out and confront the whole church. I don't know how many of them did know but it was up to the parish priest, it was his duty to come out and say it, he was more experienced and he knew his clergy.

Critical Thinking

The circumstances outlined above caused many respondents to look reflectively at the situation. In the main, this resulted in a critique of the Church even on the part of women not directly affected by the Church's position on sexuality. By critical thinking in this context, I mean the questioning of a situation or set of circumstances, leading to a new appraisal of the situation. Such a process is exemplified in the account of a woman who had been forbidden to use artificial birth control but had been sent by her confessor to the family planning service to learn of natural methods. Reflecting on these natural methods of birth control, she perceived a common underlying principle with that of artificial methods and accosted the nurse on this point: 'I said that to the one down there [isn't using natural methods avoiding it – pregnancy – too?], she said of course it is. I said why is that right and the other wrong?'

No satisfactory response being forthcoming, this respondent concluded that no significant difference existed in principle. This radicalised her position on the matter: 'Let him [the priest] buzz off so, and that was the end of it. They weren't told any more then.'

This change in practice, a coping strategy used by many respondents, would seem to indicate a transformation from the acceptance of control by others, to a greater reliance on one's own individual analysis of the situation. Allied with the changing practices in relation to confession, there is a clear movement of change in the social agencies/individual decision-making balance.

Consciousness of Control

It has been possible to discern changes in thinking and practice in the course of the quarter century between the first time these respondents were interviewed and the second. As the years moved on, a new degree of reflexivity and awareness appears to have developed; in particular an awareness of having been dominated by forces outside themselves which had far-reaching effects on some of the most intimate aspects of their lives, including fertility, sexual relations and religious practice. In the mid 1970s, answers to questions on issues relating to religion or politics, such as contraception and Church teaching, were never couched in terms of power or control. By 2000, these terms were freely used. It would seem that in the 1970s, there was a certain passive acceptance of the way things were, exemplified in such phrases as 'I'd say it was all God's will then', 'It was expected of you and you never thought of anything else'. However, a quarter of a century later, this mind-set among respondents had markedly changed, *including* among people who were still active mass-goers and supporters of the Church. People spoke of earlier expectations regarding authority and acquiescence, and compared these with life in late twentieth-century Ireland, perceiving very significant change to have taken place. 'The Church had too much control ... now they don't have the control.' One woman who expressed a lively faith, who goes to weekly mass and says the rosary nightly described her changed attitude to the clergy by saying: 'I wouldn't look up to them now for anything.' Another described the change thus: 'I think it's more open now and they [young people] can ask questions ... They're not afraid any more ... They won't be bullied by anyone like we were.'

Although there were some references to political figures, power and control were almost universally associated with religion by respondents. In relation to this, an important distinction was perceived between godly authority and Church authority. One respondent, again a very devout Catholic, who had not had problems limiting her family, as she had been able to have only one child, summed up this perspective succinctly:

> I think they made the Lord look like a very hard master, which I don't think He is myself. I think *they* were the masters.
> Interviewer: The priests?
> Yes, I wouldn't blame them either. They were only doing what the pope told the bishops and they passed that information on to them so they were only doing their job.

The awareness of domination can be identified in the above as arising from three specific aspects of the women's experience, namely: the impact of the Church position on contraception; the scandals which beset the Church in the 1990s; and the perception of previously respected leaders of society as venal and dishonest. The sense of hurt, of anger and of disillusionment experienced in response to these events has already been addressed. These feelings had significant consequences not just for these women but also for Irish society, and in particular for the Church in Irish society.

Rejection and Withdrawal

In this chapter, there have been many accounts of respondents' difficulties with the Church on the issue of attempting to limit their families. Many of these respondents perceived themselves to have been treated harshly and unfairly, especially as attempts at family limitation usually took place in the context of already having sizeable families. One of the significant outcomes of this perception was the extent to which women rejected the treatment they had suffered and withdrew from their previous roles in relation to the Church. This happened in various ways, all of which involved changes in practice.

The mildest reaction was to continue with attempts at family limitation but to stop confessing them ('They weren't told any more then'). In some cases women stopped going to confession altogether. Although mild, these reported changes in practice mark a crucial turning-point in that they indicate the beginning of a breakdown in the acceptance of Church dominance of marital sexuality. More seriously, many women ceased to go to mass or to receive sacraments. Some of these, although alienated from the Church, continued other forms of religious observance, including personal prayer, the use of holy water and veneration for statues and blessed medals:

> So, I never went back [to mass or confession]. Now I say my prayers every night … I pray for people on the streets, people without homes, people at sea, oh I do say my prayers every night.

A woman who described herself as having 'lost my religion' reported that nonetheless she would bless herself, keep statues and use medals as well as holy water. This was not unusual. The ambivalence towards religious matters manifested in this attitude is further addressed later.

Another crucial change in practices resulted from the sexual scandals which rocked the Church in the 1990s. 'Bishop Casey put the kibosh on it. He knocked all the religion out of people.' Not everyone attributed the demise to Casey; respondents were in some cases quite understanding of him, making distinctions between him and, for example, paedophile priests, abuse of authority, bullying, lack of compassion and irresponsibility. For many, these revelations irreparably changed the position of moral authority which Roman Catholicism had enjoyed up to that point. This was as true for those who continued as devout Catholics as it was for those who withdrew from the Church. 'I think everything has gone out the door with what is happening with the priests and everything else.'

Excerpts from the interviews illustrate the damage done to the credibility of the Church by these scandals. The central issue seems to have been a sense of betrayal by an institution which had been invested with enormous amounts of trust, deference and commitment on the part of its members. With the erosion of this trust, many practices which were taken for granted were called into question, and the strong position which the Church had occupied began to be subjected to scrutiny.

De-Legitimation and Non-Transmission

The mothers in the previous section clearly no longer accorded the Church the automatic legitimacy it had previously enjoyed. They withdrew acceptance of the validity of the Church's claims to authority and the willingness to be bound by this authority. Most respondents did not articulate this process so explicitly; nonetheless a major shift had taken place as a result of their analyses of the phenomena discussed, leading to new perceptions and reappraisals of earlier practices: 'I explained the situation to him [the priest], now today I would not explain anything to him.' Another respondent said: 'I think people were spastic with all the things they were telling the priest, may God forgive me.'

A shift in the locus of moral authority took place, away from the Church and towards the individual or the married couple. Such a change is illustrated in the comments of a woman who had been against contraception when interviewed in 1975. While still very religious, her position had changed:

> We were very scrupulous Catholics, we were all damned but I think the people are changing their views about the Church now. I would say the family ... should be limited, have the amount of children you think yourself that you can keep comfortably and educate.

Many respondents expressed similar views:

> I think it's between husband and wife to sort out these matters.

Expressing the view that married people were no longer listening to the Church in matters of sexuality, one of these respondents explained the situation thus:

> I would put that down to a lot of hardship, you know, in their own life, looking back. They had a lot of unnecessary hardship growing up and now

they are not going to have those enormous families that they can't keep. I
think they are going to use these contraceptives, they are using them, to
limit their families and try to educate them. It is only common sense when
you think about it.

Although she attributed this perspective to others, this woman had
spoken with great bitterness earlier of the consequences for her of
coming from a very large family; she had had to leave school very
early and work hard to support her younger siblings.

Not only did the authority of the Church come to be damaged;
for many women the legitimacy of their own positions as defenders
and transmitters of the faith was irreparably undermined, summed up
in the poignant phrase of one respondent speaking of a discussion
about the Church with her daughter: 'I hadn't the answers for her.'

In many of the families where the women's relationship with the
Church had been damaged, the traditional robustness of children's
socialisation into the Church waned. This was a crucial moment in
the Church's loss of power; some mothers no longer took the role of
transmitter and enforcer of religious practices: 'I would not put that
pressure on my children, not the way the Church turned out.'

Whether pressure to conform was exercised by parents or not,
many mothers in the interviews in 2000 said their children's practice
concerning the Church had changed very significantly.

Tensions between Discourse and Practice
It is evident that significant tensions built up in the relationship between the pressures of these women's lives, particularly in relation to
sexuality, and the Church. These tensions became untenable in many
cases and resulted in a rupture between official Church discourse and
lived practices; put simply, people's beliefs and behaviour changed in
a remarkably short period of time. This had crucial consequences for
the spread of Church discourse and practice; in many families a radi-
cal change in these areas took place in the space of one generation.

Ideological Change
Although the relationship between the Church and many of the
people in this study was seriously ruptured, it was by no means the
case that they no longer had any means of religious expression or
abandoned a spiritual dimension in their lives. Practice changed, as
has been seen above from their rejection and withdrawal. Perhaps
even more significantly, thinking changed radically also. This was

true even of those who continued to be devout in the practice of their religion, including church-going. One respondent, for example, who described herself as a religious person and was certainly a church-goer, felt able to distinguish quite clearly between allegiance to God and allegiance to the clergy. She believed that even where priests had refused women absolution, they could continue as practising Catholics. Because of education and of the problems of unlimited childbearing 'people are not as cowed down as they were where the Church is concerned'. She did not feel that this was necessarily negative or that it should result in alienation from one's faith:

> I would think it's not a bad thing. You can always hold your simple faith in God; it is not necessary to come away from your religion. Have your simple faith and hope in God, go to mass and the sacraments.

Even where priests excluded one from the sacraments, in her view a continued relationship with God was feasible: 'I would think that if you had your own faith in God you could overlook their orders a little bit and go back to your God.'

Less devout respondents who had completely given up church-going, also held a similar view: 'I believe in the one-to-one.' A clear shift took place in the basis of morality; this was a movement away from a pre-existing moral order propounded by the Church, towards a more individualistic morality based on a greater confidence in the legitimacy of one's own experience. Part of this was a movement away from an acceptance of the role of the Church as mediator between the individual and God, towards a sense of a more direct relationship between the individual and God. This is a very significant departure from the ideology of the previous quarter century described in the early part of this chapter, and more specifically a departure from the Roman Catholic Church ideology of that time in relation to married women's sexuality.

CHAPTER TWELVE

The Magdalene Experience

Patricia Burke Brogan

The first image that flashed across my mind when I was invited to write a chapter on the Magdalene laundries was the Credo Scene, Act 1, Scene 5, of my stage play, *Eclipsed*. Sister Virginia prays as she lies prostrate, then kneels before the tabernacle in the convent oratory:

Sister Virginia:	I believe in God the Father Almighty, Creator of heaven and earth and in Jesus Christ His only son Our Lord, who was conceived by the Holy Ghost – I believe in God – God? – I believe in God – I try – I believe in God the Father Almighty, Creator of heaven and earth and in Jesus Christ His only son Our Lord, who was conceived by the Holy Ghost, born of the Virgin Mary –
	(Interrupted by voices of the women)
Voice of Brigit:	Keys! My baby, Rosa! I have to find my baby!
Sister Virginia:	Born of the Virgin Mary, suffered under Pontius
	Pilate. Was crucified, died and was buried.
	(Sound of Cathy's asthmatic breathing)
Voice of Mandy:	It's Cathy! She's Chokin', Sister!
Voice of Nellie-Nora:	A Kettle! Steam! Hurry, Sister! Hurry!
Sister Virginia:	Was crucified, died and was buried. He descended into Hell.
Voice of Mother Victoria:	Mandy thought she could leave if she wasn't pregnant, so she performed an abortion on herself!
Sister Virginia:	He descended into Hell. The third day He arose from the dead.
Voice of Mother Victoria:	We gave them food, shelter and clothing. We look after their spiritual needs. No one else wants them! No one else wants them!
Sister Virginia:	The third day He arose from the dead.
Voice of Mother Victoria:	A vow of Obedience, Sister! Blind Obedience!

'Mothers for a Moment, Cloistered Forever', writes Anita Gates in her review of the off-Broadway New York production of *Eclipsed* at the Irish Repertory Theatre, November–December 1999.

The back entrance of a Dublin convent where Magdalene women are still living

The image of Eve as the seducer of man and the sinner who lost the Garden of Paradise for all of humanity, cast its shadow over women's lives. Deep within that shadow we find the Magdalene Home Laundries. From the time of the Potato Famine until the early 1970s, the 'fallen women' of Ireland, unmarried mothers, who had broken the sixth or ninth commandments, scrubbed society's dirty clothes. Betrayed by lovers, signed in by families or guardians, they lived a spartan and loveless existence. Those who became institutionalised remained inmates for life and were buried in nameless graves. Many nuns, in charge of the laundries, were trapped by Famine-guilt attitudes and by the rigidity of convent rules. Questions concerning social justice and the responsibilities of unmarried fathers were rarely asked. *Eclipsed* is set in a fictitious Magdalene Laundry, which is attached to St Paul's Convent in Killmacha. However, the repression, judgement and compassion stem from harsh reality.

One summer evening, a Mistress of Novices tells me, a white novice: 'A sister has been taken ill in one of our branch houses. You will take her place for a week. Mother Superior of our branch house will inform you of your duties.' Next afternoon, the same white novice kneels as the black-veiled Mother Superior takes a bundle of heavy keys from her office desk. 'Follow me, Sister!' She unlocks a door. We enter and she relocks the door. Keys and rosary beads rattle as we walk down a long brown-black corridor. We come to another heavy door.

This door is again relocked and bolted when we pass through. Sudden crashing noise! Steam! Grey walls pocked with moisture. Stench of bleach. Stench of sweat. Prison bars pattern the roof windows.

Under double lock within this pious cage, rows of women scrub clothes as they bend over porcelain sinks. Others seem to merge with huge womb-like washing-machines. Mother Superior turns and speaks sternly. 'Fasten these keys to your girdle, Sister! On no account are you to let any of the penitents escape. Be very careful in this laundry!'

'Why are – the women – locked away, Mother Superior?' I ask.

'These women can't be trusted. They're weak, Sister! No control! If they get out, they'll be pregnant again within a few months!'

A bell rings. Mother Superior gives me a blue-check apron and returns through locked doors to her office. Eyes, eyes, eyes! Watching, staring, watching! Young women, middle-aged women, others, white-haired and crippled with arthritis, glare at their new white-veiled jailer. My own introduction to a Magdalene Laundry.

The Galway Magdalene Laundry was established in 1875. It was demolished in 1990.

Eclipsed has a strong pagan versus Christian subtext. Early Celtic Christians, as well as pagans, respected motherhood. This changed with the arrival of Norman/Roman influences. Women lost their Brehon privileges, ownership of land, power in the family, the right to divorce their husbands. They became chattels. They and their wealth now belonged to their husbands – the patriarchal system. Killmacha, the fictitious town where I placed my Magdalene Laundry, is a combination of pagan and Christian words. 'Kill' (cill) is the Anglicisation of the Gaelic for church or cell/oratory of the early Church. Childbirth was sacred in pagan Celtic times. Macha, the sun/fertility goddess, was famous in ancient Ireland. According to tradition, the pregnant Macha, in order to save the life of her husband, had to compete in a race with two of the king's horses. She pleaded with the king and his assembly, 'Help me, for a mother bore each of you! Give me, O king, but a short delay until I am delivered.' The king refused her request and Macha put a curse on Ulster. In *Eclipsed*, Macha's plea is echoed by Sister Virginia, when she lies prostrate in prayer before the oratory altar:

> Sister Virginia: Christ Crucified, help them! For a woman bore you, carried you for nine months! Mother of Jesus, do something about Cathy, Mandy, Nellie-Nora and the others! When

you arose from that tomb, women were your first witnesses!
Your first miracle was performed at your Mother's request!
– Help us! – Help me!

Brigit Murphy, one of the characters in *Eclipsed*, is called after St
Brigit, but also after a pagan goddess. Brigit Murphy is the rebel, the
countrywoman, who refuses to accept her penance. When Christianity arrived in Ireland, it had to contend with Brigit, a folk image,
and the greatest female figure in Irish history. St Patrick, in his wisdom, incorporated pagan customs, wells and mountains into his Christian teachings. Holy wells were previously Celtic pagan places, where
the goddesses of fertility were honoured. The feast day of St Brigit is
on the first of February, the beginning of spring. The feast day of Brigit,
the pagan Celtic goddess, was also on the first of February. Brigit's
Cross is a Christian symbol superimposed on a sun-goddess symbol.
This folk image resonates in the play. Stage directions for the play
call for a St Brigit's Cross on the laundry wall-cupboard.

Despised and Rejected
These penitent women vanished from society. They were mostly buried in nameless graves. However, since *Eclipsed* was first produced in
1992, eight black marble gravestones, each bearing twelve engraved
names, have been erected in the graveyard of the Galway laundry.
Some of the named women died in the 1880s. Other engraved gravestones have been erected on the two large burial plots in the New
Cemetery, Bohermore.

In 1990, I watched the demolition of our local Magdalene Laundry. Soon afterwards, I wrote the following poem:

Make Visible the Tree

This is the place of betrayal.
Roll back the stones
Behind Madonna blue walls.
Make visible the Tree.
Above percussion of engines
from gloom of catacombs,
through a glaze of prayer,
scumble of chanting,
make visible the Tree,
its branches ragged
with washed-out linens
of a bleached shroud.

In this shattered landscape,
sharpened tongues
of sulphur yellow bulldozers
slice through wombs
of blood-soaked generations.

This is the place
where Veronica
forsaken
stares and stares
at a blank towel.

Why were these refuges for 'fallen women' called Magdalene Laundries? Mary Magdalene is not the woman of the city. St Luke's Gospel, Chapter 8 is very specific: the woman mentioned is Mary from the town of Magdala in Galilee, known today as Mejdel. She is named and mentioned fourteen times. This was very unusual for women of those times. The only woman mentioned more often is the Mother of Jesus. The woman taken in adultery, the woman with an issue of blood, not even the Samaritan woman at the well is named. Due to an early medieval confusion, sometimes attributed to Gregory the Great, Mary Magdalene became the Eve of the New Testament. The error has seldom, if ever, been officially corrected. Artists down the centuries have painted and sculpted images of Mary Magdalene as a repentant sinner. Her 'sins' have been forgiven, but stains of her sins remain. As a result, her particular apostolic work has not been recognised. Called by name, she was identified by a place and described as a leader of women who followed Jesus and supported him out of their own resources (Luke 8). A very important participant in the public life of Jesus, she saw the truth and told it. Mary Magdalene, Mary, Mother of Jesus, and the apostle, John, stood together at the foot of the cross. With other women, she went to the tomb to anoint the body of Jesus. The chosen apostles, disciples and followers had distanced themselves from his work, his teachings and his life. It was Mary Magdalene, not any of the twelve apostles, who first saw the risen Christ. She has been ECLIPSED. Even today, filmmakers and documentary makers continue to perpetrate the error.

In 1766, Lady Arabella Denny founded the earliest recorded Magdalene Asylum as a shelter for teenage Protestant unmarried mothers. They were called Mrs One, Mrs Two, Mrs Three, etc. In convent shelters/refuges, the penitents were given saints' names, but were not allowed to choose their favourite saint's name. In the nineteenth century, there were at least twenty-two refuges for penitent women in Ireland. Some of these were attached to convents. The Good Shepherd nuns ran home-laundries in Cork, Belfast, Limerick, Waterford and New Ross. The Sisters of Mercy ran home-laundries in Galway, Tralee and Dun Laoghaire. The largest home-laundry in Ireland and England was run by the Sisters of Our Lady of Charity of Refuge in Drumcondra. There were similar home-laundries in England, Scotland and Southern Italy. The children of the 'sinners' were taken from them after birth and were either adopted or placed in orphanages. Some of the orphans were fostered out to farming families.

In *Eclipsed*, Act 1, Scene 3, the asthmatic Cathy longs for Michele and Emily, her twins, housed in St Anthony's Orphanage, and asks: 'Am I ever going to be a mother to them?' Most 'penitent mothers' never knew where their babies were placed. In some cases teenage girls, who had not been adopted from the orphanages and were already institutionalised, went by choice to the home-laundries. Juliet from St Anthony's Orphanage, on her arrival in Killmacha laundry, *Eclipsed*, Act 1, Scene 4:

Sister Virginia:	You're seventeen now, Juliet. Have you been out at all – outside?
Juliet:	No, Sister! I don't want to live out there!
Sister Virginia:	Why, Juliet? Your life's ahead of you!
Juliet:	My Mammy lived here until she died. I want to stay in here!
Sister Virginia:	But you can't make a choice until you've been out!
Juliet:	I'd hate to live out there. All those men!
Sister Virginia:	What men? There are fathers and mothers, brothers and sisters – families.
Juliet:	But look what happened to Mammy! No! No babies for me!
Sister Virginia:	Most men are good, Juliet.
Juliet:	They're not! Men are oversexed! Mother Joachim said so, when I was working in the convent.
Sister Virginia:	Mother Joachim! Why did she say that?
Juliet:	When I answered the side-door. When I screamed!
Sister Virginia:	You screamed. But why? Tel me, Juliet!
Juliet:	You see, Mick, the vegetable man! He grabbed me here! Pushed me against the wall. Said he'd murder me – break my neck if I moved! Old Mother Benedict was just in time! She hit him a wallop with her big rosary beads, but Mother Joachim wouldn't believe me – that I didn't lead him on.
Sister Virginia:	He was just one man, Juliet! You mustn't stay in here! Take a job outside! Go away and see new places. Read the

great books. Earn your own money. We're on an island here!

Juliet:　　　　　But Sister, I was never on a bus or a train! I'd be afraid!

Limbo – stillborn babies were buried in outcasts' graves along with suicides and the children of unmarried mothers. The poem 'Stone Babies' in my collection *Above the Waves Calligraphy*:

'Ring a ring o'rosie
a pocket full of posy',
Thorn-trees join branches,
to shed crimson berries
on a scatter of jagged stones
on this ringfort Killeen
Do stones keep badgers
from this viridian Limbo?
Do skylarks sing lullabies
for small bones crushed
in unblessed Lisheenduff?
'A-tishoo. A-tishoo. We all fall down!'

No names,
for you are unbaptised,
born out of wedlock,
Will o'the Wisp babies!

Who covers dead babies
with daisy garlands, sings
'Ring a ring o'rosie' with you?
Who decorates small graves with quartz,
with granite fossils, limestone sea-lilies,
with metamorphosed corals?

Outcasts on this river edge
must you never cross over,
must you wait in darkness
with strangers?
Will water from Brigit's Holy Well
carry your bone-dust
to Bethlehem?
Or will you, Stone Babies,
sing 'Ring a ring o'rosie' forever?

In my stage play, *Stained Glass at Samhain*, an elderly Sister Luke returns to the convent buildings, which are being demolished during the course of the play, Act 1, Scene 1:

| Sister Luke: | You remember me, don't you? *(Highlight on Sister Luke as she writes)* Sister Luke's my name. I had to come back, come back to tell you my story – No birds sing here. Stones and bricks twitch, try to release their trapped horrors. – The pain held in the earth. |

In Act 1, Scene 7, she brings us back to Killmacha Laundry:

Sister Luke:	Now! We'll cross the outside cloister first – *(Moves behind cloister-columns and out upstage right)* Careful down these stone steps to the tunnel – Very dark in here, smell of damp, no-colour air. Tunnel air – Along through this darkness – *(Moves downstage right to left)* Unlock this huge door – Lock it carefully behind us. *(Drops big keys with a bang as she is suddenly highlighted)* And here we are in Killmacha Magdalene Laundry! – *(Stands behind row of consecrated penitents)* Can't you see the consecrated penitents sitting on that long bench? Crooning lullabies and cradling their rag-doll babies? *(Lights up a little to show a row of consecrated penitents holding rag-dolls)* No! They're not ghosts! Can't you see them? Open your eyes. Listen to them. Hear them? Sings: Seothín seo hó, mo stóir'n, mo leanbh, mo sheód gan cealg, mo chuid den tsaol mór. *(Echoed by Maura Ber backstage. She stares downstage)* You never thought about it that way? But you must know! No excuses. No! You're not too young – You sent your own dirty filthy clothes to them! To be scrubbed! *(Enter Maura Ber up right. She unfolds an old bleached apron, pulls it on over her dress. Sister Luke centre stage left)*
Sister Luke:	Maura Ber was only thirteen, still had her schoolbag on her back, when she was brought in here. Isn't that the truth, Maura Ber? – For giving cheek in school! That old bird, your step-aunt Delia beyond in Gort, was jealous of you! And signed you in!
Maura Ber:	*(Centre stage right)* Every chance I got I studied the building lay-out. For three long years! Then – one night!
Sister Luke:	One night, wearing your black canvas shoes, – you climbed that downpipe – tip-toed over this low roof –
Maura Ber:	Up the side of that V shaped roof – over and across the top – jumped across the divide between the laundry and the convent.
Sister Luke:	You slid down on the other side –
Maura Ber:	Another jump into the big field beyond the outer wall.
Sister Luke:	I spent that night in the chapel praying, praying.
Maura Ber:	There was a new moon and a few stars. Between showers of black rain – I kept running, running!

Sister Luke: My rosary beads cut into my hands as I begged God –
Maura Ber: I ran west, cross-country to Barnamore. Afterglow from
the sun, the Plough, the Milky Way and the North Star
guided me – Then I saw a light in a house off the main
road. I knocked on the farmhouse door. The farmer's wife
gave me a strange look, but the farmer himself said I was
like their collie, Bran, the time he strayed in their kitchen
door, starving and drowned wet. 'Never a bark out of our
Bran! A bad fright he must've got earlier in his life', said
the farmer. She gave me a cup of sweet tea and a salty
bacon sandwich. – Fresh bread and real bacon! I'd
forgotten what fresh bread and real bacon tasted like. The
old collie licked my wet feet, even though I only gave him
a few scraps. I was sick with hunger. When the farmer and
herself went off to bed, I lay down with my penitent
clothes spread out in front of the turn fire. – Couldn't
sleep, afraid they'd take me back to Killmacha Magdalene,
so I put on my damp clothes, gave Bran a big hug, crept
out and away through the night to my cousins beyond
Monivea. A few cars passed, but I hid deep in the ditches.
My step-aunt Delia never told my cousins and my uncles
what she'd done to me! They thought I was in boarding
school! – When my real Aunt Brigit in America heard
what happened to me, she came over immediately and
brought me back to her own home in Boston. Aunt Brigit
sent me to college, treated me like one of her own
children. I've been back here a few times.
              (Maura Ber stares downstage)
But, I could never find that farmhouse afterwards, though
I've searched and searched. I wanted to tell the farmer and
his wife my true story and to hug Bran again. My Uncle
John and my Uncle Gerry and even my Granduncle Tom
said there was no farmhouse off that road since before the
Famine – Only a few ruins? – I'm going back now to
search, search and search.
              (Maura Ber takes off apron and moves upstage right).
Sister Luke: *(Facing downstage)*
Nobody here knows the truth – I could've stopped her.
That night when I was checking the outside doorlocks and
taking a look at the stars, the Pleiades and the Milky Way,
I saw her climb that drain-pipe and on to that flat roof.
Ah, wasn't I terrified she'd slip and break her neck!

In Act 2, Scene 1, Maura Ber re-enters with questions for Sister Luke:

Sister Luke: Ah, Maura Ber! Did you find that farmhouse and the
people who gave you shelter?
Maura Ber: No, Sister Luke, but I won't give up that search! I'll go on!

Sister Luke: You'll find them. No boundaries between them and us during Samhain.

Maura Ber: I hope you're right, Sister Luke. But could you help me, please? I need more stories about the laundries for my post grad thesis in Harvard. The women won't talk to me, pretend they never met me. Chrissie and Magdalena just look through me.

Sister Luke: They want to pretend it never happened, Maura Ber – But it's always there deep down. Like a dark stain – Oozing – Oozing.

Act 1 Scene 6, 'In this scene the women try to comfort the distraught Mandy by staging a wedding between herself and Elvis – a battered shop-window dummy – that would make a stone weep with its pathos and the sense of the sweetness of life gone to waste' writes Joyce Mc Millan of *The Guardian* at the Edinburgh Festival 1992. In Act 1 Scene 3 of *Stained Glass at Samhain* we meet Sister Luke again:

Sister Luke: When I was appointed Superior in Killmacha Magdalene Laundry, I changed the so-called penitents' diet. I insisted that they got plenty of milk and fresh vegetables. The finest potatoes, cabbages and onions grew in our convent garden and we had our own milch cows. I only had to remember my own time in the Novitiate, when the smell of rashers frying for his Lordship's breakfast and for Mother Superior's favourite priest's breakfasts made my cry with hunger, made me lonely for home. I spent the laundry money on the women instead of sending it to Central Powers. I bought them tennis shoes, I took away their ugly boots, I gave them flowery aprons instead of clay-coloured overalls. 'Come over and look into the crater under this red-toothed bulldozer.
  (*She moves downstage to the crater space*)
Hundreds and hundreds of worn-out boots, torn aprons, all holding their own pain! I led the women outside to landscape the grounds, to build and decorate my Lourdes Grotto. Mary and Bernadette amidst petunias, arabis and columbines. Our Magdalena and our Katie amidst lupins and Canterbury bells! To let fresh air instead of bleach fumes into their lungs. Wasn't I right? Wouldn't Christ Himself, do the same?

One of the many images from the demolition of the local Magdalene Laundry, which I watched in 1990, resonates in my memory. A sign erected by the construction company involved in the work read, 'No Dumping'. In Act 1, Scene 3 of *Stained Glass at Samhain*, Sister Luke erects a sign with the same message, 'No Dumping'.

Chapter Thirteen

Infanticide: the Crime of Motherhood

Alexis Guilbride

In the small hours of the summer night, the residents of the big house in Dalkey were asleep in their beds. All except Mollie Byrne, who was giving birth in the servants' quarters. The year was 1925 and Mollie Byrne was about to make history of a sort. Mollie was born and reared in Cork, and orphaned by the age of fifteen. She had been sexually molested by the local doctor not long afterwards, and had moved to Dublin and found a job in a hospital. While working there, she became involved with a young man and eventually fell pregnant by him. Having left her employment in the hospital, Mollie secured a position as a domestic servant in a large house in Dalkey. Distraught over the pregnancy and abandoned by her lover, she worked through the months that followed, concealing her condition from her employer. When the baby came, she choked it before it could cry out. She buried the body in the back garden.

In an agony of remorse, she confided in her employer, who, anxious to be rid of her, gave her the train fare back to Cork. Once there, Mollie contacted a priest and told him her story. He was kind to her, and found her lodgings for the night with a sympathetic landlady who refused any payment. The following day Mollie gave herself up to the police and confessed her crime. Mollie's case was the first recorded infanticide in the Free State to appear before the Central Criminal Court on a charge of murder. She was acquitted of the murder charge but found guilty of the concealment of the birth of an infant and sentenced to eighteen months in prison. Mollie's story suggests that a degree of liberalism and tolerance with regard to such matters existed in the Ireland of the mid-1920s, although this tolerance did not extend to the apparatus of the state, which charged Mollie with a capital offence. Irish society, however, was destined to undergo enormous changes in the period which followed the gaining of independence from British rule.

A Free State, A Catholic State
Before the establishment of the Free State, the citizens of Ireland, while strongly influenced by the tenets of the dominant religion, the

Catholic Church, were subject to British laws and, largely, British social mores. Contraceptives and information concerning contraception were still available in Ireland, as was the case in Britain, and a divorce could still be obtained by a private bill in parliament (a legal right that was confined, in practice, to the privileged few).

By 1923, however, Cumann na nGaedheal, the ruling party in the new state, had sought the advice of the hierarchy on the issue of divorce, and in October 1923, their lordships, the bishops, issued a statement which proclaimed:

> The Bishops of Ireland have to say that it would be altogether unworthy of an Irish legislative body to sanction the concession of such divorce, no matter who the petitioners may be (Keogh, 1994).

By 1925, a motion was carried in the Dáil preventing the introduction of private divorce bills to the Irish parliament. So, from the very beginning, the government of a newly independent Ireland was entering into consultation with the hierarchy to seek the advice and approval of the Catholic Church with regard to how an 'Irish legislative body' (as distinct from a British legislative body) should order its affairs.

This connection between Church and State in the new Ireland did not augur well for women like Mollie Byrne, or indeed, Irish women in general. It was a connection based on a nationalist, cultural tradition located in the myth of a golden, rural past. Within this tradition, to be Gaelic was to be Catholic, and to be a woman was to be subject to the dictates of a philosophy that sanctified the primacy of the male and the subjection of the female.

Sexual morality, or the control of women's bodies, thus became one of the central political issues of the ensuing decades in the new Ireland, and it remains so up to the present day. Of course, concerns about sexual morality were by no means confined to Ireland at this time. But the economic conditions which provided the basis for a specifically Irish approach to this issue, developed in the aftermath of the Famine, which wiped out the farm labouring class as a social entity.

The tenant farmers who had survived the Famine had learned the bitter lesson: the subdivision of small farms was economically unviable. The continuing tradition of rearing large families to work the land meant that, where only one son could inherit the land and thus marry, his siblings must remain celibate or leave the country (Inglis,

1987). So, for reasons that were primarily economic, the unwed pregnant woman in post-independence Ireland became stigmatised to such a degree that she was perceived to be committing a criminal act. She could expect, if her crime was discovered, to be disowned by her family and thrown out of her home; to be expelled from her community; to lose any position of employment she might have held and, with no social welfare system to fall back on, to be reduced to prostitution or begging on the streets.

Women of the Gael

This scenario was chillingly represented in a work of social propaganda published in 1924, entitled *Women of the Gael*. The author was a Catholic priest, Fr James F. Cassidy, a prolific and widely published writer, highly regarded by his peers. Padraic Colum (a well-known Irish writer, 1881–1972) wrote the foreword to this book. Cassidy presents his readers with an image of Irish motherhood that relies heavily on a spirit of what he terms 'splendid self-denial':

> She walks along a high path of virtue, especially that of purity. She is a model of modesty, and her marked devotion to her marriage vow saves Ireland from those disgraceful scenes, which disfigure the moral and social life of so many other countries.

One of the more sinister of Cassidy's claims, however, relates to the mother who is not a wife:

> There are a lower percentage of illegitimate births in Ireland than in any other country in the world. Whenever a child is born out of wedlock, so shocked is the public sense by the very unusual occurrence that it brands with an irreparable stigma and, to a large extent excommunicates, the woman guilty of the crime.

In 1924, this vision of the lives of women in a Gaelic, Catholic Ireland, as opposed to a British-dominated Ireland, may not yet have been fully realised, but it was a vision which was to inspire those who were responsible for legislating for the new Ireland over the ensuing decades.

Legislative Misogyny

The first of a series of repressive acts passed by the state in post-independence Ireland was the Censorship of Films Act of 1923. This act paved the way for the infamous Censorship of Publications Act of 1929, which made the publishing, sale and distribution of literature advocating birth control a criminal offence. In 1935, Section 17 of the Criminal Law Amendments Act finally outlawed the importation, the sale or the distribution of contraceptive devices of any sort. The blatant misogyny enshrined in these statutes was not lost on the few remaining representatives of a more enlightened Irish cultural tradition than that which held sway in the post-independence era. This was the tradition of Wolfe Tone and the United Irishmen movement, and it was dominated by the voices of the Anglo-Irish, although its influence extended well beyond the Ascendancy (Prager, 1986). W. B. Yeats and his literary colleague, Dr Oliver St John Gogarty, personified it in the early years of the Irish senate. Both men passionately opposed the introduction of the Criminal Law Amendments Act. During a debate in the senate in 1928 on the Censorship of Publications Bill, Gogarty was moved to comment:

> I think it is high time that the people of this country find some other way of loving God than by hating women (Lyons, 1980).

One bill, which gained Gogarty's approval at this time, was the Illegitimate Children (Affiliation Orders) Bill, which came before the Senate in 1929. Senator Gogarty saw this measure as one which would reduce the incidence of infanticide around the country:

> 'There is an appalling condition of affairs in this country, and that is infanticide. Anything that will give the mother a chance and will encourage her to preserve the life of the child and not strangle it, deserves our consideration,' he told the senate (Lyons, 1980).

In practice, however, an affiliation order (one which recognised the father's relationship with the child) proved virtually impossible to pursue and, accordingly, failed to provide women in this situation with any redress, or indeed, any means of survival. From the early 1920s to the late 1950s, trial records reveal that, almost without exception, every woman who appeared before the courts on a charge of infanticide was classified as 'poor or destitute' and almost all were unmarried.

Meanwhile, it was noted by the judiciary that infanticide was on the increase. One judge, whose comments on the subject were reported in the *Cork Examiner* in 1929, claimed that:

> The number of newly-born infants in the country who were murdered by their mother at present surpassed belief. Only one out of fifty came up in

the courts, but there was a wholesale slaughter of these innocents going on through the country (Jackson, 1987).

The great majority of infanticides came before the courts as cases of concealment of the birth of an infant. These cases were heard in the district courts. Only those cases in which it could be established by the pathologist that the infant was born alive and then killed, and where the injuries sustained by the child could not have been caused by self-delivery, were dealt with in the Central Criminal Court as infanticide, or murder. The description of the offence usually referred to:

> The felonious murder of an infant child, of which she had then recently been delivered (trial records).

Infanticide, then, was clearly a woman's crime. The following case, which came before the Central Criminal Court in 1949 illustrates this point with appalling clarity.

A Woman's Crime

Frances Smith was in her late twenties, well on the way to spinsterhood, when she met and became involved with a man who was some years older than her, a widower with two sons. Frances became pregnant by this man and her family offered to pay him £200 if he would marry her. He agreed. He insisted, however, that before the marriage took place, Frances must put the baby up for adoption. Now legal adoption did not become available in Ireland until 1953 (although it had been available in England and Wales since 1926), but Frances and her putative husband were members of the Church of Ireland and Protestant-run orphanages at this time operated a system whereby they organised for the children in their care to be adopted into Protestant homes. Frances handed her baby over to one such agency, the 'Children's Fold', and two months later she was married.

Frances went to live on her husband's farm in Sligo, where her life appeared to be one of endless toil. Six months later the parson who ran the orphanage, having failed to organise an adoption, and claiming that he had received no money for the child's keep, arrived at the farm with the baby and demanded that Frances take her back. She explained to him that her husband would not allow her to keep the child, but the parson was adamant and Frances had no choice but to take the infant. From the time of their marriage there appeared to be no conjugal relationship between Frances and her husband. Her role in the household seemed to be purely servile. She slept alone in a little room at the back of the house, while her husband shared the main bedroom with his two sons from his previous marriage. Frances made up a makeshift cot in the back room and kept the child there for several days, unknown to her husband.

One day, exhausted and distraught from the terrible strain of try-ing to feed and care for the infant while keeping its presence in the house a secret, Frances dropped the child on the floor of the back room. It landed on its head and died instantly. To what extent its fall was purposeful on Frances' part, no one shall ever know. All that can be known is that she had done everything within her power to care for and protect the child, up to that fateful moment. Now that the child was dead, Frances, having told her husband what had happen-ed but receiving no help from him, took the body out to a field near the house, where she dug a shallow grave and buried it. Meanwhile, her husband reported the matter to the local gardaí who came to the house and arrested Frances. She was charged with murder.

The jury who tried her, found Frances not guilty and she was dis-charged. She had committed no crime of which they could find her guilty, and it was a travesty of justice that a case should ever have been brought against her. Frances Smith had been guilty before the law until proven innocent because she had conceived a child out of wedlock, and the child had died while in her care. It was of no con-sequence to the guardians of the law at the time that Frances had been impregnated by the man who later conferred the spurious respect-ability of marriage upon her, having been paid handsomely to do so. The title of husband allowed him to use her as a slave in his house-hold, while it also allowed him to reject the child, which he himself had fathered. And when the pressure of keeping the child's presence in the house a secret from its own father resulted in its accidental death, it was this man who reported his wife as a murderer.

Society conferred no opprobrium on the father of the child, but placed Frances Smith in the dock. The jury which found her not guilty on the basis that there was no evidence to indicate that the child's death was other than accidental, saved her from a penitentiary but returned her to the prison of her home. The case was brought against her because it was likely that a woman in such circumstances *would* have killed the baby which she was allowed neither to keep nor to give away. The role of the child in this case is indicative of the double standard in operation in Irish society with regard to the value of the life of a child. This child's life was valued by society and the state only in the circumstance of its death. While it was alive, there was lite-rally no place for it in which to exist.

Sexual Crimes and Double Standards

While infanticide was a woman's crime, the criminal justice system of the new state was controlled and operated exclusively by men. What is most striking in the legal records of infanticide cases of the period, however, is the absence of the male. The courts did not con-sider the question of who fathered the infants whose deaths were being investigated relevant. Fathers and brothers of the accused were invari-ably assumed to be ignorant of the matter, while mothers and sisters often colluded with the birth mother in the concealment of the birth and the disposal of the body. In a number of cases, it was the mother of the woman who had just given birth who was charged with the mur-der of the infant. In one such case the defence counsel for the ac-cused stated that she had done nothing more than 'attempt to con-ceal the fact that this shameful occurrence had taken place in the house'. She had placed the newborn infant of her 18-year-old daugh-ter in a bag loaded with weights and had thrown it down a well.

In 1931, Eoin O'Duffy, Garda Commissioner, told the Committee for the Report on the Criminal Law (Amendments) Bill that there had been an alarming increase in sexual crime in Ireland, a feature of which was:

> The large number of cases of criminal interference with girls and children of sixteen years and under, including many cases of children under ten years (Keogh, 1994).

A great many of these, he informed the committee, were never prosecuted (Keogh, 1994).

The case of Eily Murphy, which came before the Central Cri-minal Court in 1945, was indicative of this state of affairs. Eily, who lived on a farm in County Limerick with her parents and four young-er brothers and sisters, was only fifteen years of age when she gave birth to a baby girl at the County Home, where she stayed with her baby for ten months. There was no mention in her file as to how she became pregnant, and the question was never put to her. When the baby was ten months old, Eily's mother arranged for the baby to be taken in and reared by another woman who would receive regular payments for its keep. Eily returned to the family home and life went on as if the event had never occurred. Her father, apparently, was unaware of the existence of the baby.

One year later, in the depths of a harsh winter, the child-minder arrived at Eily's home and presented her with her daughter, a little girl of almost two years of age, claiming that the payments had ceased. Eily's father was ill in bed at the time and her mother was away visiting relatives. She kept the little girl in her bedroom for the next two days until her mother was due to return. The extent of the mental anguish she must have suffered during the course of those two days and nights is inconceivable. All that we can know is that shortly before her mother arrived home, Eily brought the child out to the shed where she tied a sock around her neck in an unsuccessful attempt at strangulation. She then covered her with wet sacks, on top of which she placed a stone weighing 16 lbs and two iron window frames weighing 40 lbs each.

Shortly after her mother returned home, Eily's five-year-old brother found the child's body in the shed. Eily's mother sent for the guards. When they arrived at the house, they found the little girl was dead, but still warm. The coroner's report stated that the cause of death was starvation and exposure. Eily was tried and sentenced to five years incarceration in the Good Shepherd Convent in Limerick, where she worked in one of the infamous Magdalene Laundries. In a report to the court, the nuns spoke well of her, referring to her as 'a good child'.

This case was typical of the state's response to infanticide and, in a wider context, the attitude expressed towards what were perceived to be sexual and moral crimes. The woman was always to blame. The representatives of the state did not concern themselves as to how Eily Murphy became pregnant, despite the fact that a crime had clearly been perpetrated in this context, given that the girl was underage. After all, the moral foundation of the new Irish State was the ethos of the Catholic Church and:

> Incontrovertible evidence that the Catholic ethos is not being upheld is usually established by referring to babies. Only females can have babies. It is therefore the single, pregnant ... Catholic female of the species who will bear the brunt of punishment ... (McCafferty, 1985).

The double standard in operation here was brought into sharp relief by the state's apparent commitment to and respect for motherhood. This found explicit expression in Article 41 of the constitution of 1937, which states:

Article 41.1: In particular, the State recognises that, by her life within the home, woman gives to the State a support without which the common good cannot be achieved.
Article 41.2: The State shall, therefore, endeavour to ensure that mothers shall not be obliged by economic necessity to engage in labour to the neglect of their duties in the home (Bunreacht na hÉireann, 1937).

As Lee (1989) indicates:

The illusion fostered by the constitution ... that Irish society placed special value on motherhood, diverted attention from the fact that social values prevented a higher proportion of women from becoming mothers than in any other European country.

A salient point here is that motherhood was dependent on marriage. Economic factors prevented women from marrying and social values prevented them from becoming mothers – but they did not prevent them from becoming pregnant.

Secrets and Silence
Throughout the 1920s and 1930s pregnant Irish women made the journey to Britain in considerable numbers, either to have abortions which, although illegal, were still more widely available there than in Ireland, or to have their babies and give them up for adoption. With the outbreak of war in Europe, however, the Emergency Powers Act came into effect in Ireland and severe restrictions were placed on travel to Britain. Consequently, the illegitimacy rate in Ireland increased significantly during the war years, as did the trade in back street abortions. But the most dramatic increase in this area was evidenced by the numbers of women appearing before the courts on charges of infanticide. From 1940 to 1946, the years of the travel ban, legal records indicate at least forty-six cases of infanticide coming before the Central Criminal Court, whereas fewer than twenty such cases were tried during the previous fifteen years.

Strict censorship of the media operated during the Emergency and a blanket of silence regarding sexual matters enveloped the country. While the courts sentenced women to hang for the murder of their babies, the rest of the population was kept in ignorance. In this era of secrets and silence there was a tragic symbolism attached to the fact that so many infants died of asphyxiation because of their mothers' attempts, not to kill them, but to silence their birth cries. Time after time, these women filled their babies' mouths with rags or clay or grass in an effort to prevent them from drawing attention to their existence.

Few women were convicted of infanticide, however; most were found guilty of the lesser crime of concealment. The great majority of these women were sentenced to periods of detention in the Magdalene Laundries, the institutions run by orders of nuns, which were founded for the purpose of rescuing 'fallen' women. Whether the women sentenced by the courts to work in the laundries were allowed to leave after they had completed their sentences is open to conjecture. The information contained in the registers of the convent laundries during the twentieth century is not available for public scrutiny.

In the case of women who received prison sentences, it is revealing of the attitudes of the judiciary that those women who could produce certificates as evidence of the fact that they had since married had their sentences quashed. They were released, as it were, into the custody of their husbands.

Not Bad, But Mad

When the war ended and the ban on travel was lifted, the number of infanticide prosecutions in Ireland began to decline, as did illegitimate births and abortion investigations. Irish women began to emigrate in such huge numbers at this time that it became a source of serious concern for the cabinet of the day. One of the measures taken to stem the tide of female emigration was the Infanticide Act of 1949.

The Infanticide Act recategorised the crime as one equivalent to manslaughter, on the grounds that the balance of a woman's mind could be disturbed by the effect of giving birth, or indeed, by lactation. Despite all the evidence that poverty and illegitimacy were the primary reasons for the deaths of infants, the policy makers were determined to classify their mothers as mentally ill, deranged by virtue of their biology. By the mid-1950s, the mental hospital had replaced the convent laundry as the appropriate place of detention for women charged with infanticide. Whereas sentences of a fixed duration were imposed on the women confined to prison or the Magdalene Laundries, incarceration in a mental hospital was often permanent.

The perception by the state of women who commit criminal acts as unstable or deranged is a convenient one, as it denies the political implications of women's crime. What the records indicate, however, is that the establishment and perpetuation of structures within society which deny women the right to control their fertility, result in an increase in infanticide. Women may be compelled to endure un-wanted pregnancies, but they cannot be forced into motherhood. The simple fact is that, throughout the history of the modern Irish state, women have killed their babies because society left them little or no alternative.

CHAPTER FOURTEEN

Motherhood Interrupted: Adoption in Ireland

Eileen Conway

Motherhood and Adoption

> Much feeling, fantasy, denial, projection and displacement are involved in the highly charged experiences of giving up a child, or not bearing a child and subsequently taking a child who was born to other parents (Andrews, 1979).

This quotation highlights the subjective and emotional experience of motherhood and adoption. Small (1987) asserts that adoptive families are structured out of loss and nowhere is this seen more clearly than when we look at the plight of the birth mother who relinquishes her child for adoption. As we will see later, the adoptive mother, too, suffers losses, although they are less immediately obvious.

Before discussing the emotional pain and loss experienced by both women, it may be helpful to look briefly at the history of motherhood interrupted by the transfer of the child from the birth mother to a substitute family.

The Historical Background to Adoption

Adoption goes back to ancient times. It is mentioned in the Bible (Moses was adopted by Pharaoh's daughter), the Greeks adopted to provide heirs and, in Ancient Rome, the adopted child was entitled to full Roman citizenship (Octavius was adopted by Julius Caesar). However, adoption was not universally practised. It was not mentioned in American law until 1851 (Cole, 1986) or in English law until 1926. Legal adoption was introduced in Ireland with the passing of the Adoption Act 1952.

The idea of giving abandoned children the right to another family life, through legal adoption, dates largely from the beginning of the twentieth century. One child in every four was known to have been abandoned in Toulouse in the late eighteenth century. Often these children were the legitimate offspring of impoverished parents (Boswell, 1988). In France, Napoleon legalised secret and irrevocable abandonment of children in 1881, by establishing the 'towers' system in which a child could be laid in a revolving device located in the exterior wall of a hospital. This revolving cradle was also a feature of Dublin's Foundling Hospital, established in 1730. Mothers who placed their children in this cradle, with the hope that they would have a better life away from their own reality of poverty and despair, were to have those hopes dashed as conditions of neglect and cruelty in the Foundling Hospital resulted in the deaths of thousands of children in the eighteenth century. Women volunteering to help babies and young children from the Foundling Hospital came forward as wet nurses. These substitute mothers offered that most fundamental element of nurturing – mother's milk. However, these children sent out 'to nurse' were subject to only the barest minimum of supervision, and many were never seen again (Robins, 1980).

The Irish Poor Relief Act in 1838 introduced the workhouse system to Ireland. Because of Ireland's dreadful poverty, these workhouses filled quickly with destitute people. The unmarried mother, ostracised by society, had to rely on 'the cold comfort of the workhouse', so that by 1854, 11.6% of women in the workhouses under fifty years of age were mothers of illegitimate children (Burke, 1987). At the close of the nineteenth century, a number of important child welfare measures were enacted in law, culminating in the 1908 Children's Act. There was also an increasing recognition of the unsuitability of the workhouse for the unmarried mother and her child. The development of Mother and Baby Homes was one of the responses to the 1906 Report on Poor Law Reform and particularly to the 1927 Report of the Commission on the Relief of the Sick and Destitute Poor, including the Insane Poor (O'Hare, et al, 1983) which referred to unmarried mothers as first offenders, second offenders, and so on, depending on the number of children they had.

These Mother and Baby Homes were run by orders of Catholic nuns (Conway, 2000). In Cork, the Guardians of St Finbarr's Workhouse, under the chairmanship of a Mr Langford, were largely responsible for bringing to Ireland the Sisters of the Sacred Heart of Jesus and Mary. This congregation had been involved in adoption work in France and England. In 1921, the bishop of Cork purchased land from a Quaker family called Pike and gave it to the Sisters to open a Mother and Baby Home. Unmarried pregnant women left the workhouse, and came to this new home in Bessboro. This was to become the Sacred Heart Adoption Society, which ceased adoption placements in 1998 but now provides a training service for adoptees and birth mothers. The sisters established two other Mother and Baby Homes: The Manor House, Castlepollard (1935–1971) and Sean Ross Abbey, Roscrea (1930–1969).

In Bessboro, the young mothers worked on the farm; before government assistance, the sale of the farm's produce helped finance the running of the home. Barrett (1952) reported that a woman entering this home was given a new name so that the women did not know each other's identity. Only first-time mothers were admitted. The young mother was free to leave at any time, providing she took her baby with her. Otherwise, she had to remain until the local authority, which had been paying her maintenance, took over the care of her baby. This sometimes meant a mother staying for up to two years in Bessboro. Another such institution was St Patrick's Mother and Baby Home on the Navan Road in Dublin, opened by the Daughters of Charity of St Vincent de Paul in 1919. Women entering St Patrick's did not change their names, and no differentiation was made between women on their first or subsequent pregnancy.

Many Irish organisations were concerned with the plight of the unmarried mother and her child, and endeavoured to arrange de facto adoptions for the children concerned. The network of Protestant children's homes arranged some of these quasi-adoptive placements. In the 1940s, it was their practice to have the mother sign an agreement not to interfere in the placement, or visit the child in the 'adoptive' home (Pasley, 1997). The main concern for Catholic organisations was the rescue of mother and child from the dangers of proselytism. Examples included St Brigid's Orphanage, founded in 1856 by a pious and concerned woman called Margaret Aylward. She organised a group of dedicated helpers, known as the Ladies of Charity, who 'rescued waifs in danger of losing the faith' (Conway, 2000), and placed them in Catholic homes. In 1883, the Pro-Cathedral in Marlborough Street, Dublin, established an adoption agency called the Rotunda Girls Aid Society, to respond to the needs of unmarried Catholic women giving birth in the Rotunda Hospital, a traditionally Protestant establishment.

The original motivation behind the setting up of the Catholic Protection and Rescue Society of Ireland in 1913 was to 'offset proselytism and babies going to England' (Conway, 2000). The society offered a meagre allowance to mothers who kept their babies, and was the first Irish adoption agency that employed a trained social worker.

In the 1960s, a repatriation scheme was introduced, in conjunction with childcare societies in England. Following the passing of the 1952 Adoption Act several new adoption agencies were established and worked with English rescue societies which were dealing with large caseloads of Irish women, usually referred to on file as p.f.i. (pregnant from Ireland).

The finding of the Kilkenny Conference in the early 1970s was that unmarried mothers in Ireland were 'regarded and treated as second class citizens and very often their own misfortune is interpreted as being of their own devising' (Kilkenny Social Services, 1972). However, rapid economic and social changes were to profoundly influence patterns of Irish family life. These changes were accompanied by a demographic transformation (Walsh, 1972). There was a decline in marital fertility (Vital Statistics, 1994) and a rise in the number of non-marital births, from 1.6% of all births in 1961, to 6% of all births in 1982 (Clancy, 1984), and to 17% of all births in 1991 (Flanagan and Richardson, 1992). Factors associated with this rise were changes in sexual mores and the growth of lone-parent families.

Significant developments in improving the status of the Irish single mother were the introduction of the Unmarried Mother's Allowance in 1973, which established her right to a regular income, and the enactment of the Unfair Dismissals Act (1977), which ensured that a woman could not be sacked from her job because of her pregnancy. By the mid-1980s, the majority of single mothers were keeping their children rather than placing them for adoption (O'Hare, et al, 1983). In 2000, only eighty non-relative adoption orders were granted in respect of children placed by their Irish birth mothers (Report of An Bord Uchtála, 2000).

From this brief look at some historical aspects of Irish adoption, it can be seen that, in the past, the woman giving birth outside marriage was powerless in most respects. She was dependent on others, in need of being 'rescued' and was agreeable, in return, to having her identity changed or concealed. Only gradually did this scenario change to one where the single mother made choices about parenting her child or choosing adoption. In the relatively rare event that she chose the latter, she had options in relation to meeting the adoptive parents and negotiating, through the placing agency, various forms of open adoption.

Having considered some historical influences on motherhood interrupted by the social transaction of adoption, the next section looks more closely at what the research literature has to tell about the unwed mother. The first thing to note is probably the terms used to describe her. While traditionally the term 'unmarried mother' was used, the description in more recent literature is 'birth mother'. This term is not always acceptable to the woman who has given birth and placed her child for adoption, and who would prefer to be known as the natural mother. However, as this implies that adoptive motherhood is in some way unnatural, most writers prefer the term 'birth mother', and this is being used in the present text.

The Birth Mother

In the past, women giving birth outside marriage were characterised as either bad or mad. Non-marital births were seen as a morality issue in the USA (Combs-Orme, 1990), with the stigma of unwed pregnancy felt by women in countries as far apart as Ireland (O'Hare, *et al*, 1983) and Australia (Shawyer, 1979). From the 1940s onwards, a shift occurred in the US literature to depicting unmarried motherhood as a manifestation of psychopathology rather than immorality. Now the woman was viewed from a psychoanalytic standpoint, as using out-of-wedlock pregnancy to heal a disturbed and neurotic emotional condition (Clothier, 1943; Littner, 1956), which resulted from early parent-child dysfunctioning (Young, 1954). This approach, described by Benet (1976) as 'pop Freudianism', was selectively applied to white, American, middle-class populations (Plionis, 1975). Social factors and moral laxity were emphasised as an explanation for single motherhood among lower class non-white women (Liben, 1969). This view of unwed motherhood reflected the fact that training for most professional social workers in the USA in the 1950s and 1960s was principally informed by psychodynamic theory. Meanwhile, professional adoption practice was slow to develop in the UK, with many untrained workers stretched to their limits, placing thousands of babies a year (Rowe, 1991). Darling (1977) indicates that in Ireland in 1970, 50% of the personnel employed in adoption work had no training in social work. It is not surprising therefore that those psychoanalytic concepts about the single mother never really held sway in the UK or Ireland. Perhaps this was positive because, as Kirk (1981) points out, 'the psychodynamic model stood in the way of the workers' understanding of quite ordinary human experiences, translating them into esoteric, transcendental terms'.

Some sociologists including Vincent (1961) in America, Schofield (1968) in Britain and Kirke (1979) in Ireland, defined unwed motherhood as a function of a woman's socio-economic position and her familial and religious affiliations. In the Irish context, no significant differences emerged in Kirke's (1979) study between the unmarried and married mothers in terms of education, work and lifestyle. However, striking differences were apparent in three areas, with the unmarried mothers showing more permissive patterns in relation to parental control of dating, attitudes to premarital sex, and less intense religious practice.

Which ever theoretical view of single motherhood prevailed, the optimum solution in the past was seen as adoption (Kirk, 1981). The woman who consented to the adoption of her child was thought to then 'make a fresh start and get on with her life'. But in the silent background were those many women who had placed a child for adoption, and who had never forgotten. For some, the pain of relinquishment had shattered their lives. The socially sanctioned denial that nothing was wrong was soon to be contradicted by emerging research on the long-term effects of relinquishment. From Australia (Winkler & Van Keppel, 1984; Condon, 1986), America (Burnell & Norfleet, 1979; Rynearson, 1982; Deykin, Campbell & Patti, 1984; Millen & Roll, 1985) and the UK (Howe, Sawbridge & Hinings, 1992) came the message that there was a relationship between parting with a baby and later impairment in psychological functioning. For many women, the loss intensified over time, linked to a lack of knowledge about the development of their child.

As well as the chronic grief suffered by so many birth mothers, the other striking feature they shared was the experience of becoming mothers in secret. Barrett (1952), writing on the subject of Irish birth mothers before the introduction of legal adoption here, said:

> The moral welfare worker must show sympathy to such a mother and render her every help in preserving her secret and protecting her from public exposure, for such exposure can only result in grave moral dangers and social ostracism for the mother.

While it was true that, in a society hostile towards single motherhood, many birth mothers needed assurances of confidentiality from helping agencies, most women wanted privacy, not secrecy. However, the birth mother was not given that choice. Having relinquished her baby for adoption, she then became part of a 'hidden population' (Berman & Bufferd, 1986). Hidden, and yet:

The memory of this life event cannot, in the long run, be wiped out and in years to come, the knowledge that someone who was part of her is breathing and growing somewhere in the world ... remains a potential torment (Raphael-Leff, 1991).

If that mother did return to the adoption agency again to hear news of her relinquished child, what groundwork had the agency done to facilitate such a search?

Irish Adoption Agency Service to the Birth Mother

I undertook a study of adoption policy and practice in Ireland in the mid-1980s. The fieldwork began in 1983, a year when 921 adoption orders were granted in respect of children placed by the adoption agencies. This figure constituted 77.8% of adoption orders granted in that year (Report of An Bord Uchtála, 1985). The study examined the nature and extent of the service provided by the nineteen registered adoption agencies to birth parents and the adoption process itself. For almost all the agencies help for the birth mother was not contingent on any particular factors. However, two of the agencies said they would refuse a service in certain circumstances. One of these said help depended on the mother's social history, her willingness to relinquish her child for adoption, and the number of previous pregnancies she had had. The second agency said they would be:

Slow to accept a birth mother who was uncooperative or if she had been difficult about giving consent on a previous pregnancy (Conway, 2000).

For those women who did receive agency help, there was a range of services available and a positive trend among five agencies to extend their work into creative schemes to help the birth mother who decided to parent her child herself. While much of the social work content of the service was in line with recommended practice, many workers were themselves concerned about the quality of the help provided. This comment illustrated their concerns:

I do not think the same emphasis is given to work with the birth mother as is given to assessment of adopters. I think the same standard of work should apply.

Excessive social work caseloads accounted for inadequate service, at times, to birth mothers in the study. Given that a figure of fifty new cases a year was the maximum recommended number for a social worker dealing exclusively with birth mothers (Advisory Council on Childcare, 1970) then at least a quarter of the seventeen social workers surveyed had too many cases. Two of these social workers had dealt with 126, and 208 birth mothers, respectively, in 1982 (Conway, 2000). All of the social workers in the study also had the job of assessing adoptive applicants, so some birth mothers must have received a superficial social work service.

Some social workers had little or no contact with the birth mother in the ante-natal period, because the referral took place so late in her pregnancy, or after the birth of the baby. Sometimes, however, a lack of flexibility on the part of the social worker resulted in only a brief encounter with the birth mother before she gave birth. This allowed for only the minimum of discussion, and no chance to build up a working relationship, before the emotional complexities of giving birth and then parting with the baby became a reality for the mother.

Sometimes, the social background of the birth mother stood in the way of her child being placed for adoption. In about a third of the agencies surveyed (Conway, 2000), this was true. Five of these agencies did not place children born as a result of incestuous relationships. In addition, one of the five did not place children where there was a history of schizophrenia in the birth family. Another one of these agencies would not consider adoption if the birth mother was a member of the Travelling community; or had epilepsy; or any psychiatric disorder; or was 'a promiscuous girl with five or six other children' or was from a 'loose living' family. The sixth agency did not place children for adoption if there was a background of schizophrenia, promiscuity or a mixed race relationship between the birth parents.

The period following placement of her baby for adoption was a time of intense grief for the birth mother, and a time when professional counselling was needed. In this study, the amount of post-placement contact varied from no contact at all to twenty meetings with the birth mother. Where a low level of social work involvement existed, this afforded the birth mothers concerned little opportunity to express their feelings of grief. Winkler and van Keppel (1984) found this to be highly significant in terms of the eventual adjustment and psychological well-being of the birth mother.

Involving the birth mother in plans for her baby was seen as helpful to the birth mother in recognising the reality of her loss (Smith, 1984; Winkler, et al, 1988). One component of this involvement was helping her think about the kind of adoptive family she wanted for her child. In four cases in the study (Conway, 2000), the birth mother had made no requests at all about the kind of family she wished for her child. This was of concern, as it may have been linked with the lack of a worker-client relationship before the birth (one case), or the social worker's expectations that the woman would make only a very generalised request about the family (three cases). Another way of encouraging the birth mother to be involved and express her feelings was to invite her to write a letter for her child explaining why she had chosen adoption. About one quarter of the agencies did not encourage the mother to write such a letter and if she did write, four agencies admitted to having sometimes erased part of that letter.

Whereas, in earlier times, the mother relinquishing her child for adoption saw it as a complete break with the past (Dukette, 1975), the birth mother who placed her baby for adoption in the 1980s might 'have no objection to the child later re-establishing contact' (Report of the Review Committee on Adoption Services, 1984). With this in mind, the seventeen social work respondents concerned were asked how the agency dealt with the expressed wish of the birth mother to meet with her child when he/she was grown. Fourteen agencies noted her wishes on file. For two of the seventeen social workers, this question had never been addressed with the birth mother. As they had not encouraged her to write a letter for her child either, it seemed they were working from a traditional adoption model, where women were counselled to go on with their lives, and where denial resulted in an unresolved sense of loss for many.

The stage was set then for a future time, when some of the thousands of Irish birth mothers who had placed their children for adoption would return to agencies to find out how those children had fared, or when others would be found by their adult children seeking the missing pieces to their identity.

The Adoptive Mother

While one mother was parting with and grieving for her baby, another woman was waiting in the wings to become a mother. About to receive joyous news, this woman had also experienced many losses. She had lost those elements so closely associated with motherhood – pregnancy, childbirth and breastfeeding. She had also missed out on society's rituals of preparation for motherhood – announcements to family and friends, the support of other pregnant women, and the cultural and medical rituals affirming pregnancy and the development of a baby. As Kirk (1964) indicates:

> in adoption, there are few signs useful to oneself or to others for underscoring the changing status which is being anticipated and worked for.

For the majority of adopting couples, the precipitating factor in their quest for an adopted child is their inability to conceive and give birth to a child of their own. Humphrey's (1969) study, of what sort of people adopt and why, showed the experience of childlessness was a raw and sensitive area for those interviewed. Wounding insinuation that the absence of children was from choice were recalled by almost three women in four. Despite demographic changes since the time of that study, it is my experience in working with infertile couples having in vitro fertilisation (IVF) treatment, that Humphrey's observations are still relevant today.

Just as the birth mother would mourn the loss of her baby, the adoptive mother grieved the loss of her fantasy child. Although the object of loss was potential and anonymous, the grief was no less acute. Stages of protest, anxiety, anger and despair were experienced before the crisis of infertility was resolved. Even with this resolution, the old feelings of sadness could be revived at various times in her life. However, if she was to turn towards adoption as a route to motherhood, she now had to put on a brave face for the adoption agency. Having lost control over her fertility, she now ceded control of her destiny to a social worker and case committee, who would decide if she would become a mother.

Irish Adoption Agency Service to the Adoptive Mother

What did the adoption agency look for in this applicant for motherhood? In my study of adoption policy and practice (Conway, 2000), agency directors and social workers were asked what kind of personal qualities they looked for in those adopting. The responses were that applicants should be caring, mature, fulfilled, warm, flexible, stable, happy, tolerant, open, empathic, in touch with their feelings, practical, humorous, maternal/paternal, understanding, traditional, honest, good communicators, intelligent, sober, kind, confident, imaginative, courteous, youthful in outlook, dependable and realistic. No director or social worker alluded to the question of how to recognise these qualities in would-be adopters. This was of concern, as some of the interpretations were very subjective. For example, two social workers prized 'traditional values', but these seemed to apply to the female applicant only:

> I look for proper role-playing, with the wife not too dominant and dressed appropriately … traditional values mean the wife dedicated to the home, and with a nice tidy house.

When it came to a policy on the new mother working outside the home, four agencies never accepted applicants where the mother intended to continue in full-time work, and one of these did not even accept a mother working part-time. Another five of the nineteen agencies surveyed said that teachers were the only group of full-time female workers accepted as adoptive parents, presumably because of their shorter working day. A typical comment was:

> we wish the mother to be family orientated, and feel she should give up work for a while to bond with the child.

Other factors affected bonding between mother and child. In their study of the bonding process of mothers and their adopted children, Smith and Sherwan (1988) said that fantasising about the child-to-be was a primary form of preparation for any child. Yet, fifty women (43%) in their study did not report any fantasies and gave as reasons the lack of time between hearing the child was available for adoption and the child's arrival, and the fear that the adoption would fall through.

Waiting for a child through adoption is hard, and the woman may feel 'pregnant without a due date' (Sandelowski, et al, 1991). Then suddenly the long-awaited call comes from the agency to say a baby is available. In my own study (Conway, 2000), seven agencies said it was usual practice to give the adoptive couple four days or less to prepare for the placement of the baby. In addition, only three agencies said it was usual for the adopters to visit the child before placement. Therefore, many mothers were not afforded the opportunity of a phased placement, which may have helped the bonding process. As the literature (Bernard, 1945; McCormick, 1948) has highlighted, the first sight of the child by the parents is highly significant, and while the woman who is pregnant has nine months to anticipate that first view of her baby, the adoptive mother faces that moment with only a few days' notice given her by the agency.

Bonding with the new baby may be affected also by the support system of the mother. Attitudes of others, which show a pre-eminence of sentiments favouring biological motherhood sometimes emerge in seemingly well-meaning comments, such as 'how good of you to adopt', or 'what do you know of the baby's background?' This suggests special risks attached to adoption and a certain second-best element to adoptive motherhood.

Questions about the baby's background were impossible for the adoptive mother to answer unless the adoption agency had given her details of her baby's birth family. In fifteen of the nineteen Irish agencies I surveyed (Conway, 2000), certain items of information were sometimes omitted from the written history given to the adoptive parents: details such as a criminal record, previous pregnancies, promiscuity or a psychiatric history in the birth mother. This was laying up problems for a time when the adopted person or birth mother might return to the agency seeking a reunion with each other. The adopted person would then have to deal with disclosure of details which she was hearing for the first time, and which contradicted what she had always believed about her own birth history.

For the new adoptive mother, the question of having information about her child's birth mother was of significance. The task of telling about adoption loomed and, as family ties strengthened, became more difficult. Adoption revelation introduced the birth mother into the family system, and threatened the exclusiveness of the relationship between the adoptive mother and child. Sometimes, then, it was easier not to strive to preserve a clear image of the birth mother and to allow her to fade from consciousness. So, when the adoption story had to be told, the format was often that of the Chosen Baby story. Many of the books written for the young adopted child focused on how the child came into the family, not how she came into the world. These and the 'chosen' stories made up by many adoptive parents shared a common characteristic. The central figure, the birth mother, was either missing (Kornitzer, 1973) or introduced in diluted form, such as 'the lady … who started you' (Rondell & Michaels, 1951; Koch, 1985). These stories did little service to either the birth or adoptive mother, because they avoided mention of loss for any of the characters involved. The birth mother was not part of the story, and the adoptive mother passed from being sad not to have a baby, to being overjoyed to have a replacement baby in the space of a few lines (Conway, 2000).

Of course, if the birth and adoptive mothers met before placement of the baby a more open approach to the whole adoption was possible. By the 1980s, this practice was gathering momentum in Ireland. I found a third of the adoption agencies arranged such meetings and that they lessened fantasies for both birth mother and adoptive parents. They allowed the birth mother to feel more in control of where her baby was going, and hence have more commitment to the placement (Conway, 2000). Since then more open forms of adoption have developed worldwide, with agencies offering birth and adoptive families the opportunity of varying forms of openness. These can range from the yearly exchange of letter and photos, to the most open of arrangements where there is full and mutual disclosure of identifying information.

The last decade has seen many changes in adoption in Ireland. These include the huge decrease in the placement of Irish babies for adoption, and the steady increase in the number of adoptive parents applying to adopt a child overseas. The birth father, previously neglected in both legislation and adoption agency practice, was afforded new rights with the passing of the 1998 Adoption Act. Requests from adoptees and birth mothers for a tracing service increased, and were noted by both the adoption agencies and the Adoption Board (Report of An Bord Uchtála, 2000). The Minister of State, Department of Health and Children, committed to introduce legislation to regulate search and reunion practice and this legislation is currently being drafted.

The proposed introduction of Irish legislation in the area of search and reunion is an important step for all of those affected by adoption. In the process of the birth mother searching for or being found by her adopted child, the circle is in a sense completed. However, the reunion is complex, as intense feelings are aroused for everyone involved. Legislation alone will not smooth out all of these complexities because as Lifton (1978) points out 'the law can set boundaries but it cannot legislate what happens in the human heart'. This will continue to remain true for all those women who became mothers, one through giving birth and then letting go and one through receiving and nurturing a child born to someone else.

CHAPTER FIFTEEN

Mothering in a Disabling Society

Goretti Horgan

The theme of this chapter is the effect that a disabling society has on motherhood, both for disabled women who are, or want to become, mothers and for the mothers of disabled children. As the mother of an only child who is physically and intellectually disabled, I am keenly aware that the lack of resources to help a disabled child reach his/her full potential and societal attitudes to disability, mean that I experience motherhood in a different way to most. While friends wish they could influence their teenage daughters' choice of friends, I am grateful for every one of the few friends mine has. While they fear the day their children assert their independence, and try to put that day off as long as possible, it seems that since my daughter started school, I have been working to make her as independent as possible.

Discussions with friends who are disabled suggest that they, too, experience motherhood differently to most. Most visibly disabled people are perceived as non-sexual beings – which does raise certain difficulties for a woman who wants to conceive a child. Mothers with significant physical disabilities, particularly one that means they require assistance with some everyday tasks, are frequently seen as not being capable of parenting a child. The chances are slim that an intellectually disabled mother will be *allowed* to parent her child.

There is little research about the lives of disabled people generally in Ireland, north or south, still less about disabled women, whether or not they are mothers (NDA, 2002). There has been some work on the effect on families of having a disabled child, but these deal with both parents or the entire family. While the focus is often on the mother as the person who is usually most involved in caring for the child, organising health care, education and other services, the concentration has tended to be on practicalities alone (Monteith, *et al*, 1997).

Research about the feelings and experiences surrounding motherhood for those women who have to deal with their own or their child's disability is sadly lacking in a country that professes to privilege mothers. There is, however, a small amount of research evidence available from Britain (Morris 1989; 1991; 1992; 1996). Mothers of disabled children have a greater risk of relationship breakdown and of becoming lone mothers and a reduced likelihood of repartnering at the same rate as other lone mothers (OPCS, 1989). This increases the likelihood that mothers with disabled children will be living in poverty. Lone mothers also have less practical support. Beresford (1995) found that the majority of those mothers of disabled children who live with a male partner identify him as the most valuable source of practical and emotional support. Despite help received from partners and others, studies show that mothers do the majority of ordinary parenting tasks and the additional work of dealing with occupational, physio- and speech therapists, paediatricians and other specialists – to say nothing of the struggle to provide an appropriate education for their child (Read, 2000).

Morris (1989; 1991; 1992; 1996) details the hostile attitudes that many people, particularly medical professionals, have towards women with disabilities having children. She emphasises that, for the mothers she spoke to, 'physical and material resources [are] major problems, and it is these things which handicap us, not our disabilities' (1989). Asch and Fine (1997) argue that the lack of these resources combined with societal attitudes mean that disabled women are less likely than non-disabled women, or disabled men 'to be nurtured and to nurture, to be lovers and to be loved, to be mothers if they desire'.

Lloyd (2001) recognises that while all disabled women have to prove that they are capable of being a mother, for women with a learning disability, 'even if sterilisation is not as routine as it once was … Pregnancy is more likely to be viewed with a mixture of fear and panic by family and professionals alike'. A mother with a significant learning disability in the US or UK (we have no information for Ireland) has a 50–50 chance of having her child taken from her (Scally, 1973; Accardo and Whitman, 1990; Booth and Booth, 1997). When learning-disabled mothers are allowed to keep their children, they face long-term surveillance from the statutory services, persistent intervention in their private lives and 'various forms of system abuse' (Booth and Booth, 1997).

Disability and women's rights activists in Britain have affirmed that many of the experiences and feelings associated with motherhood are the same whether a woman or her child is disabled (Morris, 1992). The aim of this chapter is to make that assertion in relation to mothers dealing with disability in Ireland by giving a voice to some of those mothers.

Methodology

In researching this chapter, I was aware that asking women to talk about such an intimate part of their being to a stranger was asking a lot. Time constraints and an awareness of the imperative to reduce inequalities of power between researcher and researched (Byrne and Lentin, 2000) led me to adopt an approach taken by many women's and disability rights researchers and to approach for interview, activists in the women's and/or disability rights movements, sometimes both (Shakespeare, 1997). Ten women were interviewed; five disabled mothers and five mothers of disabled children; one disabled mother was herself the mother of a disabled child, making nine mothers in all. The tenth interviewee was a disabled woman who had decided not to become a mother. Brief details about each woman can be found at the end of the chapter. All of the interviews were conducted in Northern Ireland between 2002 and 2003. Each was asked what being a mother meant to her; what being a disabled mother/the mother of a disabled child meant to her. Then each was asked to say what were the positive things about being a disabled mother/the mother of a disabled child and, finally, what were the negative things. Each was then given an opportunity to add anything they wanted to say about their experience of motherhood. I am intensely grateful for the openness and candour of all the women whose voices make up the bulk of this chapter.

Mothering a Disabled Child

Most newspaper articles, radio or television pieces on mothers of disabled children tend towards the discourse of the 'constant struggle' of the 'saintly' mother whose life has been 'turned upside down' by this disabled child. In Ireland north and south, but particularly in the republic, this approach is understandable given the lack of appropriate services for children with disabilities and their families. This view was reinforced by a focus group that I conducted with mothers of children with disabilities from the north-west for a parenting support programme. These twelve mothers, whose disabled children ranged in age from four to twenty-four and who lived in an area of multiple disadvantages, presented a very different picture to that offered by the activists below. All the discussion was about the difficulties the mothers faced in accessing appropriate services for their children. It was clear that many health and educational professionals do not see mothers as experts in relation to their own children. As a result, some mothers had spent three, four, even six years trying to convince professionals that there was 'something wrong' with their child. Even for those who received a diagnosis relatively early in the child's life, trying to get professionals to 'believe that because I was with her 24 hours a day, I knew her better' was difficult. They felt hugely unsupported by either statutory or voluntary agencies and all said that the only support they received which really met their needs, and the needs of their child, was from family and friends. These experiences are similar to those described by parents of disabled children across these islands (Read, 2000). Mothers such as these, struggling to access basic information about, and services appropriate to, their child's impairment, had little or no opportunity to see beyond the disability to the child.

Several of the activist-mothers commented that the theme of 'constant struggle', of fighting for better resources and services for their child, while reflecting the reality of their lives, annoyed them sometimes:

> I think it's a reaction against the idea that a disabled child is 'a gift from God', whereas now they're going to the other extreme and saying only how hard things are – there must be some happy medium [Eileen].

> All mothers go to extreme lengths to give their children the best lives they can. My mother did it to make sure we all got on in the world. What I'm doing for Margaret isn't all that different [Bernie].

The response to what being the mother of a disabled child means to them drew responses of 'a purpose in life'; 'responsibility'; 'a good structure to my own life'; 'gives my life a sense of purpose'; 'a mixture of joy and despair'. All went on to say quite positive things about being the mothers of disabled children, with the notion of a clearer sense of purpose to their lives than those of many other women coming through from all but one of the mothers. This idea of mothering in adverse circumstances giving a 'sense of purpose' is not unique to mothers with disabled children. Teenage mothers have voiced similar feelings (Horgan, 2000).

They were also insistent that a disabled child is first and foremost a child, although the attitudes of professionals and society in general sometimes obscure that fact:

> Professionals say to me 'you're a carer'. I say 'no I'm not, I'm a parent'. Of course there ARE parents who can be described as carers for their children

because they have to provide a level of care, like tube feeding or suctioning a tracheotomy, that other parents don't. All children need a certain level of looking after and, yes, we have to go to greater lengths but insofar as we do with our children, it's because the system, especially the education system, is so lousy [Diane].

While many of the mothers laughed at being asked what were the positive things about mothering a disabled child and suggested they would not be able to come up with an answer, all of them did have good things to say. Often, these positive things were said in the context of talking about what being a mother meant to them and they surprised themselves by how positive they were about their experiences:

> You realise that your priorities have changed. What gets you excited, what makes you proud. Of course, you're delighted when your other children pass the Eleven Plus or get good GCSEs. But when Michael came home with a certificate for having reached level one in reading and arithmetic, which is really what the average five year old can do, I was just as delighted by that as I had been by his brother's GCSEs. And that's no harm, to see that there is more to life than the boxes we're all pushed into [Christine].

All did, however, point out that they are able to be positive now that their child is older but in his/her early years, all seemed bleak and hopeless. One of the reasons given by three of the mothers for a more encouraging view now, was that their child was very unhappy and/or unwell as a younger child, with frequent hospital appointments or spells in hospital. Now that their child was happier in themselves, more 'settled' and in appropriate education, their mothers were able to be happier also.

Two of the mothers gave as a positive something which they also agreed could be a negative: while other mothers of teenagers worry about where their sons or daughters are, who they are with and what they are up to, these mothers always know where their child is, exactly who is with them and precisely what they are doing.

> When you see reports about young fellows being beaten up on the way home from nightclubs, I always think well, that's something I don't have to worry about. Michael never goes anywhere without an adult, is never unsupervised – because of his epilepsy, you know. So, we always know exactly where he is and while other mothers are worrying about what their sons are up to, we know he is tucked up in bed [Christine].

There were some striking similarities about what the mothers had to say, and which might give heart to mothers of younger disabled children. Three of the mothers, whose children are more severely disabled, spoke of the 'panic' they had felt when their children were younger:

> I was physically sick sometimes – just thinking how would I cope, the outlook was so bleak, the specialists were so negative about his potential – I just panicked.

> When he was small, it wasn't really a life, it was just an existence because he was so challenging. I would have panicked a lot about the future.

> When she was a baby and the doctors were so pessimistic, I used to take panic attacks. If I stopped to think about the future at all, I would be sick with panic.

These mothers now describe their lives as 'better than we could have hoped for, not great, but happy'; 'everyone's calmed, he's rewarding, he's happy, it's brilliant'; 'totally different, settled, still worried sometimes, but basically happy'.

Two of the mothers commented on the way the 'romance' or 'rush of feeling' they had for their disabled child had been robbed from them by the disability:

> When he was born, I had this really romantic view of motherhood. But with the autism then it didn't turn out like that. The romance went out the window, that's for sure.

> It's like I had a few months of being a 'normal' mother, having that rush of feeling, of being madly in love with her. Then it's like the disability took over and that feeling disappeared for a long time.

But both of these mothers had found those feelings returning in their children's teenage years and both attribute this to the fact that their child is now happy and settled. Both said that sometimes now they look at their child and are ready to 'burst with love'.

Unfortunately, the two other mothers were unable to share in this optimism. One felt that the level of her son's disabilities meant that he would be 'excluded from society entirely' and would not have a 'dignified or rewarding life'. The other mother, who is herself disabled, felt she is already living her son's future and it is disheartening:

> Just because of my own disability, I can't shelter him from things that I want to shelter him from ... In certain practical things, yes, I know things he is

going to come up against, maybe I pre-empt them a bit, but when it comes down to brass tacks, he still faces the same things … I know what he's feeling, how he's feeling it, when he's going to feel it and what he's up against … When you know what they're going to come up against, that is a bad thing, that you can foresee the future … like history repeating itself [Eileen].

Asked about the negative aspects of having a disabled child, the one thing all the mothers agreed on was how restricted they were in what they can do, where they can go. This was the same for all the mothers whether or not their child had the mobility difficulties associated with lack of wheelchair access:

Holidays can be a nightmare. Going to Slane or concerts in the Point or whatever are really out for us, although we've always been great rock music fans. Getting him watched just to go see a film is hard enough. I've always wanted to see Australia, thought we'd go when the kids were old enough, but I don't expect to ever get the chance now [Diane].

Two mothers of only children talked about the plans they had had – plans to give their child things they had missed out on in their own childhood and how they still regretted losing the chance to fulfil them:

I was going to be such a cool mother. I would encourage, but not dictate. All the things I never got the chance to do, she would. There would be no rows about unsuitable boyfriends, body-piercing or pink hair, no problems about dropping out to travel. It's not fair that she won't have the chance to do any of those things, not fair that I won't get to see her do them [Bernie].

All were clear, however, that the main negative things about being the mother of a disabled child were the negative things about being a mother at all:

The bad things would be similar to the bad things of having an ordinary child, the fact of your worries and fears for their future, but then multiply it – multiply it by a hundred. At least [Eileen].

Mothers with a Disability

In preparing this section, I approached five mothers with a disability. Three – all with an invisible disability – said they did not see themselves as disabled. This point is worth emphasising since it is probably the case that there are a lot more disabled mothers out there than we realise. These mothers are either trying to 'pass' as non-disabled or genuinely do not feel disabled by their impairment. All the mothers who did agree to be interviewed have disabilities that could not be ignored or easily hidden, but most of the experiences and feelings they described seemed to me just what you expect most mothers to describe.

Probably the main difference about the disabled mothers is that while society expects most women to become mothers, they are aware that society most definitely did not expect them to do so. This probably explains why, when asked what motherhood or being a disabled mother meant to them, the word 'normal' seemed to come up so much with women who would usually reject the use of the word:

> I'd never really thought about it before now but, in a word, normality, I think. When you said what your first question would be, immediately I just thought normality. It probably goes hand in hand with marriage and motherhood does normality ... yeah, it does mean normality [Eileen].

> I never thought about not being a parent. It wasn't an issue, my disability was never an issue. In hindsight, it could have been but at the time of being a teenager, I was going to fall in love, get married, have kids and that's what 'normal' people did. And that's exactly what I did ... so it never crossed my mind that I wouldn't have kids and I suppose there was some kind of statement there as well [Geri].

The 'normality' theme was quickly followed by one common to most mothers – love, joy and worry about all the little things every mother worries about. But here again, society's attitudes to disability rear their ugly head. While other mothers are reassured that their slightly-underweight baby will thrive soon or that fears around bathing a tiny baby are usual, some of the disabled mothers felt that they were expected to fail as mothers – or at least to need outside help in parenting their child. All the mothers with older children had been made to feel that their parenting skills were questioned by at least some health professionals when their children were babies. Two spoke of health visitors having a 'checklist' of issues that they wanted to satisfy themselves about:

> I remember my health visitor used to come in and she was very good but she would have said 'would you like me to cut his nails?' And I would have said 'no, I don't want you to cut his nails'. 'Who cuts his nails?' 'I cut his nails.' And I could just see her wondering about it and I used to think to myself is she writing all this down when she goes out? ... they would have been asking 'and do you measure his bottles?' and a stack of different stuff. They just assumed the worst. They had no concept of how you would have

had a regime worked out for different things … but the questions were geared for someone who is visually impaired with a young child, just like a checklist you know [Eileen].

I had thought myself about all the issues and read up on them all; all the dangers especially. I knew I should do things on the floor, like changing nappies and so on, just in case I had a seizure. And there was no way I was going to give my precious baby a bath on my own in the house, just in case. I had already thought through all these issues but she acted as if I didn't know myself, as if I was a danger to my baby. By the time I had the second one, though, she had relaxed. She could see I knew what I was doing [Helen].

One of the mothers had feared that health visitors and social workers were trying to 'trick me and that they could actually come and take him away'. Some of the mothers were unaware of their rights, and the rights of their child, in this regard. It is certainly the case that ideas and support offered by health professionals and others would have been better received if the mothers were not feeling so vulnerable and defensive. All were aware of needing to be more than just a 'good enough' mother, aware that they were likely to be judged more harshly than a non-disabled mother:

My eldest boy is 21. I remember when he was born thinking 'what if he falls over, will I be accused of neglect or whatever? And you double your efforts, you child is *always* the best turned out, *always* clean. And the minute they start misbehaving, you panic [Geri].

All the disabled mothers talked about the strategies that they developed to get around any difficulties caused by their impairment. Most had breastfed their babies and commented that this was more for the convenience of not having to sterilise, make up, and in particular carry, bottles than for the health benefits:

Getting out and about is the big thing for me, because I can drive but I need someone to lift out the wheelchair which is a pain … I had two prams, actually I had three – I borrowed a lot. It meant I had one in the house, one in the car all the time so I didn't have to lift it in and out all the time, and one in my parents' house [Kathleen].

When it came to talking about the good and bad things about being a disabled mother, most issues raised were the kind of thing every mother says – the love, the enjoyment, feeling grown-up and responsible and then the worry, the fears, feeling harassed and never having a moment to oneself. But there were, of course, other issues raised that related directly to their disability. The good things about being a mother with a disability were mainly about being able to bring their children up with a different view of the world, a more healthy, tolerant and holistic view. They said they expected their children to be 'more accepting', 'more patient' and 'more tolerant of others' because of having a parent with a disability:

> I see it as about instilling confidence into your children about difference, any kind of difference, not just disability. You know, I want them to have friends who are black and to be okay about friends who turn out to be gay and to be proud, rather than embarrassed at having a mother who is disabled [Inez].

Apart from Eileen, for whom the bad thing about being a mother with a disability was knowing what her child was going to have to go through, for the rest, the bad things were other people's attitudes. All but one felt they were viewed with suspicion as if somehow they shouldn't have a child. Two had total strangers address them in a familiar manner, asking how they came to have a child – 'I just asked if she had never heard of the birds and bees!'

> What I found as a disabled mother is that you have to balance this disability – charity – tragedy model with all of a sudden you're walking around with this big bump which PROVES you didn't deserve that. And this was quite horrific for people to take on board and I know mothers who actually had people wonder if it was the result of rape or abuse. You dealt with it [Geri].

> The stares and the personal questions [assuming] that I had Fintan before my disability, before I was ugly. I see it as that, how other people are interpreting it. This [the wheelchair] is ugly so obviously I had Fintan when I was fit and able and attractive to other people, otherwise how could I have a child [Kathleen].

Three of the mothers raised as one of the bad things about being a disabled mother, the attitude they were confronted with by some people, that their child was their carer, not the other way round. Two of them suggested that children's rights organisations and social work agencies needed to adopt a disability rights perspective when they are addressing the question of 'child carers'. 'Child carers' are now a recognised category of 'children in need' within children's services departments in Northern Ireland. But the disabled mothers were very clear that the 'problem of child carers' was a problem of lack of resources being put into support for disabled parents. If, as should be the case under the Children Order, the assessment of the child's

needs and the assessment of the parents' needs were undertaken together and co-ordinated, then the issue of children being forced to
act as carers for parents with complex needs would never arise. Instead, they felt that all children being cared for by a disabled parent
are seen as being 'victims of the disabled parent':

> People see the person who hasn't got a disability as the carer, even if they're
> a child. I'm the parent here, they're the children. I wouldn't want to have
> them involved in my personal care in any way, but I don't need them to be.
> The social workers see them as 'child carers'. It's true they can do some
> things that I can't, but I'm the carer around here [Inez].

> We should be saying if that individual with MS, or whatever, needs that
> level of care and didn't have a child, then the Social Services Trust would
> be providing it. So, society blames the parent for putting the child in that
> position, when in fact it's the Social Services Trust [Geri].

> I'm really conscious of not asking him to do anything that other children
> aren't asked to do. Like, I ask him to tidy his own toys … trying to get help
> from social services! I asked for five mornings a week, for a cleaner because
> I would find it more difficult to hoover and make beds and any big things.
> So they said they have no budget for this, but they gave me a cook. So now
> I have a woman that's five mornings a week coming in, cooking a meal for
> me – and that's something I could do. They ignored the fact I would find it
> more strenuous and tiring to do the other stuff [Kathleen].

As between a quarter and one-third of all women across these islands
now decide that they do not want to have children, it is important
to recognise that some disabled women also choose not to become
mothers. I approached Jean for interview because I thought her condition had prevented her having children. I was wrong. She has a
busy life, with many different interests and had made a positive decision not to bring a child, or at least a biological child, into that very
full life:

> I think this idea that you can have it all is a load of shite. It's about me tak-
> ing responsibility for my choices … Obviously I've been thinking about it
> a lot but I look at people who have kids and a lot of people don't seem to
> enjoy them, they don't spend time with them. It doesn't seem like a positive
> experience, like a pro-active positive experience. I have other things I want
> to do and I don't think it's possible for me to also fit kids in, really enjoy
> them and do everything else with the time I have [Jean].

This chapter can only skim the surface of the issues facing mothers
dealing with disability, since it presents the views of so few. However,
I hope it will provide some signposts to other researchers who might

explore further some of the issues raised here. Similarly, policy-makers might want to examine how their agencies might address relevant issues. There is not enough evidence from these few voices to draw any firm conclusions. However, one thing is clear: the experience of the mothers reported here has been that the negative aspects for mothers dealing with disability are due entirely to resources and attitudes. Of course, the two feed on each other – the lack of resources to enable disabled people to live their lives to their full potential allows negative stereotypes to be reinforced.

The question of resources to support mothers dealing with disability is a political one. Jenny Morris (1991) writes:

> We need to ask whether, for example, weapons of destruction are a more acceptable subject of public expenditure than developing the technology and services, which make life tolerable for one group of people.

Morris quotes a 1982 *Spare Rib* article by Micheline Mason that could be a quote from today's anti-corporate globalisation campaigners: Mason argued that there is enough wealth in the world to ensure that everyone has all they need to have a good and fulfilling life.

It is the big illusion of our time that it is the resources that we lack. The problem is some people control them, misuse them, and deny them to the majority of the rest of the world.

Mothers dealing with disability have more reason to regret this than most.

The mothers interviewed were:

Ann is a lone parent and her 17-year-old son, Danny, is autistic.

Bernie is a lone parent and her 16-year-old daughter, Margaret, has mobility and speech problems resulting from cerebral palsy.

Christine's 15-year-old son, Michael, has cerebral palsy, is learning disabled and has uncontrolled epilepsy. She lives with Michael's father and has two other children, one younger, one older than Michael.

Diane's 12-year-old son, Mark, has a rare syndrome and is physically and intellectually disabled. Diane is married and Mark is the youngest of five children.

Eileen's 17-year-old son, Jack, is visually impaired. His eye condition is the same as Eileen's, although Jack is registered partially sighted while Eileen is registered blind. Eileen is married to Jack's father. Jack is an only child.

Kathleen is a lone mother with a 4-year-old son. Her disability is progressive and she was relatively unaffected when growing up, but now uses a wheelchair.

Geri is a married mother of three children ranging in age from 12 to 21. She has cerebral palsy.

Helen is the mother of two children aged 6 and 3 and lives with their father. She has epilepsy, which is poorly controlled.

Inez is a lone mother of two teenagers. Her marriage split up about five years ago. She has cerebral palsy.

Jean is in her thirties and has decided not to become a mother. She has a life-threatening progressive condition.

CHAPTER SIXTEEN

Mothers and Poverty

Anne Coakley

> They were, in fact, sitting down to a stolen meal. Mary had come into the shop, followed by the old man, Thomsy, and a crowd who were furious because the Relief Committee was not in session that day. She had terrified Hynes by calling him a miser and demanding that he give her credit. Watching her chance, while the crowd was shouting for Hynes, she managed to slip the bacon under her cloak without being seen. 'I didn't steal it,' she said fiercely. 'I took it. A person has a right to take things to keep alive. I have to feed him that God sent me hunger' (O'Flaherty, 1984).

> That night, as she lay awake in bed, brooding over the events of the day, Mary decided to escape from the valley with her child as soon as possible. She was now convinced that the government would let the people die of hunger (O'Flaherty, 1984).

O'Flaherty's powerful fictional account of the famine in Ireland portrays Mary, a young mother, desperate, after the failure of the potato crop. She was driven to stealing food to feed her young child and older members of the household while her husband had gone into hiding from the police. Food security is the most primary aspect of poverty. The potato famine of the 1840s, during which over a million people died, shrouds our history. Globally today, food security remains a central aspect of the poverty of millions of people who die of starvation in developing countries.

Poverty is a contested and dynamic concept. In the developed world, it is generally defined relative to the standard of living in a country and its eradication is embedded in political and ideological notions about levels of social polarisation and exclusion that a society will tolerate. The objectives of the most recent European Union Action Plan against poverty and social exclusion, focus on facilitating participation in employment and access by all to resources, rights, goods and services (Social Inclusion Strategy, 2000/2001). Poverty research is crucial in providing information about groups at risk of poverty, its spatial and time dimensions, and how people enter or exit poverty over the life-course and as new social risks are generated. Gender is an important dimension of poverty particularly in relation to women as mothers and carers. Women, over the life-course, in

their capacity as mothers and as carers of other family members experience different levels of dependency on a spouse or on the state.
The level of economic independence or dependence that mothers as
carers enjoy, defines and is defined by, their relationship to the labour market, with the welfare state and within the family. The social
supports available will determine how successful the transitions are
between dependence and independence, between their role as carers
and workers and will also determine their vulnerability to poverty.
This chapter examines contemporary trends in relation to mothers
and poverty in Ireland and discusses research that locates mothers at
the centre of the experience of poverty in low-income households.

Gender and Poverty
Motherhood generates varying levels of dependency in the form of
care and nurturing over the life-course of a woman. The way a society
constructs motherhood and caring is linked to some mothers' vulnerability to poverty. The structural causes of women's poverty are to be
found 'in the interaction of economic disadvantages and risk factors
in domestic circumstances, labour markets and welfare systems' (Ruspini, 2000).

     Historically, women's responsibility for childcare and other forms
of care, and their economic dependence on men was the premise on
which the welfare state was designed in England and Ireland (Wilson, 1987; Land, 1989). Gender inequality has been the organising
concept of the Irish social welfare system from its foundation in the
nineteenth century (Yeates, 1997). Historically in both countries there
was an institutionalisation of the male breadwinner model of welfare
provision for the family. This subscribed women and mothers in particular to a dependent status (Lewis, 1992). In Ireland, women lost
many individual social rights of citizenship on marriage. The majority
were not counted as being in the formal labour market as they tended
to work in small family businesses and farms. Once married, they were
treated as dependents of their husbands' for social welfare and tax
purposes and had no entitlement to an individual social welfare income (Mahon, 1994).

     The discourse of familism, the male breadwinner model (Lewis,
1992), where the principle of maintenance prevails and married women's social rights are via their husbands (Sainsbury, 1996) dominated welfare provision for families in Ireland prior to the implementation of the EU directive on equal treatment for men and women in

social security (Council directive 79/7/EEC) in 1986. Women in Ireland only gained gradual individual citizenship rights to welfare after 1986 (Coakley, 1997). However, these rights are tied to commodification in the labour market and, while mothers caring full-time at home have formal rights to individualised payments, there are barriers to accessing such claims. Married couples are paid a 'couple rate' rather than two individual rates in the case of means-tested social assistance payments including Unemployment Assistance (UA). In addition, figures for those claiming unemployment payments indicate that a substantial proportion of women are dependents of their husbands for social welfare purposes. Just over a quarter of UA claimants in 1999 were claiming for a qualified adult (DSCFA, 1999).

The individualisation of social welfare rights to married mothers who are caring full-time continues to be the subject of debate about the boundaries between private responsibility and the public recognition of caring work (Williams, 1997). Even maternity payments' real value has been eroded over the years, as Kennedy (2002) notes, and only women in the labour market are now entitled to those payments. Earning and caring give access to different social rights, with earning being more valued than caring (Leira, 1992). The manner in which the state defines and remunerates caring work is a defining feature of the gendered aspect of welfare states. There is a strong ideological opposition in Irish state policy to the public provision of childcare and a belief that caring for children is a private responsibility in the domain of the family and of mothers.

The linking of social welfare rights to commodification in the labour market, the lack of subsidisation of childcare costs for mothers who do paid work and the cut-backs in maternity payments, exacerbate the interaction of economic disadvantages and risk factors associated with motherhood. Married mothers may become dependants of their husbands for varying degrees of time. The assumption of equal sharing of income inherent in social assistance payments for couples is central to the poverty dynamics of social welfare dependent families. The increase in lone parenthood in the last few decades often means dependency on basic rate social welfare payments.

Poverty Risks
The Government's Social Inclusion Strategy (2000/2001) has identified gender, age and membership of ethnic minorities as key factors in determining people's experience of poverty. According to the re-

port, women, children and the elderly have higher than average risks of poverty in Ireland today. Sub-groups have been identified as having particularly high risks; these are: female lone parents, children in households with three or more children and elderly women living alone (Nolan and Watson, 1998). While the majority of children in Ireland live in two-parent households, there has been a significant increase in lone-parent mother-headed households. The number of one-parent households increased by 89% in the period 1986–96 (Mc-Keown and Sweeney, 2001).

The Irish government emphasises the significant reductions in poverty from the mid-1990s. The most recent figures show that consistent poverty defined as the proportion of households with 50–60% of the average disposable household income and experiencing basic deprivation at the 60% line has fallen from 15.1% in 1994 to 8.2% in 1998 (Callan, *et al*, 1999). The figures also indicate that the rate of consistent poverty among children has reduced considerably from 25% in 1987 to 12% in 1998. However, the numbers living below relative income thresholds, such as half the average income, have not fallen. High risk of poverty is linked with social class and socio-demographic characteristics including households headed by unskilled manual workers, the unemployed and those without educational qualifications (Callan, *et al*, 1999) and local authority households (Nolan, *et al*, 1998).

The interaction of gender, class and membership of ethnic minority groups define the dynamics of poverty. Motherhood cuts across all of these variables as it is mothers who tend to be responsible for the management of poverty in low-income households. Kennedy and Murphy-Lawless' (2002) research on refugee and asylum-seeking mothers highlights their vulnerability to poverty and exclusion in relation to housing, food security, isolation from extended family, exclusion from the labour force, as well as specific problems relating to language and racism.

Active Labour Market Programmes
Government policy links the significant decrease in poverty with the reduction in welfare dependency and the expansion of labour market opportunities since the mid-1990s. The Irish state has been actively funding programmes for the re-integration of the long-term unemployed and other social welfare recipients into the labour market. Expenditure on employment supports increased from less than a quarter

of a million in 1990 to just under £200 million in 1999 (DSCFA, 1999).

Despite EU equality legislation, married mothers who are full-time at home were not eligible to participate in training or return to work programmes until the late 1990s. However, eligibility is conditional on the interchange of entitlements with husbands' and is less in the spirit of individualising the mothers' rights of access to training. It is ironic that in the recent past the state has reduced funding for such training programmes and funding for 'passport benefits' attached to such programmes including rent and mortgage supplements. Essentially many of these schemes are based in disadvantaged communities and the work is centred on children, teenagers and the elderly. Murphy-Lawless' (2002) research in an inner-city community acknowledged the usefulness of such schemes for eligible mothers and their contribution to self-development and to the communities. However, the mothers themselves were critical of the lack of progression from training courses and the failure to convert schemes into real jobs.

Mothers and the Labour Market
Mothers' lives in particular are shaped by their caring responsibilities in the family and these tasks shape their work patterns and the types of occupations in which they work. The traditional low level of participation – in particular of Irish mothers – in the formal labour market has been dramatically reversed in recent years. Women's labour force participation has been important to the growth of the Celtic Tiger. Almost 50% of women living with a husband/partner in a family unit with children were in employment in June–August 2001 compared with 43.6% three years earlier. The most notable increase in employment participation was for mothers in family units where the youngest child was aged 5 to 14. In this category, the percentage in employment increased from 47.3% to 56.2% between mid-1998 and mid-2001 (CSO, 2001). An analysis of data for the period 1991–96 shows a very strong growth in women's employment at both ends of the occupational hierarchy (Breathnach, 2002). However, despite the rapid increases in women's participation rates, women's earnings only accounted for 15% of total household income in 1994. Significantly, while increases in women's employment rates in the period 1987–94 were greatest among wives married to low-earning husbands these women have only experienced modest wage gains compared to the wives of husbands with earnings above the average

(Nolan, *et al*, 2000). Part-time work continues to be dominated by women. The quarterly national household survey (2001) notes that over 36% of women were working less than 35 hours per week compared to 7.6% of men. Dual-earner households are promoted by the Irish state in the tax system. However, it does not seem to be the case that the labour force participation of mothers in low-income households has lessened their vulnerability to poverty. The absence of state supports such as public childcare, the huge increases in property prices, as well as the loss of important secondary benefits including rent/mortgage supplements, make welfare to work transitions financially suspect.

Food and the Family
Food security and the way mothers in low-income households deal with the responsibility of food and diet in daily life provide a key insight into their experience and management of poverty (Coakley 1998). In western societies the purchase and preparation of food for the family is the major responsibility of women (Charles and Kerr, 1988; Lupton, 1996; Murcott, 1983; De Vault, 1997). Feeding work is strongly associated with women's love and caring work for their families (De Vault, 1997). Lupton points out that while motherhood is relegated to the private sphere, public institutions seek to define and regulate it. The responsibility of feeding children forms part of this regulation and there are numerous medical and public health sources advising on the best types of food from pregnancy through to adulthood.

Mothers as managers in low-income households try to ensure that their families have access to both 'healthy food' as officially defined and to food choices enjoyed by the rest of society. This can sometimes be more of an aspiration as cost constraints limit these choices on a daily basis. They still retain the prime responsibility for managing money and for shopping (Dobson, *et al*, 1994; O'Neill, 1992). They have the most detailed knowledge about the patterns of food purchasing and consumption. O'Neill (1992) notes that for women:

> The financial budget becomes one of time management. Women talked of spending hours shopping for bargains. Saving pennies here and there on over-ripe vegetables and 'sell by' date groceries.

Food Consumption
Food can occupy a contradictory position in the budgeting of low-income families. It is both the main priority for spending and the

main item that mothers may cut back on to meet other financial commitments such as clothes and bills (Graham, 1994). In the present study, there were two primary areas where this conflict of interest was evident including luxuries for children and cut-backs on food.

Luxuries

As in Dobson, *et al*'s (1994) research in Britain, mothers expressed the importance of luxuries for their children and of not depriving them of status foods that other children could have. Luxuries included snack bars, minerals, ice cream and crisps. It was a sensitive issue for some mothers as they felt their children should have 'treats'. In this sense, some mothers resisted the inadequacy of their income by trying to provide these items. However, 'luxuries' for children were also graded, cut back on and done without, depending on the demands on the housekeeping money in any particular week. In this context, luxuries occupied a contradictory position on the food list as mothers saw them as items they could economise on, but at the same time, they felt that their children should not be deprived of them:

> You get so used to doing without certain things, I buy bars for their lunch, cheap ones, certain types of biscuits, cakes and even bread I wouldn't buy, I buy the 49p pan. Once a week I'd buy a fresh turnover (M5).

Another mother noted that she only bought her two children the 10p bars on shopping days and otherwise digestive biscuits. They get minerals and bars when they visit her sister. M35 commented if she had extra money:

> I'd buy biscuits and you know I'd give the kids a little treat, because like weekly we just buy what we need, the beans, the peas.

The mothers felt that the average child had items that they defined as luxuries and they did not wish to see their children excluded from food that others in society enjoy. However, some mothers cut back on these when money was short but were unhappy about having to do this. Dobson, *et al* (1994) found that snacks were important for children and 'acceptable' meant having the same snacks as other children in school.

Cut-Backs on Food

In the present study, the outcome of competing demands on the family income meant cut-backs on food or medically prescribed diets for some family members, mainly mothers, and in some cases the children too. Previous research (Lee & Gibney, 1989) noted that in homes where resources are scarce, mothers may well cut down on their food intake to make sure that there is enough for husbands and children. Nine married women in the study noted that they used cut-backs on food or medically prescribed diets for themselves or a child as a strategy to make ends meet. Separated mothers did not mention cut-backs on food, they were more likely to do without clothes or socialising:

> If I was to scrimp and scrape I'd do without a dinner myself to feed the others ... Yeah, I'd have a bit of toast or something if I hadn't got enough (M2).

For another mother who had recently started working again the additional income meant she did not have to cut-back on her own food. Referring to the past:

> Like there was occasions like I really done without. I'd end up having a packet of crisps, you know put it on a piece of bread and that would actually be my dinner ... there was just nothing coming in (M29).

The reduction in food purchasing and consumption choices evident in low-income households is very much a mother-centred task, that often involves conflicting choices between child-friendly food and other bills. O'Neill echoes this when she describes how mothers were forced to police the family food supply:

> I'm always trying to stretch food ... I often feel like the Special Branch when I hear myself asking 'who's at the fridge? who was at the milk?' and so on.

The Intra-Household Distribution of Resources

Mothers have primary responsibility for managing poverty. This aspect of poverty has been overlooked in the structure of some welfare payments in Ireland. The familist model of welfare prioritises the rights of the man to the family payment and assumes that it is equally shared amongst family members. In addition, the household unit is traditionally used as the aggregate unit of measurement in poverty research. The transformation of money once it enters the household and the consumption process has tended to be taken for granted. However this tends to mask gender differences and the unequal access to resources in families (Glendinning and Millar, 1991; Daly, 1992).

Research on financial allocation systems in households makes an important distinction between who controls household money and who manages it (Pahl, 1989; Vogler and Pahl, 1994). Management systems are differentiated by level of household income and by women's employment. Households vulnerable to poverty, including low-income and social welfare dependent, tend to be characterised by female management of a whole wage system (Brannen and Wilson, 1987; Morris, 1993; Goode, et al, 1998). One partner, usually the wife, is responsible for managing all the household income except for the personal spending money of the husband. For households on low income either due to long-term welfare dependency or through low wages, mothers bear the brunt of managing scarce resources. Women tend to have the greatest say in households where there is least to control. Access to resources within households are structured by norms of behaviour that are an expression of dominant ideologies. The dominant ideology of man as the arbiter of family living standards was thus in force at all income levels, but among low-income women it co-existed with women's ideology which recognised that women were responsible for the well-being of the family (Wilson, 1987).

Data from the present study (Coakley, 1998) shows that while the majority of mothers were responsible for managing household money, both spouses were involved in a discourse of negotiation for financial resources in the household. Money is a contested issue and this is most clearly articulated in discussions on personal spending. Mothers largely are family centred particularly if the children are dependents (Goode, et al, 1998). Even when the children are young adults, money for mothers is mainly money for the children and the house. Women utilise a negotiation process to obtain the maximum amount of money to maintain a standard of living in the home. They are active agents engaged in an ongoing process of negotiation with their husbands around the contested issue of scarce financial resources. Some common patterns are discernible in the women's reported discourses around the contested domain of the divide between husband's personal spending money and housekeeping money. Three dominant discourses are evident: Female Control; Equality in Sharing; Male Control.

Some mothers reflected a degree of power and control in curtailing their husband's spending money. They spoke unapologetically as the managers of money in the home and demonstrated independence and self-esteem. While accepting that their husbands should have pocket money, they seem to have gained a position in the household that allows them to dictate the limits of their husband's share of the household money. A total of seven (21%) married mothers were in this group. There were twelve households (36%), where husband and wife shared control and engaged in joint decisions about expenditure. Money was predominantly for collective consumption rather than for individual needs. In just under a quarter, 24% (eight), of married households, the husband had control. The husband decided how much money to give to his wife for housekeeping and when he gave it. The amount a man retained for personal use in this group was 'elastic' and was exacerbated in cases where the man had a drinking or gambling problem.

Household Outcomes
The findings of this study show that the sharing of money had important implications in all of the key areas of household expenditure. It affected the food budget, the type of consumer durables that could be afforded, housing, the nature of debt and the type of management strategies adopted. Households fared best where a woman controlled the money. Households where a husband had financial control fared worst in that the housekeeping money tended to be the lowest, was unpredictable and mothers often had to resort to high cost strategies to keep the household going. An extensive range of strategies was evident for all groups in budgeting for food with the exception of cutbacks in food/diet which was almost exclusive to the equal-sharing and husband-control groups. It is evident that in households where mothers made decisions about finances, the outcome in terms of what the household enjoyed and the nature of ownership of utilities was generally better.

Social welfare policies that uphold the formal male breadwinner status, even when a man no longer has a substantive breadwinner role, makes the task of negotiating money more onerous in the daily life of mothers. It encourages conflict, contestation and individualism between the man, who has the status of breadwinner in name only, and the woman, who has the prescribed status of carer, but not the financial rights that go with such responsibilities.

Mothers have a central role in the dynamics of poverty in low-income households. They utilise management strategies to hide poverty from their children and from the rest of the community. They can also change the dynamics of poverty by challenging prescribed gender roles. Exits out of poverty are difficult unless social supports are provided for mothers as carers and as earners. Labour market participation in itself is not a means of exiting poverty when childcare and housing cost remain high. The traditional low-level participation of women, and in particular of mothers, in the labour market has been reversed and dual-earner households have become the norm in Ireland. The Celtic Tiger society has generated new poverty dynamics. Property poverty may be identified as central to the post-modern experience of poverty in Ireland. The dramatic rise in property prices in cities, particularly Dublin, forced many people to move to rural towns in order to buy affordable homes. It may also mean moving away from traditional sources of support including kinship and friends. People are faced with longer and longer periods of time spent commuting. Time poverty is a huge issue for working mothers as they battle to juggle paid work with care of children and the home. Time poverty may lead to social isolation and less time for community participation. A further dimension is the hegemony of consumerism and increasing polarisation between work-rich and work-poor households who are unable to access consumer goods.

The relatively rapid increase in national income in Ireland over the last decade has meant that our living standards now exceed the EU average. In the European Union, Ireland, together with the UK, belongs to the southern grouping of member states where the income gap between the richest and poorest is widest (Nolan, et al, 2000). We now have a wealthier but more unequal society. This is evident in the case of mothers in low-income households who have joined the labour market but whose earnings are not making substantial differences to household income. Mothers as carers are tied up in a complex relationship with the family, the welfare state and the labour market. Policy measures need to be supportive and sensitive to changes in this relationship. The linking of social welfare rights to commodification in the labour market, the lack of subsidisation of childcare costs for mothers who do paid work and the cutbacks in maternity payments exacerbate the interaction of economic disadvantages and risk factors associated with motherhood.

CHAPTER SEVENTEEN
Motherhood Adjourned:
the Experience of Mothers in Prison

Celesta McCann James

Studies of women's experience in the prison system have traditionally existed within a forum that has centred on criminal men. Recent issues have emerged, however, which present women's imprisonment in the context of prison regimes (lack of), provisions and gender expectations. Attention has been given to why women commit crime and why they are sentenced to prison. In Ireland, female law-breakers are acknowledged in government reports, but an analysis of their prison experiences, custodial social connections and the subsequent influence on non-prison relationships, has been absent. Based on data generated over a twelve-month research period, this chapter provides evidence of women's experiences and feelings regarding their identity as 'prisoner' and as 'mother' (McCann James, 2001). It also demonstrates that, due to present prison rules and regimes, which are based on principles of social exclusion, mothers are severely restricted from access to their children. Using case studies, autobiographical stories, poetry and views of their future, this chapter shows that most prison mothers have difficulty coming to terms with their dual roles and, as a result, develop coping mechanisms that serve to alleviate their distress. During their imprisonment, many mothers lose confidence in their maternal ability and the quality of the mother-child relationship subsequently diminishes. As women spend repeated or extended periods of time in custody, feelings of shame and guilt increase and they question their future as 'good' mothers. Most respond by re-negotiating their social and emotional identities, transferring their most meaningful attachments from non-prison relationships (i.e. mother-child) to prison peers.

Before exploring some of the circumstances and emotional consequences of custody, the following section presents a useful framework for recognising the universal significance between imprisonment and motherhood and the relevance of imprisonment to prison mothers in Ireland. (Irish prisons in this chapter refer to prisons in the Irish republic).

Profile of Mothers in Prison

A Council of Europe report (2000) acknowledged that although it is not specifically known how many babies and young children are separated from their mothers in prison, there are approximately 100,000 women in prison in European countries and there are 10,000 babies and children aged two and under who are affected by imprisoned mothers. Research findings from the UK Home Office indicate that 61% of women prisoners are mothers of children under eighteen years and one-third of those children are under five years of age (Caddle and Crisp, 1997). Nearly three-quarters of those children were living with their mother at the time of her imprisonment and were now being looked after by temporary carers (i.e. grandparents and female relations) during the mothers' incarceration. Similar findings are found in research conducted by Gabel and Schindledecker (1993) where data indicates that 75% of children of incarcerated mothers are cared for by the woman's parents or other relatives, less than 10% of children are cared for by husbands and the remaining 15% are cared for by friends or in foster homes. Although three-quarters of the mothers planned to rejoin their children after release, accommodation and employment opportunities had been lost for many while they were in prison.

Women make up approximately 10% of the international prison population, however a mere 2% of the total number of prisoners in Ireland. Despite maintaining one of the smallest female prison populations in Europe, Ireland remains dependent upon closed prison facilities, subjecting all women prisoners, regardless of their crime, to physical, social and emotional isolation. The Department of Justice, Equality and Law Reform do not routinely collect information about the number of mothers in Irish prisons and official records do not produce statistical data relevant to the issue. My in-depth research revealed, however, that 60% of the women in prison in the Irish republic are between sixteen and twenty-four years of age and the overwhelming majority (90%) are under the age of forty. With such a high number of female prisoners in the childbearing years, it is likely that many, if not most, are mothers. Prison mothers in Ireland, however, are not a group that can be generically categorised. They are made up of young and old, single, married, separated and widowed women. Their social and economic circumstances are largely similar (i.e., poor and disadvantaged) and almost two-thirds come from Dublin. The remainder are from rural Ireland, the Travelling community, foreign countries or are homeless. In addition to being a largely young and disadvantaged group, 60% of women prisoners are addicted to illegal drugs. Their addictions are directly related to their crimes and result in repeated separation from their children.

Prison Mothers' (Lack of) Interaction with their Children
Regardless of the similarities or differences in social or geographical backgrounds, all prison mothers are subject to the same prison rules and regimes, which allow for only a minimum of interaction with their children. Early committals of women to Irish prisons during the 1850s permitted children to accompany their mothers. Young children and babies were housed in a 'nursery' while their mothers were confined in 'punishment cells' on the floors above. During this period, mothers were allowed to spend Sunday afternoons with their children and children remained in the care of the prison until the age of four (Carey, 2000). At present, children do not reside on prison grounds and mothers rely upon brief half-hour visits, twice a week, to sustain and nurture the mother-child relationship. Visits with children vary for mothers, with some receiving regular weekly visits and others having a visit once every three months, or none at all. Contact with children is not only limited, but also unpredictable. During imprisonment, prison mothers rely upon grandmothers, sisters, fathers and social workers to arrange contact with their children. Some mothers are fortunate to have family or friends who regularly bring their children to the prison for visits. Others, like Suzanne (the names of prisoners throughout this chapter are fictitious), have children cared for by a family member who refuses to let the children visit their mother while she is in custody. For mothers like Suzanne, weeks and sometimes months pass without seeing her children. In other words, many mothers who were primary carers prior to imprisonment, now find themselves dependent upon a third party for maintaining contact with their children. Access to their children, therefore, is not only restricted by prison regulations, but by carers' availability and goodwill.

One case that represents the lack of influence prison mothers often have over interaction with their children is that of Darina, a young twenty-year-old woman with a three-year-old daughter. Darina is a heroin addict serving a five-year sentence for a drug-related crime. Since the birth of her child, her mother had helped care for the baby, all living in the family home. When Darina went to prison, her mother assumed primary responsibility for the child's care but had recently decided that she was unable to continue for the duration of Darina's sentence. Without any warning or consultation, Darina was notified by her social worker that she would now be receiving only four visits with her daughter per year because the child was being placed in long-term foster care. Darina expressed her anger and un-happiness at the likelihood that her daughter would no longer know her as 'Mammy' and that because of infrequent visits in prison they would be unable to have any regular mother-child contact. During subsequent months, Darina's fears became a reality. Before one of her quarterly visits, Darina expressed her feelings of increased inadequacy. She became apprehensive about visits from her daughter, stating that, 'I don't know how to be a mother any longer ... I don't know how to change her nappy or what to do if she cries.' Recalling a previous visit, Darina said that she, 'didn't know what to do or how to play with her.' With tears streaming down her face, Darina cried, 'What will I do with her when she comes to visit me tomorrow? I don't know what kind of presents to give her.'

The following afternoon, Darina was escorted to the visiting area where she met her daughter, parents and social worker. Under the supervision of a prison officer, Darina sat on a chair while her little girl played on the floor with toys brought in by the grandparents. Having spoken with her parents, Darina reluctantly moved onto the floor be-side her daughter but never spoke directly with her. Instead, she con-tinued talking with her mother about some clothes that she wanted purchased, etc. As the visit ended, Darina and her mother began to tidy up the various belongings, toys, biscuits, etc. The social worker told the child, 'Here's your coat, have your Mammy help you put it on.' The child asked, 'Is Darina coming with us?' Darina's mother answered that she wasn't coming today and the child asked 'Why?' The grandmother replied, 'Mammy's not well yet.' As the visit con-cluded, the family stood at the prison gate to exit while Darina walk-ed in the opposite direction, joining another prisoner. Being prompt-ed by the grandmother and social worker, the child called out, 'Bye-bye Darina ... I love you'. Darina turned around and shouted back, 'I love you too.' She then turned to her prison friend and headed into the laundry room where they shared a bottle of Vodka that had been smuggled in during the friend's visit.

Mothers, like Darina, regularly describe separation from their children as painful and mixed with feelings of regret, shame and fear. (Such findings are paralleled in other research which documents considerable amounts of distress, anger, anxiety, sadness, depression, shame, guilt and decreased self-esteem amongst incarcerated women who are separated from family and in particular, from children. See for example, Keavey and Zauszniewski, 1999; Pennix, 1999; and Young and Jefferson Smith, 2000.) As a form of compensation, some adorn their prison cells with photographs of their children, others store children's letters in boxes safely tucked under prison beds and crayon drawings are mounted as 'trophies' on prison walls. Despite this open display of motherly pride, women are reluctant to discuss their children candidly with one another, claiming harboured feelings of maternal inadequacy, rejection and failure.

Hannah's case is another that typifies the experience of many mothers who feel threatened by imprisonment. She is a middle-aged woman with five dependent children and was sentenced to prison for the non-payment of a fine. She cried throughout the initial intake process, mingling her tears with words of apology and concern for her children's safety. The fear she expressed was that her children would be 'disgusted by their criminal mother' and that they would subsequently 'reject' her. Emotions such as Hannah's are not uncommon during the reception process which physically strips and emotionally dismantles vulnerable women.

Like mothers of dependent children, prison mothers with adult children also feel intense shame and embarrassment. Many report that they lie to their children about their prison status. Some women, serving relatively short sentences, phone their older children and tell them that they are on holiday, while others, serving longer sentences, phone to say that they are in hospital and unable to receive visits. Prison mothers from foreign countries sometimes notify their children and tell them that they are working in Ireland and will soon be sending money to them. Regardless of the excuses and fabricated stories, many mothers of adult children find the prison experience a potential threat to their children's image of them.

Prison Mothers' Response to Maternal Alienation

In order to cope with being disenfranchised from family relationships, mothers turn to prison peers for support and establish themselves with women who share similar interests or needs. Although motherhood features as a majority attribute amongst prison women, it does not emerge as a determining factor in women's choice of prison alliances. Rather than being influenced by characteristics associated with 'motherhood', mothers arrange social connections with others who share common behaviour, attitudes and expectations. These connections take the form of small cohesive subgroups and create a vital component in the construction of the prison culture. Subgroups are organised around immediate needs such as obtaining and using illegal drugs, prison interests (e.g., school, workshops) and cultural values connected with ethnicity and nationality. (Subgroups during the research period were identified as the following: drug addicts, school attendees, mature women, Travelling women, kitchen crew, foreign women, loners [see McCann James, 2001].) What evolves then is an increased emotional distance between mothers and their children and a growing dependency upon prison subgroups. This is especially evident with prisoners who experience repeated or extended periods of custody. Non-prison relationships become less meaningful and relationships with prison peers become central to surviving custody. The two cases described below each illustrate this common occurrence among mothers in prison. The mothers struggle in completely different ways, but end up with similar relational outcomes.

The first mother is Barbara, a twenty-three-year-old serving a five-year sentence for a drug-related crime. Unlike most women in prison, Barbara had completed two years of college before she began using heroin and expresses extreme remorse for her drug involvement. At the same time, she admits that she has a serious addiction and despite several attempts to quit using, often relapses. On one particular evening, Barbara was queuing for her meal and excused herself as 'not being in the best of form'. She described herself as a 'bad' mother, citing the past two years that her young daughter had spent in foster care. During that period, Barbara had heard from a variety of individuals that she was incapable of looking after the child and was 'no good for her'. With erratic contact, no access to a comprehensive drug rehabilitation programme, no job and no meaningful support, Barbara feared an uncertain future. Describing her despair and hopelessness, she held a photograph of her daughter in one hand and a tissue in the other announcing that she had signed final adoption papers earlier that morning. Barbara spoke of the love she had for her daughter and the hope that another woman would be able to 'do better for her than her addict mother'. In the days and weeks that followed, Barbara immersed herself in the prison culture. She became content with its monotonous routine, dependent upon its often damaging environment and resigned to a desolate future.

Another case that illustrates mothers' detachment from their children due to imprisonment is Marian. She is a middle-aged woman and the mother of six children ranging in age from three to twenty. Marian is a first-time offender who was sentenced to several years in prison for a violent crime. Like many new prisoners, she did not decorate her cell, refusing to allow the prison to bear any resemblance to home. She spent her initial days and weeks quietly isolated from the rest of the prison population, declaring her innocence, and stating, 'I don't belong in a place like this'. After several weeks of solitude, infrequent family visits, and a realisation that her custodial circumstances were unlikely to change, Marian moved selectively toward other prisoners. She began associating with members of one specific subgroup and subsequently became friendly with Beverly, also serving a lengthy first-time sentence for assault. Marian and Beverly were industrious during their working hours and exchanged opinions and advice regarding personal problems in private. Their prison friendship offered a relationship with shared interests and values, as well as an emotional supplement to their limited contact with family. After a relatively short period, both women became inseparable. They defended one another as loyal and obliging friends within their chosen subgroup. Marian's attitudes about her place in prison altered. She became increasingly comfortable with prison society, conforming to its daily regimes and expanding her social connections. One year later, Beverly was released from prison, leaving Marian even more reliant upon the extended relationships she had developed within her subgroup. Marian admitted to diminished contact with her family during this period and a lack of influence in their lives. She stated that her children 'don't think of me as their mammy anymore ... they probably don't think of me at all. I can't do anything for them from here and they'll be reared by the time I'm out. What's the use ... I've a new life ... so do they.' Marian depended heavily on members in her prison subgroup for regular affirmation, while at the same time maintaining contact with Beverly through letters and phone calls. On one occasion, Beverly was present when Marian went to court, showing her support, but even more significantly, giving advice regarding the case during court recesses. This advice was highly valued by Marian, who disregarded solicitor's, husband's and children's counsel in preference to Beverly's.

Case studies such as the above demonstrate that relationships for prison mothers are likely to be re-negotiated during frequent or extended periods of custody. Such concessions result when women are reliant upon the prison culture and its resources for their relief from the physical, social and emotional deprivation that accompanies imprisonment. Relational transfers for mothers (and other women prisoners) have significant policy implications regarding the relevance and practical application of government directives in respect to the purpose of prison.

Challenges for Prison Social Policy

Out of a total of one hundred and sixty-eight hours per week in custody, only one hour is routinely allotted to visitation with family and friends from outside prison. Assuming visitors are able to travel to the prison, mothers remain dependent upon this one hour (i.e., two half-hour visits) to maintain relationships with their children and other loved ones. Despite the government's commitment to 'maintain links with families' and 'assist those in custody through programmes towards an amelioration of personal and familial difficulties', prison rules and regimes practically discourage continuity and development in the mother-child relationship. Because of the contradiction between stated objectives from the government and realistic prison practice, mothers experience inadequate opportunities for meaningful contact with their children as well as an environment that is not conducive to positive interaction. It is no wonder that mothers develop feelings of incompetence, followed by emotional detachment. Some mothers, however, continue to imagine and hope for a future in which they will be successfully and comfortably reunited with their children. They document their hopes and fears in stories and poems as they spend days and nights separated from their children. The writings that follow are but a sample of the emotional gap mothers live with during their imprisonment, despite idealised objectives from government directives:

Special Child

You came to me with a smile of gold,
So small, so precious, afraid to hold.
You yawned, you wriggled, you smiled,
And drove my emotions wild.
A day, a week, a month, a year,
You filled my life with love and fear.
Your first steps – one, two, three.
And yes, you walked straight to me.

I was part of you, you were part of me,
But that was all too good to be.
You're a boy now, growing on your own,
All because I can't go home.
I miss you dearly, I love you too.
Some day I will make it up to you.
And I pray to God above,
To keep you wrapped in my love.
By 'Niamh'

The Longest Day of my Life
The longest day I remember was when I went into hospital to have my baby. I went into the ward at two p.m. I had a lot of pain, but the baby didn't want to pop ... so I had to walk up and down the ward for five hours. The walking was to bring the baby's head down, but that wasn't working so they injected something into my back. It was to feel no pain. I can assure you ... I had a lot of pain!

But time went on and they took me into another ward. It was the ward where the gas is. It helps a bit. So, I didn't have the baby the way others would. They used the forceps on me. Ten minutes after, I had a lovely little girl in my hands. I think it was the longest and best day of my life.

I would be better if I was out with my child now. *Now this is the longest day* ... I have to wait until I get out and I don't know when that is. My baby is all I have to live for ... only for her I would be dead. She is my little blue-eyed girl.
By 'Brenda'

Most women enter prison from disadvantaged backgrounds and face obstacles to a normal life that often seem insurmountable. Despite socio-economic deprivation and insecure futures, many women benefit from meaningful familial relationships. For mothers, this includes the love they share with their children. While held in state custody, mothers are sheltered, fed, clothed and managed, however their relational needs and those of their children are largely disregarded. Despite its formal declaration of preserving and developing healthy family links, the Department of Justice, Equality and Law Reform subverts women's role as mother and diminishes their maternal influence through its use of closed prison facilities and practice of social exclusion. Mothers are systematically undermined by imprisonment, being reduced to one hour of interaction with their children per week. In addition to this physical restriction, mothers have the added fear of being portrayed as 'bad', 'incompetent', or 'inferior' to their children and subsequently losing their child's love and admiration. Rather than providing a rehabilitative structure that is conducive to healthy mother-child relationships, imprisonment adjourns motherhood by revoking women's access to their children and fostering deterioration in the relationship. As mothers perceive increased maternal insignificance, they re-negotiate their relationships and establish new identities that are valued and approved within the small community of prison peers. Mothers' understanding and experience of imprisonment contradicts criminal justice policies which currently endorse physical, social and emotional seclusion as an acceptable context for rehabilitation. There is a systematic failure on the part of government departments, prison management and society to acknowledge the immediate and long-term damage that results from penal custody for mothers in prison.

CHAPTER EIGHTEEN

Motherhood in Northern Ireland

Margaret Ward

It is not possible to think of mothers in Northern Ireland without thinking too of some of the iconic images which have emerged from thirty years of bitter civil conflict: young mothers with pushchairs, angrily confronting armed soldiers on the small streets of Derry and Belfast; women wrapped only in blankets, leading marches that called for political status for prisoners; women in Union Jack dresses and babies with 'proud to be a prod' bibs; peace women, anxious to stretch out the hand of friendship to those on 'the other side'; mothers mourning children blown up by bombs, killed by plastic bullets or by sectarian assassins (Fairweather, et al, 1984; Aretxaga, 1997; Meyer, 2000, Mulholland, 2001; Sharoni, 2001). Apart from those few, secluded in leafy suburbia, shielded from the worst of the Troubles by money and social status, 'ordinary' women, when asked about their experiences of motherhood, all start from the same place – the impact of the Troubles on themselves and their families. Throughout, the family has been a site of struggle, of resistance, of oppression – and a place of refuge from the uncertainties of the outside world. However, to concentrate solely upon heightened moments from past decades is to distort the overall picture in terms of women's experiences and their testimony of coping with everyday life in a society that has been anything but 'normal'.

This chapter is a preliminary attempt to consider different facets of Northern Irish motherhood; to discover what women feel about their role as mothers, and what they feel about the society in which they live. It incorporates the views of a range of women, from a Catholic working-class estate in West Belfast, an inner city area of Protestant South Belfast and a mixed group of Protestant and Catholic women from different areas, rural and urban. Focus groups took place in April and May 2002. The views expressed here are illustrative only, a more comprehensive study which will include rural women and women who were actively mothering during the height of the conflict, will form another stage of research.

Childhood and War

There are very few who have not been affected, in one way or another, by the experience of living in a deeply divided, impoverished, conflict-ridden society. For mothers, the task of caring for their families has taken many forms and has often been affected by external factors. Regardless of class background or community affiliation, that responsibility is linked inextricably to the reality of living in a situation where potential danger remains an ever-present threat. Many families have coped with the burden of living through war through a denial of the reality of what was occurring beyond the safety of the home:

> Yes, it's fear. Like hoping if you don't talk about it, it'll go away. At home I used to ask: 'what is the IRA?' and my family would say 'don't be talking like that in this house'.

For too many, however, the home was not inviolate:

> It got to the stage when the cops came to the door to lift him every week … To think of my mother saying 'John, you're wanted' and him just putting on his clothes and going downstairs.

For those in areas where the conflict was at its most intense, regular raids by the British army were experienced by the majority:

> We were raided loads of times because my mother had friends from everywhere … we were raided, put under house arrest, you just got on with it because it was happening to everyone else too, so it was like normal.

In such circumstances, women's protection of their children has had to take many forms. Some mothers have gone to great lengths to prevent their children from becoming involved in paramilitary activity although, given the circumstances of working-class life in ghetto areas, this often proved impossible. One woman, remembering that her brother used to go out rioting, 'when he came in my ma and da used to hit him' also recollected that every time he went out the door:

> He got battered for not giving his name and they used to spread him up against the wall and kick him and that's why I think an awful lot of kids in the Troubles got into trouble because it was like fighting back.

So difficult was life at the height of the conflict that mothers exerted great pressure to keep their children at home, although this could only be successful with the very smallest of children. Growing up in a strongly republican estate in the 1980s, one young woman saw nothing of the Troubles because she and her brother 'weren't allowed out the front gate and we weren't allowed out the back gate, we had to stay in the back or the front garden, we were prisoners'. The reason was, as her mother said, 'there were plastic bullets flying in all directions, love, and you couldn't have went anywhere.'

This fear was real. Fourteen people, including seven children, were killed by plastic bullets between the years 1974 and 1996, while many more have been seriously injured (Human Rights Watch Report, 1998). Of course, for mothers, increased disturbances meant greater confinement within the home for themselves as well as their children. The mental cost of their experiences has still to be considered. One woman, who brought up two children in a strongly loyalist estate, remembered times of intense worry, not knowing where her son might be when heavy shooting was occurring and actually leaving the house at midnight to look for him. For her, the burden was worse for mothers than it was for fathers:

> I would be quicker just to jump and go out to look for them than my husband … whenever you are afeard for your youngsters … you just want them to be safe.

While it was a 'nightmare' to rear teenagers, there was no one to turn to:

> Mothers didn't talk to each other about it, it was just going on and what could you do, just keep a check on them and ask them to ring you, but there was nobody you could go to talk about it.

Residential Segregation
One consequence of the upheavals of the past decades has been an enforced movement of population. Not only is the population of Northern Ireland highly segregated in residential terms, it is also strongly focused around the family, as those who marry stay close to their kin group. The urban inner city areas of Derry and Belfast have been described as 'matrifocal' because of the central role played by women in maintaining the strong sense of kin solidarity (McLaughlin, 1993). A number of important factors emerge from a situation where large family size and lack of social mobility have contributed to the development of social networks. In a society where conflict

has been endemic for over thirty years, such insularity has been important in maintaining a sense of community safety but for women in particular, life can be so rigidly structured around family that it prevents participation in a world outside the confines of the home. In addition, domestic responsibilities and lack of childcare has meant 'severely restricted social lives, with few able to work' (Sales, 1998). In other words, the superficially dominant role played by women in terms of kin relationships has not resulted in female empowerment. On the contrary, such family networks are likely to underpin women's oppression as the maintenance of the families' status is policed by members of the family, who ensure that community norms and conventions are respected (Edgerton, 1986). In discussion with an experienced community educator, the low take-up by women of daytime classes based in women's centres was attributed in part to their habit of visiting family members during school hours, which fulfilled the need for companionship but at the cost of self-development. Another explanation might lie in the dynamics of a relationship between a woman and her unemployed partner. In such a situation, as those involved in community-based education have observed, leaving the house in order to attend class can be much more difficult because of the reluctance of some men to see their wives and girlfriends develop in knowledge and self-confidence.

While closely-knit groups may be regarded as sources of invaluable support for women in the home, the reality is that such support is at the expense of other women. In the absence of adequate facilities within the community, mothers have relied on 'grannies' for child-minding services, elderly parents on their daughters for help, and there has been an assumption that this is part of women's role (Leonard, 1997). Male power within the family is maintained, although the majority of men have little dealings with children or with domestic affairs. While this situation persists, young mothers are finding that their own mothers are less able to act as child-minder:

> My mother is a widow, my father died three years ago and she's finding it tough as she only has £56 a week to live on so she has the opportunity to go out to work, she feels sorry for us but she had to do it when we were all young, when the men were all out working in the time of the Troubles.

One woman voiced the frustration of being a mother in a large housing estate with very little facilities with passion:

We need nurseries, mother and toddlers groups, youth facilities, parks, all this frustration is lumped onto the mother and my personal opinion of Northern Irish fathers is that they go to work, bring home their wages, the kids are yours, you get very little support there, very, very little support. You feel so alone, so trapped.

Explaining 'the Troubles'

The urge of all parents to protect the innocence of childhood soon comes into conflict with the reality that innocence is not possible in Northern Irish society, where signs of sectarian hatreds are visible on walls, pavements and lamp posts. It is primarily mothers who have to deal with the dilemmas, as they are the ones most inextricably linked with small children who begin to notice their surroundings and to ask questions. Many others echo the sentiments expressed by one woman:

> I find it very difficult to try and get a simple way of putting over the Troubles to the kids, to try to get them to understand it, because really, you don't understand it yourself sometimes.

The initial reaction appears to be to fob off questions for as long as possible, as was the case with a mother answering a four-year-old's questions concerning the proliferation of loyalist flags at an interface area:

> I'm asked who put them up and why are they there and I just say 'someone's having a party and it's not our party' ... but I know it's going to be a huge issue.

As children grow up, when they drive past unfamiliar areas, they begin to ask more questions, 'what's red, white and blue mummy', 'what's Protestants' and one mother said, with despair, 'what do you explain to your child if you are a Catholic, it's just a different culture son.' For her, it was too difficult an issue 'when it comes on the news, you turn over, you don't let them watch it.' Mothers from Protestant areas experience the same difficulties:

> If my daughter said to me, 'what's going on?' I couldn't explain what happens. So when she asks why are we not allowed up the Falls Road, why can't I play with someone who is Catholic, it's very very hard to explain to them, without coming across as bigoted.

Even when a parent might be willing to offer an explanation, there are occasions when explanations are particularly difficult, especially for those living in areas where paramilitary activity remains endemic:

> There was a wee boy got shot the other week, it was a punishment shooting and my ... nephew seen him lying, getting shot you know, and he's been wetting the bed from it, he's four years of age and what do you tell a child of four? The bad men shot the bad boy? You can't do it.

That inability to engage in any meaningful discussion with their children regarding the Troubles extends even to situations where it would appear to be in the best interest of their children to understand the circumstances, in which they live:

> My kids used to come in and say: 'why is Caroline not playing with me any more? Why can't I play in the back field now?' And I didn't want to say, you can't play in the back field 'cos Caroline might hit you.

More recently, the appointment of Martin McGuinness as Minister of Education has been a source of great contention within the Protestant community. Hostility to the prospect of McGuinness visiting schools in his ministerial capacity is compounded by a difficulty in explaining to children why he has a legitimate claim to come to their community.

Women whose experience of the education system has been limited to a secondary school education that was not academic and which provided no background to an understanding of the origin of the Troubles lack the knowledge and the vocabulary to express difficult issues to their children. One consequence is that, in attempting to keep their children safe, they have to resort to such euphemisms as 'bad people', thereby perpetuating sectarian stereotyping.

Safety and Sectarianism
Many mothers acknowledge their inability or reluctance to provide explanations for the obvious political divisions within society, admitting that what they are doing is to fob children off with answers that will shut them up, an unsatisfactory situation that 'leaves them more confused'. However, when it comes to ensuring the safety of their children, all agree that some kind of explanation is essential. Mothers of older children are adamant that it is in their children's best interest to 'equip them' so that they could avoid areas that would be dangerous. In the highly ghettoised circumstances of working-class life, it was recognised that some explanations were essential, because children would be:

> Travelling out of the area, going to be meeting different kids from different backgrounds, and so there has to be a bit of security ... to give them a bit of knowledge.

For Catholic mothers, anxious to avoid instilling sectarian attitudes, no explanation is easy:

> There are bad people and good in every area ... I would say that road's dangerous because some bad people live on it ... but there are also some Catholic areas that I wouldn't let my kids go into because it's rough.

The anxiety of worrying about the safety of their children remains a constant feature, and those who live near dangerous interface areas, the notorious 'murder miles' of the worst years of the Troubles, have found that their lives 'weren't their own' because of their insistence on driving and meeting their reluctant teenagers. Given that one square mile of north Belfast suffered 313 killings in the period 1969–1996 (North Belfast Community Internet Site) it is hardly surprising to hear the comments of one woman from that part of the city:

> I think, please God, if the peace holds, we'll not have to parent the way our parents did ... I don't think I could have parented with what my mummy and daddy had to bring us up in ... Every night, my mummy would have been advising us to be careful, and every night when we came home she'd say 'thank god'.

Despite the relative peace of the last years, worries for teenage safety remain. While there is less fear of sectarian shootings (but some residual fear remains) the worry of joy-riding, drugs and alcohol is acute:

> I have to work awful hard to keep my sons off the streets because I know if they are on the streets they are going to be in a stolen car, they are going to be standing drinking ... I have that fear constant at my front doorstep ... thank god for football, keeping them away from the bad elements.

While most of this might be similar to the experiences of mothers everywhere, who have worries about 'rough' estates and destructive influences on their children, for women in the north, the baleful effects of sectarian conflict have contributed to a deep-rooted fear of stepping outside one's own area. The effect of territorial segregation cannot be over-emphasised:

> I would be afraid to go on X road, because I've been told I can't go down it ... so it's started to make me fear it.

What I find intimidating would be going into another place, being scared, you imagine you have Catholic written on your head.

You think you are walking around with a big neon sign above you, and maybe people don't know what you are, but that's the way you feel inside.

You think you have union jack tattooed to your head if you are walking up and down, that's just the way it's perceived.

Few would venture into the territory of the 'other' and even parents who would like their children to meet those from outside their community find that concern for their children's safety overrides all other considerations. In a small, religiously mixed market town, freedom to move around is as curtailed as in segregated Belfast:

I won't let my boy go to town on Saturday as things happen in the town ... I work in the centre and it's so divided – orange on one side and green on the other. It's not that you don't want them to mix; you just want your kids to be safe. You need to teach them not to be too afraid to mix, as well as to suss out who is a threat.

For Protestants in Belfast, parts of the city centre are perceived as Catholic and therefore threatening:

I tried a wee bit to say it to my daughter ... setting out boundary lines in the town, not in Castle Place and all this ... but she can't really grasp why she can't go to certain places.

The mother of one Belfast woman had had many Protestant friends before the start of the Troubles and was reluctant to lose all contact, so she allowed her children to visit 'Protestant' areas, although only after insisting that they obeyed precautionary safety measures:

My mummy gave us a rule that you had to follow, certain meeting places if you got lost, phone numbers you had to memorise, don't say your name out loud.

Geographical segregation of residential areas has helped to reinforce stereotypes of the 'other' community. Peer pressure and the influence of their surroundings have also contributed to the development of attitudes amongst children that are often very different from those of parents who belong to a generation that grew up in a time before views became so entrenched, 'They do come out with some very bigoted statements. You can try and instil your values into them but in the end ...' One mother, raising her daughters in a village on the border, recollected that 'suddenly they were coming home with Sinn Féin scratched on their pencil cases and scratched on the desks at school'. After they joined the GAA club and experienced British helicopters flying low over the Gaelic pitch as they played, she experienced their fury, 'you know Mum, you tried to convince us that it wasn't a good thing to support Sinn Féin ... but if you don't, look at what they do to you, they walk all over you.' Children adapt quickly to radically changing circumstances and what is abnormal can, for them, quickly become the norm. One seven-year-old, currently living in the midst of a riot area in North Belfast, possesses words in her vocabulary that should not be there, 'she talks about curfew, comes running in at 8 o'clock saying "mummy is it curfew time yet?"' Commentators have criticised parents for the apparent neglect of their children, not keeping older ones under curfew, yet many mothers who have lived their lives in Belfast are more reluctant to criticise:

> I often think it is easy to sit and cast aspersions, but at the same time, when my eldest boy is out ... if we were living in North Belfast I could be seeing him on the television, you can only have so much control, they have to spread their wings and find themselves.

Another thought-provoking comment:

> If I were financially and socially poor and disadvantaged and in a fairly ghettoised area where housing was very segregated ... how could you lift yourself beyond that kind of political involvement ... to rear your kids differently to whatever everybody else was on the street?

Despite the pressures of living in a community that was rife with loyalist paramilitaries, mothers were adamant that they would not let their children join in the sectarian behaviour that was encouraged by other parents:

> At the same time, down the line it will stand you, it means there is one less boy, one less girl out there throwing petrol bombs, and slagging off Catholics and if there is one less it's a start isn't it?

Integrated Education
Integrated education has been hailed as the balm that will eventually heal the wounds inflicted by the conflict, and most mothers said they wanted their children to go to 'mixed' schools:

> Integrated ... that's what I want. They are all going to grow up, especially those years in high school, 11 to 16, that's when it happens.

Yet sending children to a school where they will meet and make friends with children from different backgrounds has its own dangers. Indeed, social attitude surveys have consistently found that the proportion of those who support the principle of integrated education is higher than the proportion choosing to send their own children to an integrated school (Stringer and Robinson, 1993). Personal testimony helps to explain why this might be the case. One mother, living in a large estate in Catholic West Belfast, sent her children to an integrated secondary school in the 1980s, believing that the 'all ability, all classes, all creeds' ethos was the 'right idea'. To her horror, she discovered that the school environment, which made children feel that 'everybody was their friend' inculcated a false sense of security because 'they had lost all sense of danger'. After an attack on her daughter, who had gone to an unfamiliar area with some of her school friends, she withdrew her children:

> Because anything could happen to them, going into these areas at night, people not knowing them and they were so innocent, everyone was their friend ... I'm not sacrificing the kids.

Another mother, coming from a working-class Protestant background and finding her local integrated primary school was located in the middle of a Catholic housing estate festooned with republican graffiti, admitted that:

> There was a certain amount of fear left over ... despite having lots of Catholic friends and knowing that it isn't the risk it was, whenever it comes to my children, if there is the slightest risk of a doubt, then it isn't good enough for my children.

Unhappy with that decision, she and her husband are considering working with other parents to establish an integrated secondary school so that their children will at least experience integrated education after the age of eleven. For others, wanting their children to fit in with their community determines choice of school. A mother who had a choice of Irish language school, integrated school or Catholic primary for her children, felt she had no choice other than the Catholic school because 'every other child in the street wears the red uniform and goes to the local school'. She admitted 'I will never be happy about the decision we took', but while society remains abnormal and people's sense of security partly emanates from neighbourhood solidarity, then the integrated route will remain a minority choice.

One mother, a Catholic married to a Protestant, had sent her children to the local state secondary school, in the belief that 'it would be a bit more inclusive'. She found it was 'the Protestant ethos really', and had to endure her teenage son calling her a 'Fenian', because that was how he had heard Catholics described by his friends at school. 'I keep trying to stop him, he is saying it for a joke, but I worry when it is not a joke.' Benefiting from the advantages of third-level education, she was determined to ensure that her children understood the history of the Troubles. As one half of a 'mixed marriage' and the product of a mixed marriage herself, her hope was that in the long run, the family, rather than peer pressure, would have the most lasting influence:

> I hope he knows that my husband and I get on well together, and our families too, they know that people can live together ... some day they will be able to say I was brought up in a mixed marriage and it worked for me, that's all I can hope.

Less than 10% of marriages are inter-religious, although this number has increased from only 6% in 1989 ('Life and Times Survey', 2001). For those living in middle-class areas, the difficulties are evident in terms of choices of schools, attitudes of their children, having to tread carefully when discussing religion and politics within the extended family circles. But for those from the ethnically segregated working-class estates, marrying outside the tribe poses other problems, including pressure from the immediate community, compounded by the difficulty of developing a real knowledge of the other community:

> My son doesn't actually know anything about Catholics ... I think if you make a difference, that's a Catholic, that's a Protestant, you are making a difference from the start, they are just people, maybe I'm being naïve, but my brother is marrying a Catholic so I don't want to make a big fuss because kids have a habit of thinking about things, and that makes you think there is a difference.

The fear that such a couple would be subjected to a campaign of intimidation was often voiced, backed up in some cases by personal experience, as in the case of a niece's engagement to a Protestant:

> My sister is constantly worried sick, they had paint thrown over their car

and had a windscreen broke and the police came out and said 'well maybe it's because you're with a Catholic.'

All believed that they would have to live in a 'different country' because 'you don't get left alone by both sides, it's not just one.' Although the religiously mixed area of South Belfast has become a favoured place to live (*Observer*, 2001), this is not an option for those who live in an environment with strong attachments to family and with limited ability to travel, 'you don't want to move, you're leaving your family and friends'. Catholics from all social classes remain more in favour of residential mixing and mixing at work than do their Protestant counterparts, yet support for mixed marriages is at a lower level for all groups, at 60% for Catholics and 38% for Protestants (Breen and Devlin, 1999).

Talking about Politics

For many women, the political arena is seen as an alien environment. The Troubles, regarded as promulgated mostly by men, are perceived as having contributed to the social and economic deprivation of their communities, 'the hatred and all the rivalry … it's stupid here, it's just mad, honest to god.' Their frustration is expressed by a woman from a nationalist area:

> This is a very political place that we live where the kids and the families and the mothers aren't (getting attention) … it's only the men fighting their ego war that stops us getting priority … and that's probably why most of the places are neglected, where money … isn't being put in where they need, because they think they have to make a stand for their religious beliefs. Me personally I would rather live without it all and just get on with it. But it's the men who still control and have the control and they are the ones who are holding us all back

This was echoed by women from the unionist community, who feel powerless to effect change because of the control exerted by paramilitaries, 'It's ok us saying we hate this, what we would like to do, but if we said anything, they would come round to our houses, we would get threatened.' Although a vain hope was expressed by Catholics that this situation could be different, 'they should kick all the men off and put the women in', no one expected that women would have the power to enter that world in order to represent their own interests. For Protestant women in a loyalist area, life without the malign influence of paramilitaries was inconceivable:

> There are always going to be the hardliners because of the drugs … it's all racketeering, and drugs, so there will always be that group, keeping things going.

Any optimism for the future lay in their children breaking away from their background:

> I always say to my daughter; be a leader, not a follower, don't just go with a crowd because they believe that. You are always going to be tempted … and there will be people saying you have to do that because you are a Protestant, but at the end of the day they have to make up their own minds.

All the mothers hoped that the situation would improve:

> You have to think that way, rather than thinking negatively. But at the same time you are wanting peace but not just the words peace, you need to see action from both sides.

Mothers in Northern Ireland have demonstrated enormous resilience at times of extreme adversity. The problems that continue to confront them are immense but the resources required to make a significant difference to their lives should not be beyond the scope of our devolved assembly. Their words in these interviews reveal a capacity to articulate their needs with great passion and insight. It is to be hoped that these voices will be heard and their needs addressed.

Acknowledgements
I am grateful to the women who responded to the 'Womenslink' discussion list call for a focus group discussion held in the offices of *Democratic Dialogue*. Many thanks to Felice Kiel of Belfast Women's Training Services for facilitating focus groups in West Belfast and South Belfast. Thanks also to Rosie Burroughs, researcher on the 'Parenting in a Divided Society' project, who provided transcripts of focus groups organised by Barnados in Newry, Lurgan and North Belfast. Unattributed quotations are taken from all the groups mentioned.

CHAPTER NINETEEN

Young Mothers

Valerie Richardson

Research in a number of countries has consistently shown that teenage mothers and their families are often at a disadvantage compared with those whose children are born in their twenties or thirties.

Teenage motherhood is of concern for both medical and socioeconomic reasons: they show higher than average risks of poor progress during pregnancy, difficulties at birth and poor health in subsequent years. A study of thirteen European countries undertaken by the Institute for Social and Economic Research in the UK (Berthoud and Robson, 2001) showed that former teenage mothers suffered a variety of disadvantages in comparison with other mothers. These disadvantages were lower educational qualifications, greater possibility of being a one-parent family, being less likely to have a job and being at higher risk of poverty. Many of these disadvantages affected former teenage mothers in all thirteen countries studied but an assessment based on all the measures analysed suggested that former teenage mothers are worst off in Ireland and are least disadvantaged, relative to other families, in Austria, Germany and Greece. Former teenage mothers in the UK and Ireland were much less likely to be married than in other countries. For example, in Ireland, 34% of women who had babies as teenagers were single and not cohabiting ten years after their first birth, compared with 7% of Irish mothers as a whole. Former teenage mothers were also likely to live in a workless family, that is, they themselves did not work and they either had no partner or one who was also unemployed. This was especially true in Ireland compared with other European countries.

Irish research has also shown consistent findings of an increased risk of poverty and welfare dependency among unmarried adolescent parents (McCashin, 1996; Wilson 1999). For example, McCashin (1993) found that over 90% of unmarried lone-parent households received 80% or more of their gross income from social welfare payments. In a further study he showed that when income data for households of different types was analysed to calculate risks of poverty, unmarried lone parents emerged as the highest risk category (McCashin,

1996). Research in the UK and the US has shown that adolescent childbirth is associated with low educational achievement, lack of employment opportunities, low socio-economic status and low self esteem, all of which contribute to the likelihood of early pregnancy as well as to the consequences of it (Phoenix, 1991; Lawson and Rhode, 1993; Berthoud & Robson, 2001).

Research conducted as part of the Moving On project, undertaken under the EU Employment Integra Initiative, indicates that pregnancy and early parenthood can lead to a sense of loss for young mothers. They feel stigmatised, they express feelings of isolation, are confused about being young parents responsible for a dependent child, their interpersonal relationships suffer and they are particularly prone to depression (Moving On: Young Mothers and Employment Project, 2002).

Demographic Trends in Teenage Births in Ireland
The table below shows the overall trend in births to women under twenty years of age over the previous four decades, 1962–2002:

Year	Unmarried No.	%	Married No.	%	Total
1962	369	28.6	922	71.4	1291
1972	681	24.0	2159	76.0	2840
1982	1618	54.3	1362	45.7	2980
1992	2435	89.5	286	10.5	2721
2002	2721	91.4	257	8.6	2978

(Department of Health, Vital Statistics for relevant years, Government Publications, Dublin)

As can be seen from the table, the total numbers of births to women under the age of 20 years has almost trebled over the past forty years. The largest total increase was between 1962 and 1972 with an increase of 140 over the next decade, followed by a drop in 1992 to below the 1972 level and then rising again in 2002 to 2778. However, the more dramatic change over this period has been the rise in the percentage of women under the age of twenty years giving birth outside marriage. In addition, the numbers of women aged 18 years or under has increased six fold from 139 in 1962 to 844 in 2002 with all but 35 of these women being unmarried. However, the rise in the number of births to unmarried mothers has not been confined to teenage mothers. In 2002, these births represented 31.1% (18,814) of all births in Ireland. (Central Statistics Office Vital Statistics, May 2003). This increase has resulted from a number of factors, mainly a change in social attitudes to non-married parenthood with a reduction in the social stigma attached to lone parenthood; financial support for lone parents in the form of social welfare payments; decrease in the popularity of marriage; and a decrease in the use of adoption as a resolution for unmarried parenthood.

Children having Children

Children having children was first highlighted as a national problem in the United States by the Alan Guttmacher Institute (1976) which referred to the increasing numbers of teenage pregnancies as an epidemic (Alan Guttmacher, 1981; Vinovski, 1988). Concerns in Britain resulted in the government commissioning a study on Teenage Mothers and their Partners (Simms and Simms, 1986). This was followed by articles in the British media such as 'Alarm over Teenage Baby Boom' (*Sunday Times*, 5 January 1992). Similar concerns were expressed in Ireland. In particular, there was a spate of media articles following the death of a 15-year-old schoolgirl who gave birth alone in an open-air grotto in the grounds of a church. In July 1990, the Eastern Health Board set up a working group to look at measures to address the increasing numbers of teenage pregnancies (1991). In addition, a number of articles were published such as Teenage Pregnancies: 'A trend that can't be stopped' (*Irish Times*, 26 July 1990) and 'Concern over Teenage Pregnancies' (*Irish Times*, 5 September 1990). The concern also resulted from an increasing number of research studies which concentrated on the aforementioned negative socio-economic consequences of adolescent pregnancy and childbearing. Children of adolescents were found to experience difficulties such as physical problems, behaviour problems and a higher risk of neglect and maltreatment.

Pregnancy in adolescence presents the young woman with the challenge of coping with multiple developmental tasks, in particular the normal psycho-social tasks of adolescence combined with the added task of coming to terms with the physical changes of pregnancy, role change and the acceptance of a dependent child when they themselves are still dependent on adults (Bloom, 1995; Richardson, 1993). One of the developmental tasks of adolescence is for the adolescent to achieve appropriate independence from parents. When adolescents become pregnant, they are presented with a situation in which their dependence on parents, particularly their own mothers, is heightened. They need emotional, physical and material support from the adults from whom they have been trying to achieve independence. Thus, the normal adolescent who is attempting to achieve a balance between dependence and independence from parents is faced with added conflict when she becomes pregnant. Scanlan (1994) in a study of single mothers parenting within their family of origin found that being both daughters and mothers had difficulties, particularly over the care and parenting of the babies. However, she concluded that the 'advantages of parenting within the family of origin outweighed the disadvantages and provided the mother with a generally positive, though challenging context within which to parent her baby'.

More recently, the literature on teenage pregnancy and parenthood has begun to question the automatic assumption that it is a problem, arguing that many of the adverse consequences associated with adolescent childbirth may also be partial causes. Lawson and Rhode (1993) asserted that the reason teenage pregnancy was constructed as a problem lay in the fact that such behaviour violated traditional assumptions about acceptable adolescent behaviour and highlighted the teenagers' sexual independence at a time when they were unable to achieve financial independence. In fact, the issues of poverty and, especially, welfare dependence, appear to be those which raise the greatest alarm. In particular, the level of public money spent on supporting teenage mothers and their children. Phoenix (1993) pointed out that because:

> good parents are socially constructed as people who make independent economic provision, those who depend on welfare payments cannot fit in with society's definition of adequate parenting.

Thus, the conclusion drawn by society is that teenage parents on welfare benefits are not good parents and are, therefore, a problem. However, no research to date has demonstrated this as being fact rather than myth. In fact, in my 2001 study, I found that the mothers were generally coping well despite the range of difficulties they might be facing. Therefore, the thrust of more recent research has been towards developing programmes of prevention and providing support services following delivery in the form of childcare and opportunities for returning to education and training.

Decision-Making by Young Mothers

Any woman who becomes pregnant outside marriage is faced with a range of options in deciding on the future of herself and her child. She may choose to have the pregnancy terminated, to marry the father of the baby, to parent her child and remain unmarried or to have the baby adopted. Therefore, the path to becoming a non-married parent is one which can be constructed as a series of decisions. Each decision the woman makes requires a further decision. This decision path is illustrated in the figure below:

Decision Path Towards becoming an Unmarried Parent

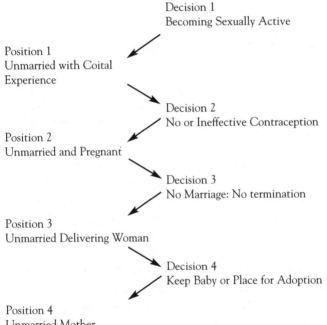

Decision 1
Becoming Sexually Active

Position 1
Unmarried with Coital
Experience

Decision 2
No or Ineffective Contraception

Position 2
Unmarried and Pregnant

Decision 3
No Marriage: No termination

Position 3
Unmarried Delivering Woman

Decision 4
Keep Baby or Place for Adoption

Position 4
Unmarried Mother

While there are a number of decisions to be made after pregnancy occurs, there are two earlier stages requiring attention. The first is the decision to become sexually active and the second is centred on the issue of contraception.

It is difficult to document the increase in sexual activity among teenagers due to the social taboos on the subject and the unreliability of survey data on sexuality among young people. There have been few Irish studies on the level of teenage sexual activity. Fitzpatrick, *et al*

(1997) in a study of 120 teenage mothers attending a public adolescent antenatal clinic, found that the mean age of first sexual intercourse was 16.5 (range 13–19) and that there was little evidence of promiscuity with over 80% of the women stating that they had had only one partner. American studies have shown increased sexual activity among young people in recent decades and at an earlier age (Cole and Cole 1996). The factors affecting the decisions of increasing numbers of adolescents to become sexually active are varied. Voydanoff and Donnelly (1990) have argued that adolescents today, compared with those of earlier decades:

> experience increased autonomy, greater opportunity for sexual activity, less negative attitudes toward sex and an increased length of time during which they are asked to be sexually inactive after they become sexually mature.

Adolescents also tend to be poor users of contraceptives. Greene, et al (1989) found that:

> lack of sex education, lack of information on contraception, poor access to contraceptive methods and social embarrassment and difficulties about the use of contraception may be important determinants of the single woman's failure to use contraception.

Fitzpatrick, et al (1997) found that while over half of the teenagers said that they had used contraception in the past the reported compliance in the majority was poor. Education, rather than availability, appeared to be a greater problem in this group. They also state that 'the psychological development of most adolescents makes them less than ideal users of contraception.' They also found that the age of first coitus, social class and education influenced fertility awareness and the use of contraception. Mahon, et al (1998) found that young women felt that they would be stigmatised for being sexually active in the eyes of their parents, doctor or other authority figure if they approached them concerning contraception and therefore they were making decisions about its use on the basis of what method carried least risk of discovery by their parents. In some cases, therefore, it meant they did not use any contraception. In addition, adolescents are known to be high-risk takers in most aspects of their lives and the use of contraception and the attitude to sexual behaviour and pregnancy is only one aspect of this high-risk behaviour. The use of contraceptives requires thinking ahead and systematic usage and this can be difficult for young adolescents who have not developed the tools of analytical thinking and who live in the 'here and now' (Jorgensen, 1981; McAnarney and Schreider, 1984; Richardson, 1993).

While abortion is not available within Ireland, an increasing number of Irish women are choosing to travel out of the jurisdiction to obtain a termination. It is impossible to obtain accurate figures on the numbers involved, although some indications can be deduced from the numbers of women giving Irish addresses who have terminations in England and Wales. Mahon, et al (1998) reported that just over 15% (686) of all abortions performed in England and Wales on women giving Irish addresses were for women under the age of 19 years. However, this number has risen sharply since that year. In just the first three months of 2002 there were 257 teenagers giving Irish addresses who received terminations in England and Wales, representing an increase of 47 over the same period in the previous year.

Once the woman has decided against termination she may decide to marry the father of the baby. However, it is clear from the statistical data available that being a teenage mother is far more likely to be synonymous with being a single parent in that the vast majority of young mothers choose to give birth to their babies as non-married women: 92.9% of teenage births were to unmarried mothers in 2001 (Vital Statistics Department of Health 2002). In 2001, I found in my sample of young mothers that marriage was of little importance to them at that time and they did not view it as being of particular interest in the future.

Once the baby is born to a non-married woman, the baby becomes eligible for adoption. There has been a rapid decrease in the number of women placing their baby for adoption over the past decade. In 1990, there were 360 adoption orders made by the Adoption Board in respect of Adoption Societies and Health Boards compared to 77 in 2000 (Reports of An Bord Uchtala, 1999 and 2000). A number of factors seem to have come together which have led to this decline in the use of adoption. Over the past three decades, there has been an increasing acceptance of cohabitation and non-married parenthood, together with a reduction in the stigma associated with being an unmarried mother. In addition, the availability of financial support through lone-parent allowances has made it feasible for unmarried mothers to support themselves and their children. A further factor may have been the negative publicity surrounding aspects of adoption (Milotte, 1997; Goulding, 1998).

In 1993, in a study of teenage mothers, I found that the mothers had very limited information or interest in adoption as an option. In addition, social workers were less likely to discuss adoption as an option than other alternatives. I also found that:

> those that stated they were thinking of adoption were taken through an exploration of this and other options, whereas those who said they were planning on keeping their babies were supported in that decision, with little or no discussion of alternatives.

Mahon, *et al* (1998) found that all the women contemplating adoption experienced their pregnancies as a great crisis in their lives. In contemplating adoption, they were 'anticipating a future without responsibility for the child, in which the responsibility would be transferred to others'. They spent a lot of time weighing up the pros and cons of this decision, which was very difficult for them.

The identification of these stages in the process of becoming an unmarried mother highlights the points at which support and help in decision-making may be appropriate. The difficulty for adolescents dealing with a crisis pregnancy is in part a developmental one. At a cognitive level, adolescents have been found to have limited ability to make rational decisions based on weighing up the pros and cons of a particular situation or of taking a long term view of the consequences of any decision they make (Richardson, 1993). As such, decisions concerning teenage crisis pregnancies may not be made by the woman herself. In fact, in 1993 I found that in the majority of the cases in my study, the decision regarding the outcome of the pregnancy was made by the mother of the pregnant girl and not the girl herself.

Irish Studies on Young Mothers

Given the increase in numbers of young mothers deciding to parent their children, recently there have been a number of small, local studies which have concentrated on listening to the women's stories to establish how best to support them in their parenting role (see for example, Richardson, 2001; McCarthy and Cronin, 2001; Dempsey, *et al*, 2002). My 2001 study examined the lived experiences of young single mothers in two local areas, one in Cork and one in Dublin.

It was very clear from the data that the young women were concerned and caring about their children and did the best they could, using the limited resources at their disposal. Poverty was a huge issue for these mothers. They were attempting to manage on low levels of income and the majority of them found it difficult to cope, particularly when extra demands were made on them at certain times such as starting school or first holy communions. All the women were on One-Parent Family Payment with no reliance on maintenance from the fathers of their children. In addition, income from employment did not figure significantly in their overall finances. In many instances, the women went without material goods and services for themselves in order to meet the needs of their children, relying on their own parents for additional finance.

Just over half of the women were working part-time; only one full-time and the remainder were unemployed. Many of them wished to work but were prevented from doing so because of inadequate childcare facilities and the need to travel out of their area to obtain work. On the other hand, some of the mothers wished to remain in the home to look after their children themselves. These mothers said they would like to return to work once their children had started school. One of the issues arising for these mothers was the lack of work experience or training, which would assist them in obtaining employment. There was a low level of educational attainment among the women together with early school-leaving. For the majority of the women, pregnancy had occurred having left school. They reported that they had disliked school and harboured negative attitudes towards it. However, most of them subsequently regretted leaving school without qualifications and expressed a wish to return to education in the future. They saw themselves returning to work or education once their children had grown up. This was one of the main aspirations for their own lives. They were adamant that they did not want their children to make the same mistakes as they had done, particularly in relation to early school-leaving and they wanted their children to remain in education and use that education to obtain good employment.

Where the young mothers were working or attending employment schemes, family members were providing the majority of the childcare arrangements. There was some ambivalence about the use of childcare facilities in that they did want good quality affordable childcare in the community but they expressed doubts about leaving their children with strangers.

Marriage was of little importance to these women either at the time of the pregnancy or in the future. They did not feel stigmatised nor did they believe that their children suffered from being part of a one-parent family. Many of their siblings and friends also had children outside marriage and they found support from this situation. The extended family played an important role in providing additional family members for the child in the lone-parent situation. The majority of them had returned to their family home immediately after the birth. However, over time this situation changed and between a quarter and one-third had moved out of home for a number of reasons: overcrowding; wishing to establish an independent life; conflict within the home; or establishing a relationship with a partner, either the father of the baby or another man. The majority of them indicated that they received emotional support from the fathers of their children during their pregnancy and immediately after the birth but, over time, this contact fell away and at the time of the study, while almost 40% of them had daily contact with the father of the child, a similar number had no contact at all.

The understanding and use of contraception before their pregnancy was limited. Much of the information obtained by the young women came from informal sources. The study found that the ability of the young women to link the fact of sexual activity with the possibility of becoming pregnant was limited and their attitude to contraception was casual. The formal sex education they had received either at home or within the school was limited. For those who had received sex education in school, over half of them felt it was of no value to them.

In terms of support in their parenting role, the young women had made little use of statutory and voluntary services in their areas, depending largely on their own families for support rather than on outside agencies. For the women who became pregnant while still at school, they felt that in particular, there was a lack of counselling and support within the school system at a time when they needed it.

A further research study on young mothers in Cork was undertaken by the Department of Nursing in University College Cork (McCarthy and Cronin, 2000). They found that the mothers of the young women were central in helping them adapt to their new role. They could not overemphasise the importance of maternal support and they cautioned against re-housing young mothers in areas separated from their families of origin. In addition, the partners were significant in providing both material and emotional support. Important support networks within the community existed and provided the young mothers with valuable social interaction and support. McCarthy and Cronin further noted that a majority of the young women suffered from varying periods of post-natal depression. The first three months after delivery were very difficult for some of the young mothers and while support was sought from various agencies or individuals, it was evident that many of them still felt they were alone. The women talked about personal stress and depression together with 'frustration at living in homes which were crowded or did not allow for personal space'. They reported that while there seemed to be support for them, the mothers still experienced a sense of loneliness and coping with lifestyle changes proved difficult.

Prevention

With a growing awareness of the long-term disadvantages for women having babies at a young age, teen pregnancy prevention programmes have begun to emerge in an attempt to reduce or postpone the numbers of young mothers becoming pregnant. Prevention programmes in the US have concentrated on a range of objectives including increasing knowledge about the impact of early pregnancy, emphasising abstinence from or delay in the onset of sexual activity, life skills and sex education together with training in effective contraceptive use. Also included have been programmes to address early school-leaving, attempts to change attitudes towards vocational and educational aspirations and individual future orientation (Franklin and Corcoran, 2000; Monahan, 2002). In Ireland, prevention programmes have concentrated on the provision of the Relationships and Sexuality Education Programme (RSE) in schools. The programme is being introduced in both primary and second level schools in an age appropriate way:

> The RSE programme is designed to equip children and young people with knowledge and understanding of human sexuality and relationships in a way that will enable them to form values and establish behaviours within a moral, spiritual and social framework (Commission on the Family, 1998).

Mahon, *et al* (1998) emphasised two factors relating to the importance of sex education for young people with regard to preventing pregnancy. Firstly, the information on the physiology of pregnancy provides knowledge of how pregnancy occurs and how it can best be avoided. Secondly:

> It gives young people a language they can use to articulate and discuss issues around sexuality with their parents and teachers, peers and sexual partners at the point where they are likely to engage in sexual intimacy.

However, Wiley and Merriman (1996) found that just under half (49%) of the women in their study had received sex education and that it was significantly related to education level:

> With the low estimate of 18% of women with just primary education having received sex education contrasting with estimates of over 70% of women with a third level qualification.

Mahon, *et al* (1998) also found that women with lower levels of education also have the poorest knowledge of the menstrual cycle and risk of pregnancy. They also found that many young women relied on informal sources of information in relation to sex and contraceptives. Wiley and Merriman (1996) stated that 10% of sexually active single women did not use any form of contraceptive and that the adequacy of family planning advice available is perceived as lowest among unemployed women. My 2001 study found that there was a wide range of responses in relation to sex education in schools. Approximately half of the women said they had had some sex education in schools and the remainder said there was virtually nothing. Those who did receive sex education said it did not make much impact on them and that it needed to be more explicit. They argued that information should include not only information on the physiology of sex but on the impact of pregnancy on their future lives, and also the implications of having a dependent child to care for. The knowledge the women had about contraception was mixed, ranging from none to those who said they knew all about it. Their sources of information were mainly informal from friends or siblings and did not figure in their sex education in schools. The overriding conclusion was that the women were casual about the use of contraception and did not make the connection between being sexually active and becoming pregnant. This latter finding was also a feature of the Cork study (2002). All the Irish studies have recommended that sexual health education programmes be delivered in a holistic, interactive and comprehensive manner and in a style that is easily understood and relevant to a teenager's experiences. Also, the development of easily accessible and widely available confidential contraceptive services at local level which link into improved sex education programmes is needed.

Support

Prevention programmes also need to be linked to provision of support for teenage parents. In Ireland, development of support services has become central to recent work with these young mothers. In particular, the establishment of three Teen Parents Support projects in Dublin, Galway and Limerick, early in 2000, supported by the Department of Health and Children and the Department of Education and Science, has been an important initiative (Acton, 2002). The unique aspect of these projects is to provide one to one support to pregnant and postnatal teens for a period up to three years, aiming to enhance their general well being and ensure that they can avail of all opportunities open to them. In addition, the projects network with local agencies in the community, working collaboratively with them to respond to the needs of the client group. One important aspect is the focus on involving young fathers and valuing their role in supporting the mother and the baby. For all the projects, the lack of suitable housing for young parents presents a major problem. Overcrowding is common where young mothers remain with their family of origin. However, they cannot join the housing list until they are 18 years and when there, they can remain on the list for long periods. When they are finally re-housed they need to remain close to the vital support networks of their extended families.

Employment is seen as the main route out of poverty for young mothers. However, access to employment depends largely on marketable skills and the availability of good quality affordable childcare. Therefore, the projects emphasise the need for completion of secondary education, continuing work training where possible and supporting them in doing so with the provision of childcare arrangements and financial support for books, fees and childminding. The Moving On: Young Mothers and Employment project was established in 1996 to enable young mothers to gain access to employment, education and training by developing and delivering needs based, accredited, prevocational training. It was set up as a response to research evidence of young mothers experiencing high levels of isolation together with low levels of formal educational qualifications (Ryan, 1998: Moving On Consortium 2002). Complementary to these projects, the Agreed Programme for Government between Fianna Fáil and the Progressive Democrats (June, 2002) states that:

> Over the next five years, we will develop adult education services to a stage where we will offer ... every person who left school without completing the junior cycle at second level ... the chance to participate on an adult education course.

The Limerick project has been working with secondary schools to devise a protocol of good practice for schools to encourage students to remain in education. These relate to support at the time of disclosure, during the pregnancy, at the time of birth and postnatal support. What has emerged from all the projects is that where services are in place, young mothers will use them when given a little guidance and encouragement (Acton, 2002).

With the increasing numbers of young mothers, teenage pregnancy and parenting are issues which need to be addressed at the level of both prevention and support. At the level of prevention, there is a need to develop comprehensive relationship and sex education programmes in schools, delivered in such a way that they will help young people to make rational decisions about their sexual behaviour. A peer-led approach that encourages teenagers to consider the consequences of their behaviour together with access to contraceptive advice and provision at local level is needed. Such programmes should be focused on both sexes. In addition, they might be more effective if they were supported by a confidential social work counselling service within the schools which would allow young people the opportunity of discussing issues with individuals outside the teaching environment.

At the level of support, teen parents need help in continuing education, employment opportunities, the provision of affordable and accessible childcare and housing. There is also a real need to introduce specific services to support teenage fathers who in turn provide supports for the young mothers. In addition, all the research has shown the vital supportive role of the extended family. Therefore, support services for the families, particularly the mothers of the teen parents, should be factored into any provisions. The central issue in policy discussion has now become teen parenting rather than teen pregnancy and it is at the level of parenting that future initiatives should be focused together with preventative programmes.

CHAPTER TWENTY

Traveller Mothers

Pavee Point Primary Health Care for
Travellers Project *and* Patricia Kennedy

In July 2002, I met with a group of twelve Traveller mothers, some
also grandmothers and some great-grandmothers, at Pavee Point in
Dublin. The women were all Primary Health Care Workers working
and living in the Dublin area. The project co-ordinator was also present. We discussed the symbolism and experience of motherhood in
Traveller culture from their knowledge and experience. In October
2002, I went back to Pavee Point for further discussions with three
of the women and the project co-ordinator. In 2003, I met with three
generations of one family, a ten-year-old girl, her mother and grandmother, in their home in a group housing scheme in Dublin. What
follows is an unedited version of the women's words. Some sub-head-
ings and contextual information have been added for clarity in co-
operation with the women concerned.

Health Status of Travellers
Quirke from Pavee Point states that: 'issues around health are inextricably linked to issues regarding appropriate accommodation provision for Travellers and further to the social and economic exclusion
of this community within contemporary Irish society' (Pavee Point,
2002). Accommodation is perceived as the major issue for Travellers
with constant demands being made for access to suitable accommodation. Crowley (1999) outlines how accommodation for Travellers
has been characterised by: inadequate provision, with one-quarter of
families living on the side of the road without access to basic facilities; its unsuitability for the traditional organisation of economic activities around family and home; its inadequacy for transient Travellers; and the over-crowded and under-resourced temporary sites.

The 2000 Department of the Environment and Local Govern-
ment/Local Authority count of Traveller families indicates that there
were 4,898 Traveller families in that year (Department of Health and
Children, 2002). Of this number, 1,353 live in the Eastern Region
Health Authority (ERHA) region.

Quirke (Pavee Point, 2002) indicates that some research carried out since the latest national study on Travellers' health (conducted in 1989) indicates that 'the health status of Travellers has not improved, and more alarmingly may have deteriorated'. A statistic she presents which is particularly relevant here is that the rate of sudden infant death among Travellers is twelve times that of the settled population (ISIDA, 1999). Over a decade ago, the broad figures on fertility and mortality for Travellers were:

- A fertility rate of 164.2 per 1,000, compared to 70.1 per 1,000 of the settled community.
- Infant mortality rate of 18.1 per 1,000 live births, compared to the national average of 7.4.
- Travellers reaching (by time of study in 1989) the life expectancy of that achieved by settled people in Ireland since the 1940s.
- A low uptake of maternity services, with less than a third of mothers attending hospital by the end of the first half of pregnancy.
- A low uptake (less than 59%) of infant health services, immunisations and attendance at development check clinics.
- High mobility of the Traveller community with only 50% to 60% of infants located by the public health nurse at the child's first birthday (Barry, 1989).

Traveller women are doubly discriminated against as women and as Travellers. Therefore, it is no surprise that their health status suffers as a result. The unpublished study, *The Health of Traveller Women* (O'Reilly, 1997) indicates:

- 46% of the women surveyed described their own health as 'poor' or 'fair'.
- 34% had been ill in the four months before the survey.
- 60% had been prescribed medicine by a doctor at least once in the previous year.
- 33% said that they suffered from long-term depression.
- 10% had taken anti-depressants prescribed by their GP in the previous year.
- 32.6% had had a cervical smear test.
- 55.1% had never done breast self-examination (compared with 38.7% of the general female population).
- While 69.1% believed ante-natal classes were a good idea, less than 1% had attended.
- 51.5% of the women who had children did not attend post-natal check-ups for themselves after the birth of their last child.
- 73.4% did bring the baby for a six-week check-up.
- 88% preferred to attend female practitioners for their health.
- 68% said that being able to plan the spacing of their children was important.
- The ideal number of children was judged to be four.
- 50.3% had never had family planning advice or service.

As regards methods of family planning that had been used, women reported as follows: the contraceptive pill, 46%; intra-uterine device (IUD), 19%; and DepoProvera (an injectable drug, whose use is controversial), 10%.

Culture

Travellers form Ireland's oldest ethnic minority group and are characterised by their nomadic way of life. They identify themselves as a distinct community with their own culture and traditions and their own language, 'the cant'. One young mother explained her understanding of Traveller culture:

> All Travelling women, we don't think the same. We don't know every Traveller woman in the country just like every settled woman would not know every settled woman. The Travelling culture is still there but more with the Traveller girls than with the Traveller boys. I am a Traveller but I never travelled once. I did live in a trailer for five years. My family is Traveller. I was born a Traveller. I was brought up a Traveller. You could live in a palace and be still a Traveller. The culture is your name, the way you are brought up, your own crack, your tradition, your own language. For example, if I fill the washing machine with clothes, I wouldn't put one tea towel in it. We wash them separately with bleach. We have our own stories and the language, the cant. Long ago it was used more as a secret code when we were at the side of the road. My mother says 'You're not a right old Traveller; travelling on the road, making flowers, selling things out of baskets. You never did that'. I wouldn't go hawking to save my life. If I did, I would cry. I respect it but I couldn't do it.

However, her mother explained that she herself, regretfully, does not 'hawk' now due to lack of transport and a lack of willingness of her family to drive her:

> When I could get out I would get a basket and go out hawking but I can't go now without transport. I would sell hairbrushes and pegs and toothbrushes and things like that. I go on 'call backs' now. There are particular houses I go to every month and they trust me and bring me in and give me tea. My grandchild has been doing it since three years of age.

The granddaughter enthusiastically piped up:

> I love it. I'll keep on doing it always.

Another Traveller woman described life on the road:

Molly Collins from Pavee Point visiting a prayer garden in Cork, August 2002

If the younger generation had to live the life my mother had I don't think they would survive. She lived fifty-five years on the road and served the whole family on the road and has lived in group housing for the last thirty years with her family around her. My mother is still alive now. She is eighty-five this year. She is in Dublin in her own little house. My father was a wagon maker. He worked with the farmers and with the bog and made a bit of money and then he started making wagons. When he'd build them he'd sell them. The farmers down around the Midlands then were very good. They'd give you work. You'd pick potatoes and pull beet and they'd give you your dinner. You'd start in April and you wouldn't finish until June or July and you'd make a few pounds and you could go in and buy a few messages.

My mother had eighteen kids and that's all she ever did. She'd go in for the night and she'd be out around the country again the next day calling. There was no money, no dole, and she used to have to go begging for the other children. That was their life. That was their lifestyle. The farmers were very good that time. The relationship was great. They'd bring you in and give you tea and a few potatoes and a bit of meat. I often saw my mother now and she'd sit down and she'd give a bit to whoever was with her. The kids would be dying to go to get a feed. In the line of food, there was loads. You would never be short. People were very good that time. God was very good to the Travellers. It was always good food. She might bring one or two of them along with her with maybe no boots on their feet, just walking along. She used to breastfeed. She breastfed every one of them.

Another woman referred to the changes that have come about since she was a child:

My father used to make buckets and saucepans and he would give them to us to go around to the houses to sell them and he would bring home buckets from the farmer and put new bounds on them. He'd bring them back and the farmer would give him maybe two shillings or a half a crown; but since plastic came in all of that is wiped out. Snagging the turnips and the beet, all that is all gone now too because they have machines.

The younger women continued to explain other aspects of Traveller culture:

Traveller mothers are strict, more strict than settled women even though with the younger generation it is dying out. My mother was very strict. My first child was a girl and I said I would not be as strict with her as my own mother was with me but now that she is growing up – she is ten – I find I am being strict with her. By strict I mean not mixing with boys, going out with them before marriage, hanging around the place. My daughter goes to the local school and mixes well but I wouldn't leave her go to sleepovers. That is the Traveller way. I was brought up like that. My husband wouldn't allow it either. We were too afraid. I explained it to the settled woman but she looked at me funny. When I was young we would stay around home. We would have lots of chores to do. The boys would have jobs too but different jobs. The girls would have more to do. They were more or less responsible. They would keep the house clean and keep everything in order. They would replace the mother. Nowadays we wouldn't put as much responsibility on our daughters but with my daughter, now that she is ten, I would ask her to keep an eye on her younger brother or to do the dishes. At her age, I did a lot more. I was brought up in England so I went to school. I had to go to school but I would still do all my chores too.

The young mother explained how their kinship patterns favour marrying within their own community and at a young age:

You wouldn't leave home until you got married. The marriage was arranged. We didn't meet one another until we got married, until the wedding day. For example, we didn't go out together to the pictures or anything. It didn't bother me. With my daughter, I will leave her go out a little bit more but I still won't let her go here, there and everywhere. I won't pick her husband. That has changed big time. They are making their own marriages now. We tend to turn a blind eye to the younger generation, even though we know when they are going out with one another secretly.

They are still marrying young, eighteen or nineteen. Eighteen, as soon as it is legal. They are having fewer children. They know all about contraception and some of them are even planning their families. It is acceptable now with the younger generations. The men are involved in it more. The majority of Traveller women are having smaller families. They are stopping after three and four. Most of my friends who are aged thirty-one or thirty-two are sterilised. They discuss it with their husbands.

Another young mother explained:

> In England you are passed as a 'Paddy'. I could go to school and get a job no
> problem. When I came back here I was asked in the dole office if I was an
> itinerant. I didn't know what it meant. In England, I was never asked that
> question. Here they knew by my accent and my name. When I moved back
> here first, Travellers would have to sign on at a certain time but that is
> changed now. But still they put Travellers to extra trouble.

Her mother added:

> when I was in England, I worked in different jobs, childminding and in fac-
> tories, for example. Only for I started in Pavee Point I wouldn't be employ-
> ed by the Health Board today. It is contract, part-time work.

A younger woman explained some of the difficulties for Traveller
women in gaining employment:

> we are not well enough qualified. We didn't have the same opportunities as
> settled people. We are only starting now and we have children and all, so
> it is harder. I hope that my daughter will do all her education before she gets
> married. I would love to see her do that. Most of the women are on FÁS
> courses, part-time; that causes problems. They are caught. They can only
> work certain hours because of the social and they might lose their medical
> card. Traveller women would have big problems if they lost their medical
> card. Most Travellers know that they have more illness than the settled
> people and use the health service more. They need their medical card. They
> couldn't afford to be sick. So the women are caught between trying to do
> the FÁS courses and not lose their benefits as well. It doesn't cause a prob-
> lem for the men. They love to see the women going off in the morning with
> the children. In the past men wouldn't mind children but now they would.
> That has changed an awful lot. They are more involved.

This was different in the past as one older woman explained:

> that time the fathers had to be very supportive because there was nothing
> there. He was always the boss but she was always looking after the children,
> getting food for the children, making beds for the children, making sure the
> straw was got for the beds for the children. God love them the mothers put
> everyone before themselves. The mother had a hard life, a hard, hard, hard
> life. The fathers would get the sticks all right and the water. Or if there was
> a bale of straw needed for the bed, he'd go up to the farmer's house and get
> the straw but she'd have to shake in the straw. He would throw it beside the
> tent. She would have to cut the twine off it. She'd make it nice. It wasn't that
> they were being bad but that the women would do a nicer job. She would
> shake it out. You'd hear them say 'There may be fleas in that now if the hens

were up on it'. It would be shook, shook, shook, shook and would be left there for a half an hour, maybe an hour, and then it would be put into the tent. The blankets would be put over it and that was the bed. You'd have no pillows. You could have a wet coat, a drowning wet coat. That is why I think we all have arthritis.

Preparing for Childbirth

They wouldn't talk about babies that time in front of girls. They would not tell girls anything. You would hear the odd thing going around. When my mother had twins I heard them saying 'there was five minutes in between' but you wouldn't know what that meant. They didn't tell girls, I don't know why. It was supposed to be protecting us but it meant when we got married we didn't know anything. The way I didn't.

There used to be a nun in Rathangan and no matter how far the woman was she would always get her maternity powders (powders taken by Traveller women which are believed to help with the labour). And they would hold that there until they got sick. The nuns would give you the powders. The women still use it. The nurses don't approve. There is someone in the north of Ireland who has them. Men don't mind and drive you for the powders and maternity blessing. They believe in it too.

They would go up to the priest and get the maternity blessing and that was more than good.

A younger mother explained that this was still common practice for Traveller women:

Traveller women go to the priest for a maternity blessing or to the nuns in Tallaght for the powder; St Teresa's powder. It comes from Spain. When you go into labour, you put it on your tongue. Now the nurses in the hospital think it is drugs and take it off you so you take it before you go into hospital.

Another older woman described how unprepared she was for childbirth:

I was having my first baby. They started asking questions when you go in for the first check-up. They'd give you a fair idea then when you would be having the baby but when I actually went to have my baby I hadn't a clue. I definitely had no idea whatsoever. I was going for my check-up. Everything was fine. Everything was great. That was it. But nobody sat down and explained anything to me. Nobody told me how the baby was going to be born. I think an awful lot of women back then, settled women as well, their mothers didn't tell them. I was often talking to settled women and they did not know. We thought it was only our mothers. We were getting married and we didn't know anything. The only thing we relied on really was when another woman was having a baby and you'd be kept out. I went to England

and that is where I missed out. If I had been at home and was travelling there would be another woman there who would have had her first baby and that woman would explain to me and she'd talk to me. That is the only way that we would get information, from friends. I was more isolated because I went to England.

We were only a day married. We were mad to get away. I thought it was grand. It was lovely. I was going to something wonderful. I was on the boat for my first time. Married as well, like. I was fifteen and a half. It was all excitement and things at that stage. But my sister was over there and she'd come down and talk to me a bit but still never explain everything to me. I don't know if it was embarrassment or not about the actual birth and how I was going to have the baby and everything. I think she actually thought I knew it. I got married on 29 December and I had my first baby 12 months after the new year. I was about sixteen and a half. My husband was 21.

She described the resourcefulness of Traveller women in the past:

The settled women would give you bits and pieces of clothes. They'd give you shirts and you'd get a scissors and make nappies out of them. There was no nappies. They'd take them out and wash them in very cold water and they'd always get a bar of red soap and they'd wash them out. The babies never got nappy rash. They'd use a powder, borax powder and they would spread that on the baby. I don't ever remember seeing a baby the way you would see them now, red raw.

The first of mine was born here and then the next fellow was born in London. I had only five altogether but it was plenty for me. I have an older sister that was married and it was very, very hard. They would never talk about it and they would keep themselves covered. You'd see them now with their big bumps sticking out. They wouldn't do that. They would have an apron and that apron would cover over them half-way. Then they would have a jumper over it. So you could swear that there was never anything there and the only way you would know then is that – they wouldn't go to any clinic, any doctors – I'd hear my father saying: 'I'm going back down towards Tullamore'. And one man would say to the other; 'well do in the name of God now because she'll be soon going in' and that would be the only way that we would know. We would move camp.

Maybe you would be out in the country where there would be no hospitals no place and they wouldn't attend any doctors for the whole nine months and the night then that she would get sick they would call for an ambulance and she would go in then and she would have her baby. When her labour would start, he'd run down for a doctor or a nurse or else they would ring an ambulance. She would go in on her own and have her baby in the morning. They'd ring in and that was the only way you would know.

I remember my mother having children at the door of the tent. I didn't see her having them but she'd have them in the tent. You'd be run off down the road at ninety miles an hour. I remember my mother having two and by the time the nurse got to her, they were already born. My father would get up and would bring my mother to a town with a nurse in it. She would know the nurse because she would be after having a child there before. I remember one particular day. The women were gone away. One woman wanted to stay. She didn't want to leave my mother. I didn't know why she didn't want to leave my mother. She was saying 'Oh go on. I'll be all right.' I didn't understand why. I didn't know what was wrong. The particular woman was gone off and I remember us getting run: 'Go down the road and don't come back and bring the other children with you and tell your father I want him. Quick.' We still didn't have a clue but he didn't go back to her. He ran for the nurse because he knew. We didn't know why he didn't go back to her. He came back up with the nurse and stood outside. We were looking at him standing outside. But afterwards I heard the baby was already born when the nurse got there. I often wondered how she did that. She must've picked the child up. She knew the nurse was coming. I hadn't a clue what was going on.

Another older woman recalled:

I remember back one time. My mother went out and she came back very early. My grandmother was a great nurse. She told us to go down the road and the next thing we heard the child screaming. She came out of the tent with the child in her arms. After seeing the child and hearing her screaming we still didn't know where she came from.

However, younger mothers remarked on how things had changed:

For myself now, when I was pregnant for the first time, I went to the doctor at six weeks and I kept attending the hospitals but when I had her she had bronchitis and she was in and out of hospital. A year later, I had a boy. He was heavy. He was nearly ten pounds. I was living in a chalet with three bedrooms. I started having twins and I didn't even go to the doctor. I said I was all right with the first two so I'll be all right with this fellow. When I was five months pregnant, I took a terrible pain. I thought it was a kidney infection. I rang the hospital and they told me come in. The doctor told me the baby was breech and he gave out to me over not attending the clinic. The doctor told me that if I didn't stop smoking they would be very, very small. The more he frightened me, the more I smoked. They were born six weeks premature, one was 6lbs 8ozs and the other was 6lbs 4ozs. The doctors couldn't believe it. They are 24, 23 and the twins are 21 and the others are 18 and 12. I was nearly 21 when I got married. I was old enough. There was no complaints. I didn't breastfeed any of them. Times had changed. For the first one I used to get the towel nappies and for all the rest of them, the disposable nappies were there. I had it a lot easier.

Traveller women are now better informed about what lies ahead:

When I was in hospital I stayed for the whole five days and I enjoyed it. Women nowadays, they know everything; every twist and turn, but women in my time, they didn't know anything. I was 23 or 24, I didn't know anything about having the baby.

Another woman explained:

> With my first baby I knew what to expect because I went to school in England and there you get all the information. It wasn't from my mother, indeed! Traveller women now talk about having children but not in front of the men or the children. Before you are married, you wouldn't talk but once you are married you would talk about having children. But not before you got married. Nowadays, Traveller women go to hospital when they are pregnant. They have more information, from school. Once you are into the system, you keep going and get to know the services around you. There are still a lot of Traveller women who do not go to hospitals. Here we know because we live together.

A younger woman described how fathers had become more involved in supporting the mother in childbirth:

> Some men even go into the labour wards. They won't talk about it but you would hear a mother chatting about it. I was treated well in hospital with my first two children but the last time I didn't find I was treated at all well. After I had the baby, the nurse was so busy she couldn't help me. The hospitals seem much busier and there are lots of refugees having babies here now, so the nurses are busier with them too. I became friends with settled women in the hospital and I still visit them.

Birth Complications

In the past, maternal mortality was a reality for many women:

> There was women who died in childbirth. We didn't know at that time. It wasn't easy for women.

Many experienced miscarriage and stillbirth:

> I lived in England when I had my children. I had seventeen alive and three dead. One was a twin and that boy now is almost 40 years of age. The little girl died. They were born two months before time and I didn't know I was having twins. That was the thing then. They didn't have scans. I definitely used to go in for my check-ups. I was in England that time and the nurses used to come around to you an awful lot when you had young babies. And they told me to go for my check-ups, which I did. I used to go for check-ups but they never told me I was having twins. Plus, I was very small. When I was having my children, I could wear the one skirt, all the way through nearly. The waist would be the same but I'd have a little bump below it. The bigger women who would come … I think they would be checking them for twins when they saw them so big. Because I was so small, they just didn't bother checking me. They were just checking the baby's heart, sort of thing. Whatever way the babies were lying, one on top of the other. They didn't know

so when I went to have my baby, as I thought, it was two months before. The baby was born straight away and he was five pounds in weight. I knew it was two months early. He wasn't to be born until February and he was born at Christmas.

I had to go back into labour all over again which I hadn't a clue about because nobody really explained anything to me and told me anything. I was knocked out, put asleep. I knew before I fell asleep that there was another baby there. When I woke up, I was only nineteen at the time, it was my third pregnancy, I assumed that my baby was born. When they told me that there was another baby and I had to go through the whole thing again I was not able. I wasn't able to move ... I wasn't able to have another baby at that stage. I had to go through the whole thing again and it wasn't a few minutes in between. When my mother had her twins, I never forgot it, five minutes; she told me there was in between the twins. There were actually hours between mine. There would be sections or something now.

The boy was born first. He lived. I had him during the day of a Friday. The girl was born in the early hours of the Saturday. That is how long I was in labour. I was so young then I never went into detail, what happened, why it happened. They just said to me they were so premature. They were so premature at the time that the boy was kept in actually for weeks after. I was ten days in hospital. The only one I got support from was my own husband. That time he was working. He took time off. And he took weeks off work. My other child was 10 months and the other was a year and ten months. I have two birthdays now in the one year. I was only a child myself at the time. I found it hard. I would love if the twins had lived. I really would. I often thought about it. I never knew I was having twins but as the years went on, I started worrying about it.

They didn't talk to me about the baby. I was very ill at the time. The reason they gave me was that it was very immature and I often thought that there must've been something they could do to bring that labour on quicker. It was forty years ago. I think women shouldn't be let as long. There has to be something better. You were just left there to die. I never forgot that twin. Nor in my life, I don't think I ever will. Like I said, at the time it came as a shock more than anything else and a shock to my husband. Neither him nor me knew we were having twins. I won't say the doctors were wrong or they didn't help me. They were all very nice and they were doing their best with me because I had all my children in one hospital and they were very, very good to me and they were very generous and I couldn't say one word wrong about the hospital. It was just that they weren't well up that time.

I had a girl born when I was six months pregnant. She was three pounds in weight. I saw her and I christened her and I'll never forget her as long as I live. I went in and I was pretty young as well when I had her. She came after the twins. She lived for one day. I was able to go in and see her but I didn't take it into my head that she was dying, that she was going to go. They advised me to have her christened, which I did. My husband and all came in. They wanted to know what name would I call a girl. I called her after my mother with the opinion that she was going to live. That night around ten o'clock, I don't think I'll ever forget it. She died. I was in and

out to her but at the time she died I wasn't there. I had three small babies.
I was still in hospital at that stage when she died. Looking back on it now
I don't think I realised that she was dying.

I came on then and I had a girl after that baby died. When I went into
the hospital in labour, the nurse that was delivering my baby, knew me well
from going in and out, said to me 'you have a girl' and they had to calm me
down, not because I was excited or anything because I wanted a girl. I had
three boys at home now. It wasn't the idea that I was having a girl that was
exciting. I assumed that if she was a girl, she would die. That was the idea
I took into my head that if I was going to have a girl she was going to die.
And I went hysterical. The nurse tried to calm me down but I don't think
she understood what I was roaring about. I was still screaming, saying 'no,
no, no, not a girl'. It stood with me until I got out of the hospital but I think
once I got her into my arms and brought her home … I knew now because
they checked her out and said everything was perfect. It was great. But that
left me then. I was very protective about her. I didn't want to leave her with
anyone or go anywhere. She is actually married now with ten children herself. I got over that. After that, it didn't worry me. I had her now and she
was alive and I assumed it wasn't going to happen again to me. All I had
was four girls anyway. If they all lived, I would have 14 boys and 6 girls.

I had no mother over there (England) and I think if you have a mother
or a mother-in-law who will go in and ask questions … I knew I was going
to the hospital but I was only going in and doing what I was told. The nurses
just told me 'Go in and get your check-ups done' and I did it because the
nurse told me, not because I knew it was important. Now that was the truth
because I didn't know one way or another. I just was going because I was told
it was the best thing to do but I think if I had a mother or a mother-in-law
around who would talk to me, or advise me, or tell me something, it might
have been better because I might have looked after myself better. I was so
young myself. I was always going. I would never sit down. I would never take
the time. Like we talk now about relaxing or sitting down for five minutes.
Look after myself. I never did it. I was just in a room that time. We didn't
have a house. It was just one room with a little kitchen with a little cooker.
I was never a big eater. A very small dinner would do me at any stage and
I could go for hours without eating. But I cooked the dinners and everything. I was never one for drinking milk or anything like that. That time I
couldn't. Milk would disgust me.

Post-Natal Care
One young woman explained:

I wouldn't breastfeed now. Some would while they are in hospital because
they had privacy but when they come home they would not have privacy.
Even though I know the advantages of breastfeeding I still wouldn't do it.
Some would but the lack of privacy now stops them.

However, in the past it was different:

Breastfeeding. That is what they used to do. No bottles. She'd spend one day in the hospital then. Maybe two days if there was something wrong. They'd want to come home as soon as that baby was born. They had no caravans or anything. All they had was tents at the side of the road. He'd light a big fire … a cold tent to be coming home to. They would be dying to come home to the other kids … and the following day she'd have to go off to the farmers' houses with the child in her arms. She'd have a can in her hand looking for spuds or bacon or anything she'd get. They'd have just a bed of straw. There were no mattresses … just a bed of straw. I'm talking now about forty years ago. Things have changed an awful lot lately. For the women of today it has changed. But for the women that time it was a lot harder.

Traveller women used feed their child for a year and a half or two years because they thought that while they were feeding the children they would not get pregnant. It did work for them. It was a form of birth control. All the women that time used to breastfeed. When my mother had the twins, she had to put them on bottles. Why I don't know. She had the little bottles with the two teats on it, a twin bottle shaped like a boat. The food they used to feed the children would not be bought. They would mash food. I saw women cooking porridge. They would drain the water off it and put it down to boil again and it turned to a cream with no lumps or anything in it. They would put that in a bottle. They would cook it on the fire on a few lumps of red coal. Another thing was bread and milk. They would whisk it up until it was real, real fine. There was no such thing as baby dinners.

You'd see the women sticking the baby's clothes, a little shift, down in their bosom and that would warm it. They would wear it there until it was dry.

Cures and Remedies

A feature of Traveller culture is the strong oral tradition. This facilitates the passing on of knowledge, including cures and remedies. Some of which the women described:

> If a child had thrush they would go for the cure. They would go to the man or woman who would have a cure. It could be a Traveller or a settled person. It would all depend … maybe they would blow down their throat. It would be gone. Not like some of the kids today that are pampered. Those children God love them they didn't have a stitch of clothes. That wasn't one child. It was all children. I remember some women when they would come home from the hospitals they would tie a thing called a bellyband around them to keep the bellybutton pure. They would put a bit of powder on it and a soft cloth. They would never look back. When they had that baby they would get on their feet and that would be it. They might be a bit weak for the first day or two but after that you would see them coming back and there was nothing that they couldn't do.

Young mothers today still believe in the value of these cures:

to cure thrush, you go to a boy whose father died before his birth. He takes him into a room. He won't do it in front of you. You have to have the faith.

Some beliefs are strongly linked to Catholicism:

that time, it would only be one or two days and you'd get the baby christened. As soon as the women would come out of the hospital, they would go straight to the priest next day. They would go into the church and get the child christened and themselves churched, that was blessed and from that day on, they would never look back. In the old days, they wouldn't touch the food, the old women until they were churched, because they did not believe that the food would do them any good and it wasn't right to eat the food until the woman was churched.

Mothers of all generations referred to the custom of tying something red to the hair of a child who was getting too much attention, for his protection:

If there was a nice little child born, they were all lovely children but you'd see a child with nice hair, or curly hair or something and a woman would come up to you, maybe an older woman and say 'Get a bit of a red string and tie it in that child's hair'. You would tie the child's hair with the string or you'd wrap it around it. The red ribbon or a bit of red cord for the protection of the child. They'd have a little white cap, knitted, with a bit of red thread through it for the Sacred Heart and a bit of blue for the Virgin Mary'.

If you went into a house and a woman would say, 'That is a beautiful child'. You'd be thinking. You would go back to the woman and you would say, 'I want you to say, "God bless that child", that is my belief.' The women would say 'God bless that child'. Otherwise, she might be crossing the child with bad luck. That was only the Travellers.

For toilet training, the children, even boys, would often wear dresses. If the child had nappy rash, a scalded bottom, you would burn a white blanket piece and put the brown ash on the baby's bottom.

Several women mentioned the cure for whooping cough:

To cure whooping cough you would go to a couple married, with the same name but not related. They give you a piece of dry bread and you give it to the child to eat a few times. Or you could go to a seventh son of a seventh son or a seventh daughter of a seventh daughter. They will give the cure to settled people but you have to have the belief.

Conclusion
While the women agreed that there had been many positive changes in their lifestyles over the last fifty years, they also believed that there

had been losses. They lamented the closeness with settled families which had previously existed, particularly in rural areas.

They were all agreed that women's access to health services had improved and took pride in the fact that Travellers were becoming more assertive and vocal on their own behalf:

> There are more Travellers starting to speak now. Travellers never had the courage to speak up but now they have.

They agreed that this was due to the establishment of organisations like Pavee Point but also due to co-operation between Travellers and settled people:

> Pavee Point is a partnership of Travellers and settled people and it would not work without that mix. The Primary Health Care Project has helped women as mothers, going to the sites, giving them information. We have done marvellous work. We got women to go for smears, breast checks, hearing tests for kids, to the Well Women. We block book on a particular afternoon and we go along with them and now they are starting to make their own way there. We did all the foundation for the welfare, doctors, etc., to go in where they wouldn't go before. We laid all of those foundations.
>
> There are many on the side of the road with no water, toilets or electricity. This is due to discrimination. It is also due to being put in a bay in a site where there is a place but where you do not want to be because you do not get on with some people there. It may not be suitable. You have no say as to where you go. There is no place for the children to play, no grass, so they are constantly being shouted at. There are loads of pylons and some make so much noise it is hard to sleep at night. We waited seventeen years for them to build these houses. They are houses for Traveller families – group housing it is called – where the people in the site are mostly related. I campaigned for better conditions with other people and they (the corporation) finally listened to us. Before we were living in wooden or metal chalets with rats as big as dogs running around you. These houses are nice and warm and have central heating and all, but there is no place for the children to play ... Some sites were for a certain number of families but they keep building more on them and we are all squashed in together. That is not healthy either. Maybe some Travellers do not want to live in houses, they still want to live in trailers. Some halting sites are very badly designed, they are still building metal chalets for kitchens and toilets on halting sites where children get their fingers caught in the doors. These places are freezing in the winter and you wouldn't be inclined to have a shower there on a cold morning. Travellers can help design what they want too.
>
> Just because you are a Traveller doesn't mean you deserve less.

CHAPTER TWENTY-ONE

Mother Courage?
Irish Mothers and Emigration to North America

Grace Neville

The numbers are notorious, the sheer scale unimaginable: between 1885 and 1920, an estimated seven hundred thousand Irishwomen emigrated to the United States. Most of them never returned (Nolan, 1989; Miller, 1985; Diner, 1983; Arensberg and Kimball, 1940). Every individual among these emigrants had a story to tell; so did their families left behind in Ireland. Studies of Irish emigration often emphasise trends and statistics more than the fate of individuals or of groups. Taking its cue from recent French historical analyses of marginal social groups, this chapter focuses on mothers and emigration, particularly on the effect emigration had on mothers (Le Goff, 1978; Bertaux, 1997; Geremek, 1987; Rossiaud, 1988). The source material analysed will be mainly non-literary accounts of emigration from rural Ireland to North America in the late nineteenth and early twentieth centuries.

Among the various groups of mothers affected by emigration, the most commonly cited is that of the mothers left behind by emigrant children. Such mothers rarely if ever speak in their own voices; instead, others generally present them in the texts under discussion here. As such, they are depicted primarily as victims of emigration, having little or no influence on what was happening around them, reactive more than proactive. They are the *locus* of grief, to the extent that some emigrant songs imagine them dying of sorrow for their departed children [IFC 1411:49 (Archives from the Irish Folklore Collection, housed in Roinn Bhéaloideas Éireann/Department of Irish Folklore, UCD, hereafter IFC. These extraordinarily rich archives in Irish and English contain lengthy interviews on a very wide range of topics, including emigration, with elderly people living mainly in rural Ireland in the 1930s and thereafter)]. Like some *pietà* figure, these mothers are usually depicted mourning their lost children:

one old woman had three daughters, all of whom had gone to America, and the poor old woman was making herself ill with weeping and mourning for them [IFC 1430:213].

One emigrant song conjures up the discrepant situation of a child who dies before the parent, of a mother who does not lament over her dead child's grave, who is not there to fulfil the supremely female *mediatrix* function of smoothing the path of the deceased to the next world:

No kind mother's tears will flow oer my grave
On the shores of Americay [IFC 1409:90].

Even before their child leaves or dies, these mothers are remembered above all for the extremism of their emotions at 'American' wakes:

the mother was always the lone-liest [*sic*, IFC 1409:123–4].

One reads of a mother who had accompanied her departing daughter to the train station:

she had never seen a train before. The train came into the station blowing its horn, and the woman began cursing it: 'Bad luck to you [...] you're taking me daughter away from me' [IFC 1430:229].

Their body language conveys their utter desolation at the impending loss:

Then the saying goodbye would start [...] the mother would put her arms round their neck and sometimes hold on and on until somebody would take her away [IFC 1411:224–5].

At a train station on the journey from Kerry to Cork, the writer J. M. Synge (1871–1909) remembers:

At one place an old woman was seized with such a passion of regret, when she saw her daughters moving away from her for ever, that she made a wild rush after the train; and when I looked out for a moment I could see her writhing and struggling on the platform, *with her hair over her face*, and two men holding her by the arms (my italics, Synge, 1979).

Elsewhere, Synge describes an old Aran Island woman who has just received a letter from her emigrant son in America:

All the evening afterwards the old woman sat on her stool at the corner of the fire *with her shawl over her head*, keening piteously to herself. America appeared far away, yet she seems to have felt that, after all, it was only the other edge of the Atlantic, and now when she hears them talking of railroads and inland cities where there is no sea, things she cannot understand, it comes home to her that her son is gone for ever (my italics, Synge, 1977).

The mother of the immigrants [sic] *threw her apron over her head* and started to bewail her Poor Johnny or Biddy [my italics, IFC 1409:315].

It is significant that, here as elsewhere, the wailing mother is represented with her face covered, like the *pleureuses* of medieval France, for she is now lost to her companions, cut off and alone in a tiny private world of her own, entirely consumed by her intense grief. She is, indeed, the *mater dolorosa*.

These extravagant displays of distress may have been, in part, a choreographed response to the expectations of the community. At the same time, the functions of such maternal grieving are many and varied. These mothers acted as a kind of lightning conductor for the grief of the whole community, their female gender and high status as mothers allowing them to express pain in ways that might have been deemed excessive in others. They thus fulfilled a cathartic function in assuaging the grief of others, in accomplishing what the French (*pace* Freud) call *le travail du deuil*. Furthermore, those emigrating may have needed their last memories of home to be these extreme physical and verbal displays of loss on the part of the person arguably closest to them: their mother. Individuals already waked, poised on the brink of the unknown, about to enter a new life (after-life?) across an ocean in a huge new world may have needed to believe that they mattered so much that their absence could trigger off intense pain and even death in their mothers, that their absence could turn light into darkness. In a rare first-person statement, we hear the Blasket Island nurse, American-born Méiní O'Shea (1876–1967) recalling the impact on her of her daughter's departure for America:

She explained movingly to Mike Pheig her sorrow at her daughter's departure. 'That was the first time,' she said, 'that the island became dark around me' (Matson, 1996).

Such verbal and physical expressions of grief fulfil a vital function: they convince the departing offspring that absence does not mean oblivion, that they will continue to exist even after being waked, that they are not likely to be forgotten. In imparting such messages

Mother of Emigrant Children
© *Caroline Canning*

to their offspring, these mothers were good mothers: they enabled their children to leave them.

An interesting variant on the above leave-takings is found in the material below, when mothers faced with the departure of their children are depicted as utterly impassive. Commentators leave us in no doubt as to the agony of these women, implying that they hid their anguish from their departing children in order not to add to their distress. In other words, in denying themselves a space for self-expression, these mothers are deemed to be sublimating their own needs in the relentless interest of their children. Journalist John Healy describes his grandparents who had just bid farewell to their children who were leaving Mayo for America in the early twentieth century. His grandmother:

> now walking back up the road to the thatched cottage, could be a mother again. No one would see her tears and her face would be dried in the

shower-of-hailstones apron before she climbed the hill to the house and the rest of her children (Healy, 1978).

No one would see? But someone must have, for her grandson, John Healy, recorded the moment (that predated his birth) for posterity. Perhaps, then, such reports tell us more about the observers' *mentalité* than about anything else, especially their assumption that all mothers embody selflessness to the point of being marginal even to the major events of their own lives. For while commentators often unquestioningly interpret such maternal impassivity as proof of self-abnegation, cynics might wonder why maternal anguish was not always so effectively hidden after all.

At all events, another large group affected by emigration were the mothers left behind by husbands whose departure for America left them stranded in a kind of temporary widowhood. The emigrant husband's role initially was to send home money that would enable his wife and children to survive in his absence:

> a lot of poor women at that time were glad to see the Yankee letter with the money in it coming for they would then be able to pay the bill, that they nearly all owed, at the local shop [IFC 1411:143].

After a lapse of time that could stretch to several years, these husbands usually sent home the passage money for the rest of the family:

> the usual practice was that the father emigrated first, and as soon as he could arrange, his wife and children joined him and set up a new home [IFC 1409:276].

A more extreme example of such arrangements concerns mothers who emigrated from Ireland to Australia from whence their men folk left for America, leaving them and their children stranded between two worlds [IFC 1409:317]. Mothers thus left behind had to cope without their husbands for several years while they waited for the call to cross to America, *de facto* widows although their husbands were still alive, mother *and* father to their young children. Not that such paradoxes were surprising in a situation already rich in paradoxes, for how else could one explain the widespread custom of holding a wake for people still alive? In the absence of their men folk, mothers in such situations sometimes strayed out into the male preserve that was the public sphere, even to the extent of making poitín (to earn money?) and being imprisoned for so doing. They were now without husband or children. The transgressive nature of these women's activities was invoked by a sympathetic magistrate as mitigating circumstances:

> he said he thought that because these women had large families and their men away that they should be let off a little earlier [IFC 1411:232].

The presiding judge was not convinced:

> every woman had to serve three full months in jail [IFC 1411:233].

Husbands/fathers were not the only people whose presence was traded for fistfuls of dollars, of course. Mothers lost their children, too, and traded the comfort and companionship of their presence in similar pacts:

> every month after that girl landed the pound note came to [her mother]. [The mother] used to say 'we're getting a pound a month: we can put on the kettle now'. Another girl emigrated: the monthly amount increased to two pounds. Others went. The family house was slated and general improvements were made [IFC 1411:399].

Supreme irony: these arrangements, extreme as they were, did not always produce the expected results. Money was not always forthcoming even from well-meaning absent husbands/fathers/children [IFC 1409:119]. Even when it was, one cannot help thinking that a cruel price was exacted for a field or a few cows:

> one boy went to America to the father, and there is one boy at home with the mother. They have built up a lovely home, with Stanley 9 Range in the Kitchen Bath Room and a lot of nice stabling about 200 sheep on the mountain and about 20 head of cattle and they also bought more land [IFC 1409: 120].

Each of these arrangements was undoubtedly different, unique even, but accounts of them usually portray the mothers involved as passive, waiting in a kind of limbo, mothers without children, wives without husbands, eternal Penelopes, their lives on hold, awaiting a call that in some cases never came:

> He never returned nor she never heard anything more about him [IFC 1411:319].

Alongside the *topos* of the mother left behind by emigration, others exist. A lesser-acknowledged fact is that mothers became emigrants too. Emigration sometimes offered women a degree of control over their actions, a space in which to make decisions: one reads of a woman who sold her farm to a neighbour before leaving with her daughter for America. Eight years later, she returned and bought back the farm [IFC 1411:151]. Significantly, no husband is mentioned. Equally, widows sometimes emigrated with their children, a decision based presumably on the calculation that life in the new world would be kinder than life in their homeland. We read of a widow whose husband and two sons were drowned and who emigrated to America, presumably seeking a fresh start, although her landlord had offered her free rent on her home [IFC 1411:70]. Of another widow we read:

> Some of her children were in America, when her husband died [...] the family in America sent their passages to the two sons, and the mother went with them to America. She would not remain in Ireland when all her family were gone [IFC 1409:245].

In other words, the mother saw her home as being with her children, albeit in another continent. Paradoxes abound here as everywhere in these emigration narratives: we read of an evicted widow who was brought out to America by her daughter already in the New World: the child, in effect, rescuing her mother [IFC 1409:74].

Other mothers emigrated. Emigration could be seen as a 'solution' for unwanted motherhood. The mother of an illegitimate baby might emigrate under pressure from her ashamed family [IFC 1411:377]. The child's father might be prepared to marry her in America though not in Ireland because of this shame [IFC 1411: 396]. Indeed, one sometimes suspects that scare stories were circulated with the aim of dissuading young unmarried women in Ireland from becoming pregnant and using emigration to America a 'solution' to their situation; stating that pregnant girls were not allowed to enter the US, one commentator recalls:

> I was told that girls were made to stand on ice and from that they could tell someway whether they were in the family way or not [IFC 1411:392].

Similarly, discouraging tales are told of women giving birth on the sea journey westwards and of the lack of support for them even from other women who felt pressured into giving them some of their scarce money [IFC 1411:393]. Even without the incriminating evidence of a baby, single young mothers were still anxious that they might not be allowed to land in America, their childless motherhood rendering them untouchable in two continents [IFC 1411:414].

Emigration deprived mothers of their children in many ways. Some mothers emigrated and, in so doing, left their children behind in Ireland (or later sent them back to Ireland from America). Of a mother who emigrated to Boston, we read:

> she had a little daughter and the little daughter went out two years later [IFC 1409:202].

Similarly:

> during the period of the evictions all of those evicted who could possibly emigrate did so. The small children, if any, were left at home in the care of relatives until arrangements could be made to take them over [to America] [IFC 1409:279].

Arguably, the most famous of these emigrant mothers was the mother of President Eamon de Valera. De Valera was born in New York in 1882. Following his father's death, his mother sent him home to be reared by her family in Limerick:

> Following the early disappearance of his father, he would have become especially dependent on his mother, and his subsequent separation from her would undoubtedly have had a profound effect on him. Not only did she remain on in the United States, but the uncle who had brought him to Bruree soon returned to America, to be followed shortly by the boy's aunt, Hannie, to whom he had become attached [...] His mother visited Bruree briefly in 1887, before returning to the United States, leaving the boy to be reared by her mother and her brother, Pat Coll. She was planning to remarry and de Valera pleaded with her to take him back, but she refused. One can only imagine the scarring consequences of being rejected by his mother, especially when the rejection fuelled speculation about his legitimacy (Dwyer, 1991).

According to the above account, de Valera was barely five years old at the time of this initial refusal. The young boy's longing to be reunited with his absent mother did not fade with time. When he was thirteen years old:

> clearly disillusioned with life in Bruree, he wrote to Hannie in January 1896 pleading with her to intercede with his mother to allow him to return to America, but his efforts were in vain (Dwyer, 1991).

It is tempting, therefore, to see his powerful 1937 constitution as his attempt to place his elusive mother at the heart of matter, immured by words, statements, laws, aspirations, never to escape again. While tantalisingly little information is available about the de Valera case, a memorable first-hand account of the impact such disappearing emigrant mothers had on their young offspring is provided by poet John Montague. He remembers being sent as a young child from Brooklyn (where he was born in 1929) to live with relatives in rural Ireland, away from his mother who was struggling with health and family problems. It is surely significant that among Montague's earliest memories, one of the most vivid remains the trauma he experienced at school in Tyrone for speaking a different mother tongue from his peers. He was marked out as different and bullied to the point of speechlessness for his American English. In other words, the 'gifts' bestowed on him by emigration were perverse: not only did emigration rob him of his mother but, supreme irony, in her place, it gave him the 'wrong' mother tongue. In his life, emigration truly was the bad fairy (Montague, 1984, 1991).

One of the most interesting groups of mothers affected by emigration concerns returned emigrants, women who, prior to marriage, had worked in America, before returning home to Ireland to settle down and rear a family. While most of the women who left for America stayed there (Schrier, 1958), the presence of those who returned to Ireland was inescapable:

> when I was young, the townland of Ballyhillion (the most northern townland in Ireland) was always referred to as Boston there were so many Yankees in it. All these people *mostly women* had been in the U.S.A. for a number of years and had come home and married and settled down. To this day most of the people in Ballyhillion have been in America for some time [my italics, IFC 1411:237].

Tantalising glimpses can be snatched of how their American years moulded these women's lives subsequently, of their impact particularly on their mothering philosophy. The ambition and focus of many of these mothers are evident over a wide range of examples. We read of an Irish woman who had worked as a domestic servant in America before marrying a widower there. She was remembered, significantly, as 'more than good to her step-sons and encouraged them to save to get a small boat of their own' [IFC 1411:409]. They took her advice, made a fortune and 'ended up buying one of the Vanderbuilt [sic] homes' [IFC 1411:409]. Back in Ireland, mothers who had spent some time in America were remarkable for their work ethic:

> such brides are very common in this area, and they are mostly good hard-working women who try to urge their husbands to make the most of their resources. They have the reputation of being economical and that generosity holds no place in their lives [IFC 1409:295].

One of the most vivid accounts of the influence on a mother of her 'American years' is provided by journalist John Healy in his portrait of his mother in his memoir, *Nineteen Acres* (Healy, 1978). Healy's mother had emigrated to New York early in the twentieth century and had trained and worked there as a nurse before returning to Ireland where she married, reared a family and worked as a much-appreciated district midwife. Healy presents her as a determined, feisty, intelligent woman, with little sentiment or patience for anyone, least of all herself:

> she was not a sentimental woman: she had seen death too many times in her life. She had seen it in New York in the plague of the Spanish Lady: the great flu epidemic which reached in and took her sister. She knew how to set her face against: you worked and you did not sit around moping, as she'd say. Life had to go on and life went on at an increased pace so you didn't have time to think about it. She despised the weakness of self-pity (Healy, 1978).

America had taught her alternatives to scraping a living on poor land in the west of Ireland and she was determined to apply this lesson of the American dream to her own children. Her unwavering resolve that they get an education, her steely focus on scholarships and schooling, were born of her 'American years' where she had witnessed the life-changing experience that was night-school education:

> her own early struggles in Brooklyn imprinted on her the value of an education: she had to make up a tremendous deficiency when she went to America, and was determined that her children would not have to make the same struggle (Healy, 1978).

The supreme value she placed on education led this fearless woman to withstand community pressure and to support her son's plans to work on a bog in order to finance his education, protecting him against the taunts of those who would despise such low-status work:

if you had any doubts about your townie status or being worried about being
called a 'bogman', my mother straightened you out. 'Better men than ye went
on the bog in their day. There's nothing wrong with it: it's good money.
And when you have an education, you can travel the world. Off with you
on Monday morning and I'll put it a-by for ye and you'll get a schooling yet'
(Healy, 1978).

Along with a rigorous work ethic and a respect for education, America had taught her other values that she transmitted to her children.
Her spirited defence of victims of prejudice whom she had met in America clearly influenced her son who recalls with pride her periodic
warning born of the years when, like her sister, she had worked as a
nurse for highly-appreciative Jewish doctors in New York:

No child of mine should ever say anything against the Jews for they put
many a penny my way in my time (Healy, 1978).

America had taught her new customs and practices, new ways of
operating in the world. It taught her a passion for hygiene, and her
supply of carbolic soap served her well in her long career as a midwife much sought-after because of her unbeaten record in delivering
safely the babies of the settled and Travelling communities. Her dread
of dance halls and cinemas was due less to a fear of sins than of germs,
for her experience as a nurse working in Brooklyn through the 1919–
20 flu epidemic had shown her that the surest way of avoiding infection of any kind was to avoid crowds:

my mother wanted the minimum of public contact and only the parish
church was deemed safe (Healy, 1978).

America had moulded her personality; it had toughened her:

my mother held that he [her husband] was 'too soft' and that she would not
be like that: every time she was called on 'a case', she had her fee. She stood
for 'no nonsense' with patients in the district and they knew where they were
with her. If they wanted her, they'd pay for her, she wasn't cycling the hills
at all hours of day and night without getting paid (Healy, 1978).

It is tempting to see Healy's mother's experience of emigration as the
impetus behind Healy's own dynamism and determination, qualities
that ultimately made him into a leading national figure. His memoirs
in which his mother plays such a defining role are valuable for many
reasons, one of which is their rarity value, for Healy's experience as

the son of a mother who was herself a returned emigrant was replicated many thousands of times, over many generations, but has been documented by just a handful of witnesses.

Emigration widened and redefined the concept of motherhood. It made grandmothers into the mothers of young children orphaned through emigration, children left behind by mothers who had left for America, for instance. In *An tOileánach*, the author recalls how his widowed sister emigrated to America, leaving her young son in the care of her extended family on the Blaskets. She returned from America for him three years later before remarrying and staying on the Blaskets (Ó Criomhtháin, 1978). Elsewhere, Ó Criomhtháin recalls how his widowed brother emigrated to America leaving his two young children in the care of his own mother, the children's grandmother. When her daughter-in-law had died:

> the youngest was only three months old and my mother had to set about bringing him up when she'd finished with her own clutch (1978)

Similarly, at the 'American wakes' held before departure, the concept of mothering was widened to embrace all the women of the community as they brought gifts of food for the festivities:

> the women brought presents of tea, sugar, eggs, perhaps a roll of butter [IFC 1409:247]

and for the long journey westwards:

> they [the emigrants] had to take their food with them [for the sea crossing] and for weeks before all the neighbouring women would be coming to the house with oaten bread or butter or something of that sort to put in their barrel [IFC 1411:113].

It is interesting to note the role played here by that most maternal of gifts, milk:

> The women would bring presents of new milk, and buttermilk for baking [IFC 1409:47].

Similarly, a local 'wise woman' might try to help the departing emigrants by providing them with a drink that could cure sea-sickness:

> I have heard that in the 1860s and 1870s, those travelling (to America)] were provided with some concoction made up from herbs by the local 'Wise Woman' [IFC 1409:291–2].

Such nurturing contrasts sharply with the role of the neighbouring men at such rituals: they usually brought the alcohol, which they then proceeded to drink!

> The men supplied the drink only [IFC 1430:2216].

Accounts abound of aunts who brought nieces and nephews out to America. Indeed, women frequently 'rescued' young people who were neither family nor even acquaintances and enabled them to start a new life in America. Even when they married and became mothers in America, some of these women still managed to send money home, in effect mothering young and old in their extended families on both sides of the Atlantic [IFC 1409:117].

Emigration, which deprived so many mothers of their children, at least brought some joy to other lives. It enabled women without children to experience motherhood. A very young child went to America to be adopted by his childless maternal aunt and her husband [IFC 1409:304–5]. A young woman, whose baby was born and died on the transatlantic crossing, was hired, on arrival in New York, as a wet-nurse for a widower's child: an arrangement that evidently suited all parties [IFC 1411:414].

It would be tempting but simplistic to see the mothers who left as powerful and those who remained in Ireland as powerless. In fact, the opposite could be the case. In the texts under discussion here, emigration often appears less like the result of any considered decision than as an inevitable move, a right of passage as unavoidable as puberty. On the other hand, it often required great strength of character or a defining life event such as marriage to foil emigration and remain at home. In particular, mothers who remained in Ireland had a significant influence on those who left, at several levels. Many of the women who emigrated to North America worked there as servant girls in the homes of wealthy families, a profession generally eschewed by other European immigrant women. Under their mother's guidance at home in Ireland, they had already served a lengthy apprenticeship that later facilitated their massive entry into this profession, albeit in another continent:

> The girls helped in the house, knitting and spinning and making clothes. They learned these trades from their mothers and grandmothers [IFC 1409: 202].

Despite their awareness of their impending loss, mothers themselves often encouraged chain emigration by exhorting each departing child to pay the passage to America of a younger sibling. In her farewell to her various daughters who were leaving for America, John Healy's grandmother used to enjoin each of them to send the passage money for one of their sisters still at home (Healy, 1978).

Few first-hand accounts remain of attitudes of emigrants to their mothers left behind in Ireland. In this context, the Hurley letters (Foster, 2000) provide many valuable and often moving insights into a standard experience for countless Irish people over many generations. Spanning 67 years from 1871 to 1936, this corpus of 123 letters was written to family members near Clonakilty in West Cork, by two brothers, Denis and Michael Hurley, emigrants to Nevada in the 1870s. They both died in America, never having even once returned home. Many of these letters are addressed to their mother. What strikes the reader throughout is the deep affection, care and respect of these emigrants for their ageing mother:

> When I saw in the Eagle [*The Skibereen Eagle* newspaper] that a great many were sick in West Cork I was afraid you would be found also in the lists. I am glad mother had strength and vitality enough to shake off that nasty illness [Denis Hurley to his mother, 18 February 1892, Hurley papers B. 12].

From halfway across the world, they try to lighten her spirits and convince her that she is indeed well by confronting her with evidence of her good health from a reliable source: Denis quotes a priest he had met who had recently met Mrs Hurley:

> he says you are lively enough to live several years yet [1 December 1896, Hurley papers, B. 20].

When it is clear that her health is, indeed, failing, Denis is honest in his account to her of the effect this news had on him:

> your sickness was rather a dampener on the Xmas occasion [24 February 1899, Hurley papers B. 26].

Letters are always coded, and the sub-text of these letters conveys carefully formulated messages to the doubtless many family readers of these texts on how they should treat the woman in question. In other words, the sons try to manage their mother's life, albeit at an unavoidably long distance, through the potent mixture of exhortation and flattery they heap on those close at hand:

> Christmas is coming and I am writhing [sic] to you to have a little money
> in your private purse [...] it is just one week's pay. I hope you do not want
> for anything and that brother John and his wife are kind to you. I believe
> he was too good a man to doubt his affection for his poor old mother. And
> your daughter-in-law sprung from respectable people must be equally good
> [Denis Hurley, 5 December 1891, Hurley papers, B. 11].

The alleged behaviour of their sister is the subject of constant criticism over the decades:

> Sister Kate must be a very busy woman not to find time to come to see her
> poor mother. It is good to be industrious and economical, but we should not
> allow the pursuit of making money and putting it in the bank, to turn our
> minds from other duties [Denis Hurley, 29 September 1898, Hurley papers,
> B. 24].

Here too, such remarks, with their dual blend of criticism (for alleged
dereliction of daughterly duty) and praise (for hard work and thrift)
may have been carefully crafted in the expectation that they would
be reported back to the erring party in whom they may have awaken-
ed an appropriate sense of duty.

 Some letters to their mother emphasise their identity as children
and hers as mother. Writing to both parents, the young emigrant,
Michael Hurley, stresses:

> The meat of New York and Boston is very palatable, my mother need not
> fear that I am not able to eat it. They use it here at every meal [Denis Hur-
> ley, 21 April 1873, Hurley papers, B. 1].

They praise her in her role as mother, source of sound advice:

> I went to see a doctor, too a good Irishman, and among other things he re-
> commended to me to take some cod liver oil. I said that was about the last
> piece of advice I got from my mother. He said her sons would do worse than
> to mind what their mothers tell them [Denis Hurley, 29 September 1898,
> Hurley papers, B. 24].

Their attempts to help their mother imagine what they now look like
are worthy of note. One could argue that they are here trying to help
her maintain her role as mother for, though absent, her children are
not invisible/she is still a mother. Thus, along with lengthy hand-
written letters and photos, they provide her with other signs of their
absent physicality:

Michael weighgs [*sic*] 192 lbs and I about 132 [Denis Hurley, 29 September 1898, Hurley papers, B. 24].

One imagines the ageing mother in West Cork trying to visualise from the people around her what men of 132 and 192 pounds would look like. A more startling and moving instance of these attempts at visualisation occurs elsewhere in two of these letters:

> Mother, you must be jesting when you speak of some grey hairs in your head. I suppose they are all grey and white [Denis Hurley, 6 September 1895, Hurley papers, B. 16];
>
> your welcome letter received [...] the lock of your hair surprised us. I thought you must be joking. My wife says I must be taking after you in that respect as I am old enough now to be getting pretty grey like so many who are younger get in this country [Denis Hurley to his mother, 2 December 1895, Hurley papers, B. 17].

This playful tone (flattering in the second extract which seems to suggest that the old woman's hair is not yet white and that her son, in this too, is her faithful child) speaks volumes for the affection in which this absent mother was still held, despite not having been seen by her sons now for several decades.

However, as years slip by, the relationship between sons and mother is somehow redefined, the emigrant sons treating their mother as if she were their child, their responsibility. Less than two years before her death, we read:

> That was an awful thunder storm! Did it scare you? [Denis Hurley, 29 September 1898, Hurley papers, B. 24].

They are solicitous even about the detail of their ageing mother's life:

> Do not overtax yourself in trying to walk to church. Barrack Hill used to be pretty steep [Denis Hurley, 2 December 1895, Hurley papers, B. 17].

Five thousand miles away, they find a solution to this mobility problem:

> I hope dear Mother that you have got confidence in John's horse and that you ride to church now [Denis Hurley, 9 March 1896, Hurley papers B. 18].

They do not hesitate to reprimand her for what they see as a foolish financial transaction, a land purchase for £750:

I think you must have been out of your mind. No wonder times would be hard in Ireland when people are that foolish to pay so much for such a place and such rent after [Michael Hurley, 13 January 1891, Hurley papers, A. 4].

Advice on food and health flows from sons on the other side of the Atlantic to their mother in West Cork:

If circumstances could enable you to drink a little stout and have some light nutritious food suitable to your condition [Denis Hurley, 24 February 1899, Hurley papers, B. 26];

Have a little jug of good whiskey and take a good joram when you feel cold or feeble and then you can recite your rosary more briskly and fondle your grandchildren with more zest [Denis Hurley, 2 December 1895, Hurley papers B. 17]

They even offer their mother advice on dying:

don't be afraid of death – you were devoted to the Rosary and the B.V. [Blessed Virgin] will protect you [Denis Hurley, 3 March 1899, Hurley papers, B. 27].

More than just one person, she gradually comes to personify qualities such as hard work, a laudable attribute for the emigrant letter-writer in the New World. Writing to his niece in West Cork decades after his mother's death, Denis Hurley remarks:

your children keep you pretty busy although your grandmother with double three in the family did a good deal of work. Some mothers here with one baby think they have their hands full and send their washing to a laundry and other parts of the house hold work are done on the outside [Denis Hurley to his niece, 2 March 1930, Hurley papers, E. 2].

She embodies other central elements in their lives, such as religion:

She was devoted to the Rosary in the days of yore. Many a time poor Father would want to be excused from saying it because he was very tired and sleepy. But it was no go: she insisted [see 6 January 1900, Hurley papers, M. 8].

She becomes Everymother: a *locus* of respect in an uncertain world, a link between past and future:

I am glad your daughter-in-law is so kind to you and so agreeable. May the Lord reward her and hope when it comes to her turn to be old and feeble that she may receive the same kindness [Denis Hurley, 2 December 1895, Hurley papers, B. 17].

She is respected not just because she is their mother but because all mothers are worthy of respect and attention. In a letter to his niece, some time after his own mother had died, Denis Hurley remarks:

> you don't speak of your mother's health. I hope it is good [6 January 1924, Hurley papers, D. 6].

Motherhood, rather than any one individual mother, becomes the focus; when sending money to his mother, Denis wryly remarks:

> I have a mother-in-law too, and to keep the peace in the family we send her a similar amount [Denis Hurley, 3 December 1897, Hurley papers, B. 23].

Elsewhere, in Peig Sayers' son's hesitation over his decision to emigrate to America, the mother similarly becomes a cipher for something more than just one woman: the individual's duty to seek the greater good and to follow the 'natural' order of things:

> How could I leave my mother behind all on her own on an Island in the sea? [...] I was going against God, surely, to leave her on her own on the island without anyone to look after her (O'Guiheen, 1982).

Traces emerge of the same idealisation of the long-absent mother that one finds in John Healy's memoirs: writing to his niece, Denis Hurley notes:

> Your family is increasing in numbers. I hope you will do as well as your grandmother. There was less modern improvements then. She had a pretty hard struggle at times to make ends meet [Denis Hurley, 2 May 1930, Hurley papers, D. 18].

For the devoted Hurley sons, in their wish but also their need for her to be well, their mother comes to represent the happiness and stability they clearly enjoyed in their youth alongside her:

> I am sorry to see by it [a letter] that you are confined to bed. I hope that with the advent of fine weather you would be able to be around frisking with the little ones and picking noneens [daisies] [Denis Hurley, 3 March 1899, Hurley papers, B. 27].

More than one woman, the mother bereaved by emigration becomes a cipher for something much bigger such as the homeland, youth, the idyllic past which may – or may not – have existed:

Eight years Pádraig had spent in America when he got a longing to pay a visit home. He wrote to my mother saying that he would be back with her before long, that he wanted to see his own beautiful sun-village again, and especially his mother, the person he loved most in the world. My mother laughed and cried while she was reading that letter (O'Guiheen, 1982).

In many of these texts, the mother of emigrants, more than anyone else, comes to embody loneliness, the passing of time, loss of control and of purpose, the terror of ageing and of death. Onlookers vividly project these inevitable realities of the human condition onto her frail person:

I was inside with an old widow a few night ago, that grey woman you used [to] see in the middle of the village [...] her children are all in America only her son that's a man here, but not in her house. Imagine her sitting in the corner alone thinking and looking at her empty house [in] which her grand-children should be playing and she know that she will never see her dear ones again. Do you know how her heart is, she told me she sometimes don't know where she is atall or what's going to happen her and she sleeps very very little. Then when storms come she is frightened to death that the fairly big house will fall down on her (Ní Shúilleabháin, 1978).

In this context, it is significant that the frustration and negativity of some returned emigrants are vented on the mother. We read of a young woman who had dinner in a local hotel during her trip home from America:

she said, she could not eat it at home, as there was not enough of service [IFC 1409:147].

Similarly, the mother tongue, Irish, becomes the focus of occasional public repudiation. An apocryphal story tells how a mother refers to an '*ubh*' [egg], whereupon her returned emigrant son asks her 'o mother what is an ubh?' [IFC 1430:220]. One could surmise what is at work in these anecdotes. More than just one woman, the mother embodies nourishment, hospitality, the home, the past, Ireland, old ways of doing things. She is an easy (inevitable?) target for anyone desperately trying to fashion a new identity for themselves: the old are rejected and crushed, and the young emerge.

In the texts under discussion here, mothers more than fathers seem to express regret at the near-Faustian pacts involved in trading children for material comfort: we read of a mother praising the generosity of an emigrant daughter 'through her tears' [IFC 1409:236], whereas a father complains that letters from his emigrant children contain photos of themselves instead of photos of Abraham Lincoln i.e., dollars [IFC 1409:297]! Such gender differences are all too obvious to one emigrant daughter:

> You would laugh if you could see the letters my Father writes to me, of course for money on the sly, I always send it to him. He tells me [he does] be always watching for the postman for fear my Mother would get it (from letter in author's possession written to my grandmother, Grace Neville, Cork City in 1907 by her friend Cissie [surname unknown] who was a servant girl in Riverside Drive, New York City).

While it would be impossible to generalise, it would seem that mothers more than fathers were missed by their emigrant children. On his train journey from Kerry to Cork, J. M. Synge recalls a fellow passenger:

> a returned American girl, who was on her way to Mallow, to get the train for Queenstown. When her mother was lost sight of the young girl broke out into tears, and the returned American and myself had trouble to quiet her (Synge, 1979).

Insofar as memory lines were maintained with departed children, mothers usually did this:

> it was nearly always the mother who wrote these letters and if she could not write some of the family or a neighbour wrote for her and put down exactly what she told them [IFC 1411:240].

At the same time, it is surely significant that 'American letters' seem to have been addressed to mothers rather than to fathers. Indeed, to illustrate the formulaic nature of these writings, one commentator says that they usually started with the salutation 'My dear Mother' [IFC 11411:139]. Interestingly, responsibility for sharing the contents of these letters everywhere throughout the community seems to have often been assumed by mothers:

> when night would come the house would be full to hear Johnny's letter [...] the woman had read the letter so often that she would know it off by heart [...] so well was she practised [IFC 1411:124–5].

One could thus argue that mothers in this context were *lieux de mémoire par excellence* (Nora, 1984–1992).

Stereotypical views of rural Ireland and of male behaviour are constantly challenged in these (largely male-authored) emigration narratives. While mothers are depicted as the main embodiments of the grief felt at departing children, they did not have a monopoly on the expression of such grief:

> I saw fathers and mothers whose sons or daughters were going away stretched on the floor lifeless with grief [IFC 1409:232–3].

Synge remembers the scene at train stations on his way from Kerry to Cork:

> parties of old men and women wailing with anguish on the platform (1979).

One commentator (born in 1889) remembers a young schoolmate who was reared in Ireland by an uncle after his widowed mother remarried. He was subsequently brought out to America by another uncle:

> the uncle who reared him cried over him for three days [IFC 1409:227].

Nor did time assuage such grief. If anything, for some men, the passage of time intensified such feelings of loss: in the last years of his life, Seán Eoghain, husband of Blasket nurse, Méiní, still 'pined' for his children in America:

> the letters that Peig read to him were but a feeble consolation, even when one of them brought news of a second son for Máire and Austin in Springfield. As Méiní said, 'There was nothing now in the bed but a skeleton paying no attention to what was going on' (Matson, 1996).

An anecdote worthy of Maupassant tells of an emigrant widower who spent a whole lifetime in America, earning money for his sons back on the Blaskets, before returning home impoverished and in ill health to his by now indifferent children:

> the sum of the whole matter is that not a one of those two has ever asked after him since (Ó Criomhtháin, 1978).

In America, they were distant from him but not as distant as when he returned home to reclaim them. He had lost out on all counts. Thus, while mothers are usually depicted as the victims of emigration, the suffering of fathers is not denied in the texts under discussion here.

Whatever about visible mothers in these texts, the absence at the heart of these emigrant narratives surely concerns missing mothers. In fact, the 'absent presence' of generations of missing mothers haunts these texts (de Certeau, 1984). For while emigration enabled some women to put together the price of the dowry that enabled them to return to Ireland, marry and become mothers, at the same time one could argue that, since so few of them actually returned, emigration drained the country of young women over succeeding generations. Hundreds of thousands of Irish-born women became mothers in a new place, America, where their children were often soon lost to them. This cry of rage and frustration of one commentator at his son is worth recalling:

> He's nothing but a bloody Yankee. I wanted him to go home with me to Ireland but he wouldn't come. He said America was good enough for him. These damn Yankees are no good. The Irish blood goes out of them in the first generation [IFC 1430:238].

Some undoubtedly coped well with the challenges of motherhood in a new land far removed from the support systems of home, others not at all. In this context, the eponymous Angela, Frank McCourt's mother, would deserve a study devoted entirely to herself (McCourt, 1997). At all events, the texts under discussion here offer an interesting and perhaps useful counterpoint to the depictions of mothers that fill Irish fiction of the same period, which covers such luminaries as Synge, Joyce and O'Casey (Weekes, 2000; Ward, 2001). In particular, it is interesting to note that the figure of the missing mother still haunts contemporary Irish fiction: witness award-winning Colum McCann's haunting novel, *Songdogs*, which tells of an Irish son's futile search for his runaway Mexican mother (McCann, 1995; Wall, 2000).

In these texts as elsewhere, the figure of the mother is a kind of palimpsest upon which various kinds of mothering/nurturing are inscribed. Emigrant mothers/mothers of emigrants are, of course, just one variant of the *topos* of the Great Mother, others of which include the Virgin Mary and Mother Ireland (O'Brien, 1976). It is surely significant that the concept of motherhood is accordingly widened in these emigrant texts to include other maternal icons such as Ireland:

> I hope this will be a better year with the people of poor Ireland than the last. And hope that the time will soon come, when her *children* will be able to live at home in peace and comfort [my italics, Denis Hurley, 24 June 1873, Hurley papers, B. 2].

One could argue that Ireland is a country that still offers multiple and contradictory versions of motherhood. On the one hand, motherhood is highly valued and respected to the point of being en-shrined in the Irish constitution, whereas even a cursory comparison of maternity entitlements and childcare services in Ireland with those of other EU countries reveals a chasm between ideal and reality (Rich, 1977). One might be tempted to suggest that the rhetorical flourishes that marked discussions of motherhood, especially in the political sphere in the context of recent referendums, amount to no more than trite compensation for shortcomings in everyday reality (Rich, 1977). In particular, the contention that the nuclear family was ever the norm in Ireland is challenged in the texts analysed here through their repeated depictions of mothers and children being rent asunder by emigration over successive generations, with consequences that we are only now, very belatedly, beginning to address (Gray, http://migration.ucc.ie/oralarchive/). Much of the fascination and the richness of the various texts under discussion in this article stems from their ability to focus our minds on important issues such as these.

I wish to acknowledge with deep gratitude the generous permission granted to me by: the Head of the Department of Irish Folklore, University College Dublin, to use material from the Irish Folklore Collection in this article; and the Cork Archives Institute for permission to use materials from their collections.

BIOGRAPHICAL DETAILS

BRESNIHAN, VALERIE is a freelance consultant and social researcher. Her recent research projects concern the mentally ill in prison: *Out of Mind, Out of Sight, Solitary Confinement of Mentally Ill Prisoners* (April 2001) and *The Politics of Prison Medicine* (February 2002). In 1997 she completed a PhD entitled *Irish Political Culture, a Symbolic Analysis*. She is currently chairperson of the Irish Penal Reform Trust and is serving on the board of the Dublin Rape Crisis Centre. She was a NUI candidate in the 2002 Senate elections.

BURKE BROGAN, PATRICIA is a painter, poet and playwright. She was born in Co. Clare and lives in Galway city. She has won many awards for her poems, etchings and short stories. Her paintings and graphics have been shown in the Oireachtas Exhibition at The Municipal Gallery; with Listowel International Biennale 1978; at the Douglas Hyde Gallery, Trinity College; with Listowel International Exhibitions 1980 and 1982; and in selected International Exhibitions in Spain, Hawaii and Japan. She has had many solo exhibitions in Galway, Spiddal and Dublin. A retrospective exhibition of her paintings, graphics and collages was shown at the Kenny Art Gallery, Galway in January 1999. *Above the Waves Calligraphy*, her collection of poems and etchings, was published by Salmon Publishing in 1994. The script of her stage play, *Eclipsed*, was published by Salmon Publishing in 1994. *Eclipsed*, first produced in Galway in 1992, was an immediate success. It has won many international awards including a Fringe First at Edinburgh Theatre Festival 1992; the USA Moss Hart Theatre Award 1994; and two awards from the USA Newspaper Dramalogue 1995. It was selected as Critics Choice and Best of the Weekend by *The Los Angeles Times* 1995 and Best of the Fringe at Seattle 1995. To date there have been forty productions of *Eclipsed* worldwide. The second play of the trilogy, *Clarenda's Mirror*, was chosen for a rehearsed staged reading as part of the Irish Showcase at the Fourth International Women Playwrights Conference in NUIG, June 1995. *Stained Glass at Samhain*, Patricia's new play, was produced at the Town Hall Theatre, Galway in October 2002. Patricia was awarded an Arts Council Creative Writing Bursary in 1993 and a European Script Writer's Bursary in 1994. Work-in-progress includes a new collection of poems and a novel.

CALLARY, HELEN S. is originally from Wales, but now lives and works in Dublin.

CANNING, CAROLINE is an artist who works in her kitchen in Dublin and in the wilds of Connemara. She is the mother of Libby, Michilín and Ben.

COAKLEY, ANNE is a lecturer in the Department of Sociology at the NUI, Maynooth. She has developed expertise in the area of family finances, patterns of distribution and expenditure. She has published in the area of mothers and social welfare: 'Gendered Citizenship; The Social Construction of Mothers in Ireland in Social Welfare' in A. Byrne and M. Leonard (eds) (1997) *Women and Irish Society: A Sociological Profile* (Belfast: Beyond the Pale Publications); and on work and social welfare; 'The Social Citizenship of Mothers in Ireland: Perspectives on Paid and Unpaid Work' in R. Oikonomou (ed) (1998) *The Gender of Rights* (Diotima, University of Athens). Her most recent publication is on food and health policies: 'Healthy Eating: Food and Diet in Low Income Households' (2001)in *Administration* vol. 49, no. 3.

CONROY, PAULINE is a social policy analyst with Ralaheen Ltd and guest lecturer in European Social Policy in the Departments of Social Science at UCD. She was technical editor of the *European Commission's Annual Report on Equal Opportunities for Women and Men in the European Union (1997–2000)* and is closely associated with the European Commission's initiatives on combating violence against women and children. She has been published on the history of backstreet abortion in Ireland; Irish women emigrants; clothing outworkers in the underground economy in Italy; and women's employment in a single European market. Her analysis of social policy in Ireland during the last fifty years has appeared in *Irish Social Policy in Context*, published by UCD Press in 1999.

CONWAY, EILEEN completed a PhD in the Department of Social Policy and Social Work on adoption in Ireland. She is employed by the ERHA as a social worker and also works part-time in the infertility clinic in the Rotunda Hospital.

DE BUITLÉAR, ROISÍN is a glass artist who lives and works in Dublin. She graduated from National College of Art and Design (NCAD) in 1983 with a first class honours in glass design. Her blown work is in private and public collections in Ireland and abroad. On a larger scale, her architectural glass work has been commissioned by the OPW and the National Museum of Northern Ireland. In 2001, Róisín won a scholarship to attend the Pilchuck Glass School in Seattle, USA and was nominated for the Corning Glass Prize for the work she carried out there. She has been a lecturer in NCAD for over 15 years where she is a vital member of the glass department. Through extensive travel she has built a network of contacts with contemporary glass artists and has been instrumental in attracting many of them to come to Ireland. In 1998, she helped to found the Glass Society of Ireland Contemporary Makers who meet regularly to discuss, learn about and promote, contemporary glass issues. Róisín was primarily involved in the internationally acclaimed Millenium Glass Conference which was held in Dublin in 2000. She has lectured in Britain, USA and Ireland on contemporary Irish glass. She is currently on the board of selectors for the Golden Fleece Award. She is a regular contributor of articles for the Glass Society of Ireland magazine.

DELANEY, FLO works as the Education Officer at the Women's Education Research and Resource Centre (WERRC) at UCD. She has researched the reality of women's experiences of infertility in Ireland for her MA thesis in Women's Studies. She worked in the USA as a registered nurse for ten years and now lives in the Wicklow hills with her husband, Christopher.

DILLON HURNEY, PAULINE completed an MA in Women's Studies at UCD in 1997. The thesis she presented, entitled *Breast or Bottle: Choice or Coercion?*, is a contemporary exploration of women's experience of infant-feeding. She is currently doing a PhD at the Department of Social Policy and Social Work at UCD and is researching the infant-feeding practices of working-class Dublin mothers in the early decades of the twentieth century.

GUILBRIDE, ALEXIS is a writer and adult educator. She is also the mother of two teenage children. She has seen a number of her articles and essays published in the *Irish Times*. Her creative work, in short story form, has also appeared in the pages of several magazines and anthologies. She is particularly proud of her contributions to *Dublin Stories*, an almost annual collection published by the Inkwell Writers' Group, of which she is a committee member. The four collections produced so far have had considerable critical and commercial success, and a fifth is in the pipeline. Alexis was co-author of the well-received play, *These Obstreperous Lassies*, which was commissioned by the ICTU as part of its centennial celebrations in 1994. She has also worked as a script consultant to Peter Sheridan. Her research into infanticide in post-independence Ireland was the subject of a short film, *They Went Away in Silence*, directed by Nicola Lafferty in 1997. In addition to teaching creative writing, Alexis reviews books for *Gay News* and *Books Ireland* and is currently working on a novel of her own.

HENSEY, MAREE is a textile artist. Born in Ireland in 1962, she trained as a midwife and moved to Scotland to work. In 1987, she studied printed textiles/painted textiles at Galashiels College of Textiles from which she graduated in 1992 with a first class degree and was awarded the Dr Oliver Medal for Design Excellence. She was one of thirty design graduates to represent Ireland at Texprint-Frankfurt, Germany. In 1993, she returned to Dublin when her work formed a major part in the identity of the new Brown Thomas. Maree was involved in designs for rugs and textiles, illustration for print, packaging and window display. Maree was commissioned by John Rocha to produce designs for printed textiles for several collections. Maree has worked with the Irish Rug Company and is currently with McMurray Carpets producing artwork for individually commissioned handtufted rugs and carpets. Recent Commissions include: OPW boardroom rug, Tánaiste's office carpet, reception area rugs for the Great Southern Hotel, Dublin Airport, Towers Hotel, Waterford and many private clients. She is also a part-time lecturer at the National College of Art and Design and visiting lecturer at the Faculty of Art and Design, Belfast. Maree continues to draw and paint and has two children, Ella and Conor.

HILLIARD, BETTY has been a lecturer in Sociology at UCD since 1988, prior to which she worked in research and evaluation for the EU and semi-state sector. She is director of the masters programmes in Sociology at UCD, and chairperson of the Social Science Research Centre there. In 1998–99 she spent time as a visiting scholar in the Centre for Work and Families at the Institute for the Study of Social Change attached to the Department of Sociology at Berkeley. She has published on change and the family, theoretical issues in the study of the family, and gender issues, as well as contributing to comparative work on European families and research on the Irish language.

HORGAN, GORETTI is a Research Associate in the School of Policy Studies, University of Ulster at Magee. She has a particular interest in participatory research and has published studies on the views and experiences of teenage mothers, young disabled people and children in the care system. An active socialist, she has been involved in the struggle for reproductive rights since the late 1970s, and in 1982–83 was the national organiser of the Anti-Amendment campaign. She lives in Derry with her partner and their teenage daughter.

McCANN JAMES, CELESTA is a lecturer and co-ordinator for Applied Social Studies (Social Care) at the Institute of Technology, Blanchardstown. She received her primary degree in California, USA and her MA in Women's Studies at NUI, Dublin. She was awarded her PhD in sociology from NUI Galway, where she researched oppression and the social world of women in prison in the Irish Republic. Additional research interests and publications focus upon social policies regarding paid work and family initiatives for women; experiences of adult women returning to formal education; and the professional provision of social care to ethnic minorities in Ireland. Celesta's unpaid work includes active participation in community development, campaigning work as a board member with the Irish Penal Reform Trust, and the rewarding experience of mothering four children.

McCARTHY, ÁINE is a writer and an international writing tutor and mentor. She has contributed hundreds of articles and book reviews to the Irish and British press and currently teaches women's studies and creative practice at the Women's Education Research and Resource Centre (WERRC) at University College Dublin (UCD). She recently completed her first novel, Going Under (Penguin, 2005) an examination of ideas of freedom and autonomy through the lens of the Irish Civil War; and is at work on a second novel, a fictionalised depiction of the life of Iseult Gonne. Both novels explore aspects of 'the passionate conflicts and ambiguities of the mother/daughter relationship'.

MHAC AN TSAOI, MÁIRE (Marie Cruise O'Brien) was born in Dublin in 1922. She was educated at Dublin and Dún Chaoin. Her third-level education was extensive and varied: BA in Celtic Studies and modern languages (UCD); King's Inn, Dublin, called to the bar in 1944; in 1945, she received an MA in classical modern Irish. From 1942–45 she was a Scholar at the Dublin Institute for Advanced Studies and published Two Irish Arthurian Romances (1946). She studied at the Institute des Hautes Etudes en Sorbonne (1945–47). She entered the Department of Foreign Affairs as a Third Secretary in 1947 and served in Paris and Madrid from 1949–1951. She served as Secretary of the Irish Cultural Relations Committee, 1951–52. She was seconded to the Ministry of Education to work on the compilation of a modern English/Gaelic dictionary. From 1956– 1961 she served at the International Organisations Desk in the Ministry of Foreign Affairs and from 1957–1960 was a member of the Irish Delegation to the General Assembly of the United Nations. In 1961, she was appointed permanent Representative of Ireland to the Council of Europe and resigned to marry Conor Cruise O'Brien in 1962. She accompanied him during his periods of residence in Africa, London and the United States. The couple adopted two part-African/ part-Irish children. She also taught Irish at various levels in Ireland and abroad and taught a course on the Gaelic background to Anglo-Irish literature at Queen's College, New York, 1969–1970. Máire is a distinguished poet and has published three volumes of poetry in Irish, a selection of translations from classical Gaelic poetry, a monograph on the life and work of Gerald Fitzgerald, the Third Earl of Desmond. Her collected poetry was published under the title An Cion go dTí Seo in 1988 and her work has been translated into French, Japanese and Hebrew.

MOYNIHAN, MARY works as an actor, director and drama facilitator. In the latter role, she has worked with professional and community-based drama groups, women's groups, children, older people and foreign students. Mary is a founding member and artistic director of Smashing Times Theatre Company Ltd, a professional theatre company that specialises in community arts. Mary has an MA in Film Production from the Dublin Institute of Technology and a BA in Drama and Theatre Studies from Trinity College, Dublin. As an actor she has appeared in numerous film, television and theatre productions such as *Fair City* and *The House of Bernarda Alba* (Focus Theatre). Mary trained in the Stanislavski system at the Focus Theatre under the direction of her friend and mentor, the late Deirdre O'Connell. Mary is the mother of three young boys, Féilim, Naoise and Éanna.

NEVILLE, GRACE completed a BA in French and Irish from University College Cork; an MA in French from NUI; a doctorate from l'Université de Lille. She has studied and taught in France at the universities of Lille, Caen and Metz. She has been awarded scholarships and research grants from various sources including the French government, the French embassy, the CNRS (Centre National de la Recherche Scientifique), the British Council. Currently statutory lecturer in French, University College Cork, where she is an elected member of the UCC Governing Body. Her research and publications are in the following areas: French literature, the history of the French language, Franco-Irish relations from the medireview to the modern period, the literature of emigration, women's studies. She has presented her research at the French Senate, the College de France, the Sorbonne, Harvard University and Ann Arbor.

RICHARDSON, VALERIE is a senior lecturer in the Department of Social Policy and Social Work in University College Dublin. She has published in the area of child-care policy and practice and in the area of lone parenthood and in particular teenage parenting. Other interests centre on family policy, particularly the integration of work and family roles. During the 1990s she was one of the two representatives on the European Observatory on National Family Policies. She is currently carrying out research in the area of child custody and family breakdown.

WARD, MARGARET is the assistant director of the Belfast-based think tank Democratic Dialogue. She grew up in Belfast, graduated in Political Science from Queen's University Belfast and received a PhD from the University of the West of England. She was a founder member of many feminist groups in the early years of feminist politics in Belfast, including the Socialist Women's Group, the Belfast Women's Collective and the Northern Ireland Abortion Law Reform Association. In the mid 1980s she was women's officer in the Community Services Department of Belfast City Council. Her research interests include the current position of women in public life in Northern Ireland. As a feminist historian, she has also taught in universities in Northern Ireland and England. Her publications include *Unmanageable Revolutionaries: women and Irish nationalism*; biographies of Maud Gonne and Hanna Sheehy Skeffington and an edited collection of documents, *In Their Own Voice*. She is the mother of two children, Fintan and Medbh.

APPENDIX 1
SELECTED EVENTS IN THE LEGALISATION OF CONTRACEPTION 1922–1992

Date	Key Legal Events	Results
1922–1935	Contraception Legal	
1929	Censorship of Publications Act	
1935	Criminal Law Amendment Act	Prostitution and contraception banned under this act, which made it an offence to sell, offer, advertise, import or attempt to import any contraceptives
1946	Censorship of Publications Act	
1969	Ireland's first Fertility Guidance Clinic opened in Dublin	
1970	Irish Family Planning Association begins to provide talks on contraception to women's groups	
	Irish Women's Liberation Movement (Contraceptive Train) began – women went to Belfast and purchased contraceptives. They challenged customs officers to arrest them on their return but they allowed the women through	
1971	Criminal Law (Amendment Bill)	Bill prepared by Mary Robinson, to legalise contraception. Her Senate supporters her parents and herself became the target of public abuse
1971	First private members bill to change the law on contraception is placed on the order book of the Senate by Mary Robinson	She did not get the six Senate votes which would have ensured at least the publication of the bill
	She proposed to repeal section 17 (3) of the Criminal Law Amendment Act, 1935, sections 16 and 17 of the Censorship of Publications Acts 1929 and sections 7 and 9 of the Censorship of Publications Acts of 1946	Refused a first reading
1971	Bill given a first reading without any prior notice	Defeated by 25 votes to 14
1971	M. Robinson given leave to introduce another private members bill, amending the 1952 and 1964 Adoption Acts	This bill would allow couples in mixed marriages to apply to adopt a child
1972	Mary Robinsons private members bill, Adoption Amendment Bill 1971 given a second reading	She withdrew her bill when Minister for Justice promised government would bring in its own bill to deal with discrimination against mixed marriages in adoption matters

1972	M. Robinson versus An Bord Úchtala led to Adoption (Amendment Act) Act 1974	Challenged the constitutionality of the religious clauses in the Adoption Acts which led to their removal
1972	Mary McGee was defeated in High Court in her case to prove that the confiscation of her contraceptives at customs had been unconstitutional	
1973	Mary Robinson's second private members bill, the Family Planning Bill, 1973 passed its first stage	Senate agrees by 27 votes to 12 that her bill should proceed to second stage (Senate Debates, 14 Nov 1973, cols 3–12)
		First full debate on contraception in Irish Parliament 1974 (Senate Debates, 20–21 February 1974, cols 205–406)
1973	McGee [1974] IR 284	Courts had forced the government to act – Supreme Court decided 12 Dec 1973 that Mrs Mary McGee had the right to import contraceptives for her own use and that the law that stopped her was unconstitutional – an invasion of her right to privacy under Article 50 of the constitution and 17(3) of the Criminal Law Amendment Act 1935
1973	First vasectomy operation performed at IFPA in Mountjoy Square, Dublin 2	
1974	IFPA was able to import condoms, diaphragms and creams and distribute them by donation at the clinics	
1974	IFPA was charged under the 1935 Criminal Law (Amendment) Act with the promotion of unnatural methods of contraception in a booklet The case was dismissed.	
1974	Debate on Mary Robinson's Family Planning Bill, 1973	Defeated 32 votes to 10
1974	M. Robinson introduces Illegitimate Children Maintenance and Succession Bill in Senate	Bill withdrawn when government promises to introduce its own bill: The Family Law (Maintenance of Spouses and Children) Act, 1976
1974	Third private members bill, Family Planning Bill, 1974 granted first reading and published	Finally defeated by 23 votes to 20. Mary Robinson had pushed for this bill to be under the Dept of Health and not the Dept of Justice
1976	IFPA booklet Family Planning was banned by the Censorship Board	
1977	High Court declared banning of the booklet Family Planning null and void. An appeal was lodged against this	

decision by the Attorney General
and the Censorship Board

1978	Supreme Court upheld the decision of the High Court on the booklet *Family Planning*	
1979	Irish Family Planning Association versus Ryan (1979) IR 295	Mary Robinson represented IFPA when their booklet on contraception was banned and won – having pursued the Censorship Board to the Supreme Court
1979	Family Planning (Health) Act, 1979 enacted	Provided for contraceptives including condoms, to be made available on prescription from a doctor for medical reasons, or for *bona fide* family planning purposes, to married couples with a prescription. Despite its limitations, it made contraceptives available
1981	First IFPA course on Sex Education and Personal Relationships was held. The courses were designed to assist those working with young people in the area of sexuality and personal development	
1983	First case taken under the (Health) Family Planning Act against Dr Andrew Rynne for supplying ten condoms directly to a patient He was fined £500 but the fine was later lifted	
1985	Health (Family Planning) (Amendment) Act, 1979	Amended to permit sale of condoms to persons aged 18 years + (without a prescription from a range of named outlets)
1986	European Court of Human Rights, Case of Johnston & Others V Ireland, decision of 23 January 1986, Series A No 112	A child born outside marriage was classed as illegitimate. The court decided this child should be legally and socially in the same position as a legitimate child
1992	Health (Family Planning) (Amendment) Act, 1992	Legally obliged health boards to provide family planning services.
1992	Sale of condoms was deregulated	

APPENDIX 2
TEXTS OF FIVE REFERENDA ON ABORTION, 1983–2002*

Referendum	Text	% Poll	% in Favour	% Against
8th Amendment 1983: The right to life of the unborn	'The State acknowledges the right to life of the unborn and, with due regard to the equal right to life of the mother, guarantees in its laws to respect, and as far as practicable, by its laws to defend and vindicate that right'	53.7	66.4	33.5
12th Amendment 1992: The right to life	'It shall be lawful to terminate the life of an unborn unless such termination is necessary to save the life, as distinct from the health, of the mother where there is an illness or disorder of the mother giving rise to a real and substantial risk to her life, not being a risk of self–destruction'	68.2	33.0	70.0
13th Amendment 1992: The right to travel	'This subsection shall not limit freedom to travel between the State and another state'	68.2	59.7	40.3
14th Amendment 1992: Information	'This subsection shall not limit freedom to obtain or make available, in the State, subject to such conditions as may be laid down by law, information relating to services lawfully available in another state'	68.1	57.3	42.7
25th Amendment 2002: Protection of Human Life in Pregnancy	'In particular, the life of the unborn in the womb shall be protected in accordance with the provisions of the Protection of Human Life in Pregnancy Act, 2002. The Provisions of section 2 of Article 46 and sections 1, 3 and 4 of Article 47 of this Constitution shall apply to any Bill passed or deemed to have been passed by both houses of the Oireachtas containing a proposal to amend the Protection of Human Life in Pregnancy Act, 2002, as they apply to a Bill containing a proposal or proposals for the amendment of this Constitution and any such Bill shall be signed by the President forthwith upon his being satisfied that the Bill has been duly approved by the people in accordance with the provisions of Section 1 of Article 47 of this Constitution and shall be duly promulgated by the President as law'	42.9	49.6	50.4

* Taken from *Referendums in Ireland*, Stationery Office, Dublin, Sept 2000 and *The Irish Times*, Dublin, 8 March 2002, p. 1.

FURTHER READING
(Note: Women's Education and Research Resource Centre = WERRC)

CREATION I

INFANT-FEEDING (pp. 37–47)
Pauline Dillon Hurney

Armstrong, S. (2000) 'Public Health Nursing' in Robins, J. (ed) *Nursing and Midwifery in Ireland in the 20th Century*, Dublin: An Bord Altranais, pp. 125–139.
Apple, Rima D. (1987) *Mothers and Medicine: A Social History of Infant-feeding 1890–1950*, Wisconsin: University of Wisconsin Press.
Barrington, R. (1987) *Health, Medicine and Politics in Ireland 1900–1970*, Dublin: Institute of Public Administration.
Blum, Linda M. (1999) *At the Breast: Ideologies of Breastfeeding and Motherhood in the Contemporary United States*, Boston: Beacon Press.
Browne, A. (ed) (1995) *Masters, Midwives and Ladies-in-Waiting*, Dublin: A. & A. Farmar.
Cameron, C. (1904) *How the Poor Live*, Dublin: Privately Printed.
– (1910) *Report upon the State of Public Health in the City of Dublin for the Year Ended 1909*, Dublin: Gilbert Library.
– (1911) *Report upon the State of Public Health in the City of Dublin for Year Ended 1910*, Dublin: Gilbert Library.
Carter, P. (1995) *Feminism, Breasts and Breastfeeding*, Hampshire & London: Macmillan Press.
Centre for Health Promotion Studies (1999) *Knowledge of and Attitudes to Breastfeeding in the Eastern Health Board with Special Reference to Community Care Area 1: Final Report*, Galway: Centre for Health Promotion Studies, NUI.
Clarke, T. A. and Matthews, T. G. (1995) 'The Development of Neonatal Paediatrics at the Rotunda' in Browne, A. (ed) *Masters, Midwives and Ladies-in-Waiting*, Dublin: A. & A. Farmar.
Clear, C. (2000) *Women of the House: Women's Household Work in Ireland 1922–1961*, Dublin: Irish Academic Press.
Coey Bigger, Sir Edward (1917) *Report on the Physical Welfare of Mothers and Children: Volume IV–Ireland*, London: Carnegie United Kingdom Trust.
Collis, W. R. F. (ed) (1938) *Clinical Paediatrics: The Baby*, London: Heinemann.
– (1938) 'Management of the Normal Infant during the First Week' in Collis, W. R. F. (ed) *Clinical Paediatrics: The Baby*, London: Heinemann.
– (1938) 'Breastfeeding' in Collis, W. R. F. (ed) *Clinical Paediatrics: The Baby*, London: Heinemann.
– (ed) (1958) *Neo-Natal Paediatrics*, London: Heinemann.
Crichton, Brian (1925) 'Infant Mortality in Dublin' in *Irish Journal of Medical Science*, 5th series, no. 42, July 1925.
– (n/d c.1930) *The Infant: A Handbook for Students and Nurses*, Dublin: Fannin and Co.
Department of Health (1992) *Perinatal Statistics*, Dublin: Department of Health.
– (1994) *A National Breastfeeding Policy for Ireland*, Dublin: Dept of Health.
Department of Local Government and Public Health Reports, 1925–1937. Dublin: Stationery Office.
Dockeray, G. C. and Fearon, W. R. (1939) 'Ante-Natal Nutrition in Dublin: A Preliminary Survey' in *Irish Journal of Medical Science*, 6th series, no. 157, January 1939.

Ehrenreich, B. and English, D. (1979) *For Her Own Good: 150 Years of the Experts' Advice to Women*, New York: Anchor.

Farmar, T. (1994) *Holles Street 1984–1994, The National Maternity Hospital – A Centenary History*, Dublin: A. & A. Farmar.

Foucault, Michel (1991) 'The Politics of Health in the Eighteenth Century' in Rabinow, Paul (ed) *The Foucault Reader: An Introduction to Foucault's Thought*, London: Penguin.

Freeman, Valerie E. (1996) *A Longitudinal Study of Growth, Feeding Practices and Irons Status in Health of Children from Birth to Aged Two Years*, PhD thesis, Dublin: TCD

Germon, J. and Williams, L. (eds) (1999) *A Sociology of Food and Nutrition: The Social Appetite*, Oxford: Oxford University Press.

Goulding, J. (1998) *The Light in the Window*, Dublin: Poolbeg.

Kearns, K. (1996) *Dublin Tenement Life: An Oral History*, Dublin: Gill & Macmillan.

Kennedy, F. (2001) *Cottage to Crèche: Family Change in Ireland*, Dublin: Institute of Public Administration.

Langford Symes, W. (1899) *Notes on the Feeding of Infants*, Dublin, Fannin & Co.

Lumsden, J. (1897) *Hints to Mothers in the Management of their Homes, the Feeding of their Children and the Prevention of Disease*, Dublin: G. F. Healy (2nd ed 1906; 3rd ed 1909).

Mac Clancy, P. C. D. (1958) 'Management of Infant-feeding' in Collis, W. R. F. (ed) *Neo-Natal Paediatrics*, London: Heinemann.

Maher, V. (ed) (1992) *The Anthropology of Breastfeeding: Natural Law or Social Construct*, Oxford: Berg.

McSweeney, M. and Kevany, J. (1982) *Infant-feeding Practices in Ireland*, Dublin: Health Education Bureau.

McSweeney, M. (1986) *National Survey of Infant-Feeding Practices*, Dublin: Health Promotion Unit.

Moran, M. (1958) 'Management of the Normal New-Born Baby' in Collis, W. R. F. (ed) *Neo-Natal Paediatrics*, London: Heinemann.

Murphy, E., Parker, S. and Phipps, C. (1999) 'Motherhood, Morality and Infant-feeding' in Germon, J. and Williams, L. (eds) *A Sociology of Food and Nutrition: The Social Appetite*, Oxford: Oxford University Press.

O'Brien, J. V. (1982) *Dear Dirty Dublin, A City in Distress 1899–1916*, California: University of California Press.

O'Dwyer, I. and Mulhall, A. L. (2000) 'Midwifery' in Robins, J. (ed) *Nursing and Midwifery in Ireland in the Twentieth Century*, Dublin: An Bord Altranais.

Prunty, J. (1998) *Dublin Slums, 1800–1925: A Study in Urban Geography*, Dublin: Irish Academic Press.

Rabinow, Paul (ed) (1991) *The Foucault Reader: An Introduction to Foucault's Thought*, London: Penguin.

Raphael, D. (1976) *The Tender Gift: Breastfeeding, Mothering the Mother – the Way to Successful Breastfeeding*, New York: Schocken Books.

Reddin, K. (1934) 'Prenatal Work and Child Welfare in Dublin' in *Irish Journal of Medical Science*, 6th series, no. 99, March 1934.

– (1938) 'Infant Mortality and Child Welfare' in Collis, W. R. F. (ed) *Clinical Paediatrics: The Baby*, London: Heinemann.

Robins, J. (1995). 'Public Policy and the Maternity Services in Ireland during the Twentieth Century' in Browne, A. (ed) *Masters, Midwives and Ladies-in-Waiting: The Rotunda Hospital 1745–1995*, Dublin: A. & A. Farmar.

– (ed) (2000) *Nursing and Midwifery in Ireland in the Twentieth Century*, Dublin: An Bord Altranais.

– (2000) 'Bord Altranais 1950–1970' in Robins, J. (ed) *Nursing and Midwifery in Ireland in the Twentieth Century*, Dublin: An Bord Altranais.

Ryan, G. (1996) 'Breast is Best' in Ms.Chief, No. 11, p. 4.

Thompson, W. (1905) 'Infantile Mortality' in *Dublin Journal of Medical Science*, vol. 120, pp. 460–471, December 1905.

(Unattributed) (1901) 'Section of State Medicine, Medical Miscellany: "On the Mortality of Infants under one year from Improper or Imperfect Feeding, with Suggestions for Public Instruction to Parents and Nurses on the Subject"' in *Dublin Journal of Medical Science*, vol. 112, pp. 378–386, November 1901.

(Unattributed) (1902) 'Periscope: "Care and Feeding of Infants"' in *Dublin Journal of Medical Science*, vol. 113, pp. 318–319, April 1902.

Van Esterik, P. (1989) *Motherpower and Infant-Feeding*, London: Zed Books.

Wiley, Miriam & Merriman, Barry (1996) *Women and Health Care in Ireland*, Dublin: Oak Tree Press.

Women's National Health Association of Ireland (1911) *Fourth Annual Report*, pp. 46–47.

DEATH OF A MOTHER (pp. 48–63)
Mary Moynihan

Kennedy, P. (2002) *Maternity in Ireland: a Woman-Centred Perspective*, Dublin: The Liffey Press.

Murphy-Lawless, J. (1998) 'Women Dying in Childbirth: "Safe Motherhood" in the International Context' in Kennedy, P., Murphy-Lawless, J. (eds) *Returning Birth to Women: Challenging Policy and Practice*, Dublin: WERRC, UCD and Centre for Women's Studies, TCD, pp. 41–55.

– (1998) *Reading Birth and Death: A History of Obstetric Thinking*, Cork: Cork University Press.

O'Donoghue, J. (1997) *Anam Cara, Spiritual Wisdom from the Celtic World*, London: Bantam

Why Mothers Die, Report on Confidential Enquiries into Maternal Deaths in the United Kingdom 1994–1996 (1998) London: Bantam.

INFERTILITY: THE SILENT PERIOD (pp. 64–76)
Flo Delaney

Bartlett, J. (1994) *Will You Be Mother?* London: Virago.

Belenky, M., Clinchy, B., Goldberger, N., Tarule, J. (1986) *Women's Ways of Knowing, The Development of Self, Voice & Mind*, USA: Basic Books Inc.

Burch, B. (1989) 'Mourning and Failure to Mourn, An Object-Relations View' in *Contemporary Psychoanalysis* vol. 15, pp. 608–623.

Byrne, M. (1992) *In Vitro Fertilisation, A Cure for Infertility?* Dublin: Unpublished MA Thesis (Women's Studies), WERRC, UCD.

Campbell, E. (1985) *The Childless Marriage*, London: Virago.

Carter, J. W. & Carter, M. (1989) *Sweet Grapes: How to Stop Being Infertile and Start Living Again*, Indianna: Perspectives Press.

Coliver, S. (ed) (1995) *The Right to Know: Human Rights and Access to Reproductive Health Information*, Pennsylvania: University of Pennsylvania Press.

Cooper-Hilbert, B. (1998) *Infertility & Involuntary Childlessness: Helping Couples Cope*, NY: W. W. Norton & Co.

Doyal, L. (1987) 'Infertility–a Life Sentence? Women and the National Health

Service' in Stanworth, Michelle (ed) *Reproductive Technologies: Gender Motherhood and Medicine*, Oxford: Polity Press.

Eck Menning, B. (1977) *Infertility: A Guide For The Childless Couple*, New Jersey: Prentice Hall.

Harkness, C. (1992) *The Infertility Book*, California: First Celestial Arts Publishing.

Ireland, M. S. (1993) *Reconceiving Women: Separating Motherhood from Female Identity*, London: Guilford Press.

Kubler-Ross, E. (1969) *On Death and Dying*, New York: Touchstone.

Monarch, J. H. (1993) *Childless No Choice: The Experience of Involuntary Childlessness*, London: Routledge.

Morell, C. (1994) *Unwomanly Conduct–Childlessness, the Psychological Aspects*, London: Routledge.

O'Donnell, M. (1990) *Reading the Sunflowers in September*, Galway: Salmon Publishing

Personal Narratives Group (ed) (1989) *Interpreting Women's Lives; Feminist Theory & Personal Narratives*, Indianna: Indianna University Press.

Pfeffer, N. (1987) 'Artificial Insemination, In Vitro Fertilisation and the Stigma of Infertility' in Stanworth, Michelle (ed) *Reproductive Technologies: Gender, Motherhood and Medicine*, Oxford: Polity Press.

Poovey, M. (1998) 'Feminism and Deconstruction' in *Feminist Studies*, vol. 14, no. 1, pp. 51–65.

Richardson, D. (1993) *Women, Motherhood & Childrearing*, London: Macmillan.

Veevers, J. E. (1980) *Childless by Choice*, Toronto: Butterworths.

– (1983) 'Voluntary Childlessness: A critical assessment of the research' in Macklin, E. D., Rubin, R. J. (eds) *Contemporary Families and Alternative Lifestyles*, Beverly Hills: Sage Publications.

Wolf, N. (1993) *Fire with Fire*, London: Random House.

CHILDBIRTH IN IRELAND (pp. 77–86)
Patricia Kennedy

Balaskas A. J. (1979) *New Life: The Book of Exercises for Childbirth*, London: Anchor Press.

Central Statistics Office (1997) *Women in The Workforce*, Statistical Release, September 1997, Dublin and Cork.

– *Census of Population 1991*, Dublin: Stationery Office.

Chamberlain, G. (1995) *Obstetrics by Ten Teachers*, London: Arnold (16th ed).

Conroy Jackson, P. (1993) 'Managing the Mothers: The Case of Ireland' in Lewis, J. (ed) *Women and Social Policies in Europe: Work, Family and the State*, New York: Edward Elgar.

– (1997) 'Lone Mothers: The Case of Ireland' in Lewis, J. (ed) *Lone Mothers in European Welfare Regimes, Shifting Policy Logics*, London: Jessica Kingsley.

Department of Health (1991) *Perinatal Statistics*, Dublin: Stationery Office.

Department of Health (1994) *A National Breastfeeding Policy for Ireland*, Dublin: Stationery Office.

Flanagan, N., Richardson, V. (1992) *Unmarried Mothers: A Sociological Profile*, Dublin: Department of Social Policy and Social Work/Social Work Research Unit, National Maternity Hospital.

Glazener, C. M. A., *et al* (1995) 'Postnatal Maternal Morbidity; Extent, Causes, Prevention and Treatment' in *British Journal of Obstetrics and Gynaecology*, vol. 102, pp. 282–287, April 1995.

Kennedy, P. (1998) 'Between the Lines' in Kennedy, P., Murphy-Lawless, J. (eds)

Returning Birth to Women: Challenging Policy and Practice, Dublin: WERRC, UCD and Centre for Women's Studies, TCD.

Kennedy, P., Murphy-Lawless, J. (2002) *The Maternity Care Needs of Refugee and Asylum-Seeking Women in Ireland*, Dublin: Women's Health Unit, Northern Area Health Board.

Kennedy, P. (2002) *Maternity in Ireland; a Woman-Centred Perspective*, Dublin: The Liffey Press.

Kitzinger, S. (1978) *Women as Mothers*, Great Britain: Fontana.

– (1988) 'Why Women Need Midwives' in Kitzinger, S. (ed) *The Midwife Challenge*, London: Pandora Press.

– (1993) *Ourselves as Mothers*, London: Bantam.

Leboyer, F. (1975) *Birth Without Violence* (translated copy), London: Wildwood House Ltd.

– (1991) *Birth Without Violence* (2nd ed), London: Mandarin.

Mahon, E., Conlon, C., Dillon, L. (1998) *Women and Crisis Pregnancy*, Dublin: Stationery Office.

McCarthy, I. C. (1995) 'Introduction' in McCarthy, I. C. (ed) *Irish Family Studies: Selected Papers*, Dublin: Family Studies Centre, UCD.

Oakley, A. (1979) *Becoming a Mother*, Oxford: Martin Robertson.

Odent, M. (1984) *Birth Reborn*, New York: Pantheon.

Richardson, V. (2001) *Young Mothers*, Dublin: Vincentian Partnership for Justice and Social Science Research Centre, UCD.

Smyth, A. (ed) (1993) *Irish Women's Studies Reader*, Dublin: Attic.

Tew, M. (1995) *Safer Childbirth A Critical History of Maternity Care*, London: Chapman and Hall (2nd ed).

Wagner, M. (1994) *Pursuing the Birth Machine: The Search for Appropriate Birth Technology*, Sevenoaks, Kent: ACE Graphics.

CREATION II

MOTHERHOOD IN GAELIC IRELAND (pp. 89–94)
Máire Mhac an tSaoi

Chenivix Trench, C. (1986) *The Great Dan: a Biography of Daniel O'Connell*, London: Triad.

de Brún, Breandán, Ó Buachalla, P., Ó Concheanainn, T. (eds) (1971) *Nua-Dhuanaire*, Bhaile Átha Cliath: Institúid Ardléinn.

Greene, D. and O'Connor, F. (ed) (1967) *A Golden Treasury of Irish Poetry*, AD 600 to 1200, London: Macmillan.

Hartnett, M. (1985) *Ó Bruadair: Selected Poems of Dáibhí Ó Bruadair*, Dublin: Gallery Press.

MacAingil, A. in de Brún, Ó Buachalla and Ó Concheanainn (eds) (1971) *Nua Dhuanaire 1*, Bhaile Átha Cliath: Institiúid Ardléinn.

MacErlean, J. (ed) (1910) *Duanaire Dháibhidh Uí Bhruadair, Part 1*, London: Irish Texts Society.

McCartney, D. (ed) (1980) *The World of Daniel O'Connell*, Dublin: Published for the Cultural Relations Committee of Ireland by Mercier.

Ó Coileáin, S. (ed) (2002) *An t-Oileánach/Tomás Ó Criomhtháin*, Baile Átha Cliath: Cló Talbóid.

Ó Criomhtháin, T. (1967) *An t-Oileánach: scéal a bheatha féin*, an ceathrú cló, Baile Átha Cliath: Clólucht na Tálbóidigh.

Ó Grianna, S. (1934) *Caisleáin Óir/Máire*, Baile Átha Cliath: Comhartha na dTrí gCoinneal Teó.

O'Rahilly, T. F. (ed) (1927) *Measgra Dánta, miscellaneous Irish poems*, Cork: Cork UP.

Osborn, B. (1918) *Studies, an Irish quarterly review*, Dublin: Irish Jesuits.

'OH MOTHER, WHERE ART THOU?'
IRISH MOTHERS AND IRISH FICTION IN THE TWENTIETH CENTURY (pp. 95–107)
Áine McCarthy

Atwood, M. (2002) *Negotiating With The Dead: A Writer on Writing*, Cambridge: Cambridge University Press.

Boland, E. (1995) *Object Lessons: The Life of the Woman and the Poet in Our Time*, Manchester: Carcenet.

Boylan, C. (1987) 'Introduction' to Molly Keane's *Conversation Piece*, London: Virago.

Brown, T. (1985) *Ireland: A Social and Cultural History 1922–1985*, London: Fontana.

Carlson, J. (1990) *Banned in Ireland: Censorship and the Irish Writer*, London: Routledge.

Devlin, P. (1982) 'Introduction' to Molly Keane's *Conversation Piece*, London, Virago.

Doyle, R. (1996) *The Woman Who Walked Into Doors*, London: Jonathan Cape.

Farrell, J. T. (1932) *Young Lonigan*, New York: Prairie Press.

Innes, C. L. (1993) *Woman and Nation: Women in Irish Literature and Society, 1880–1935*, London: Harvester Wheatsheaf.

Johnston, J. (1991) *The Invisible Worm*, London: Sinclair Stevenson.

Keane, Molly (1982) 'Introduction: Interview with Polly Devlin' in *Conversation Piece*, London: Virago.

Lavin, M. (1969) *The Collected Short Stories*, London: Constable.

McIntyre, T. (1977) 'Review of The Shrine and Other Stories' in *Books Ireland*, 16 September, pp. 171–2.

Morrissey, M. (1996) *Mother of Pearl*, London: Jonathan Cape.

Ní Dhomhnaill, N. (1992) 'What Foremothers?' in *Poetry Ireland Review*, Autumn 1992, pp. 18–31.

Nolan, J. A. (1990) *Ourselves Alone: Women's Emigration from Ireland 1885–1920*, Lexington: University of Kentucky Press.

O'Brien, E. (1968) *The Love Object*, London: Weidenfeld and Nicolson.

– (1970) *A Pagan Place*, London: Weidenfeld and Nicolson.

– (1972) *Night*, London: Weidenfeld and Nicolson.

– (1977) *Johnny I Hardly Knew You*, London: Weidenfeld and Nicolson.

– (1992) *Time and Tide*, London: Weidenfeld and Nicolson.

– (1996) *Down by the River*, London: Weidenfeld and Nicolson.

– (2001) *In the Forest*, London: Weidenfeld and Nicolson.

O'Faolain, J. (1980) *No Country for Young Men*, London: Weidenfeld and Nicolson.

Olsen, T. (1972) *Silences*, London: Virago.

Rich, A. (1979) *On Lies, Secrets and Silence, selected prose 1966–1978*, New York: W. W. Norton.

– (1976) *Of Woman Born: Motherhood as Experience and Institution*, New York: W. W. Norton & Co.

Roth, P. (1984) 'A Conversation with Edna O'Brien' in *New York Times*, 18 November.

Smyth, G. (1997) *The Novel and the Nation: Studies in the New Irish Fiction*, London: Pluto.

Tóibín, C. (1999) *The Penguin Book of Irish Fiction*, London: Penguin.

Weekes, A. Owens (2000) 'Figuring the Mother in Contemporary Irish Fiction' in Harte, Liam and Parker, Michael, *Contemporary Irish Fiction: Themes, Tropes, Theories*, London: Macmillan.
– (1992) *Irish Women Writers, Seeking a Tradition*, Dublin: Attic Press.
Woolf, V. (1923) *A Room of One's Own*, London: Penguin.
Yeats, W. B. (1888) 'The Poet of Ballyshannon' in Reynolds, Horace (ed) *Letters to the New Island*, Cambridge, Mass: Harvard University Press.

CONTEXT

MIND-MAPS: MOTHERHOOD AND POLITICAL SYMBOLISM IN THE IRISH PRO-LIFE MOVEMENT (pp. 117–126)
Valerie Bresnihan

Barber, B. (1984) *Strong Democracy: Participatory Politics for a New Age*, Berkeley and London: University of California.
Bresnihan, V. (1997) *Irish Political Culture: a Symbolic Analysis*, Dublin: Equality Studies Centre, UCD.
– (1999) 'The Family in the Politics of Nitro-Glycerine Containment' in *The Irish Journal of Feminist Studies (IJFS)*, Autumn 1999.
Chubb, B. (1982) *The Government and Politics of Ireland*, London: Longman Group.
Coole, D. (1993) *Women in Political Theory, from ancient misogyny to contemporary feminism*, 2nd ed, New York and London: Harvester Wheatsheaf.
Dryzek, J. S. and Berejikian, J. (1993) 'Reconstructive Democratic Theory' in *American Political Science Review*, vol. 87.
Edelman, M. (1971) *Politics as Symbolic Action*, Chicago: Markan Publishing Co.
Geertz, C. (1975) *The Interpretation of Cultures*, London: Hutchinson.
Honahan, I. (1997) 'Republican and the Common Good' (paper presented to the Irish Philosophical Society).
Levis-Strauss, C. (1966) *The Raw and the Cooked*, New York: Harper and Row.
Lloyd, G. (1993) *The Man of Reason*, London: Routledge.
Pitkin, H. (1987) *Fortune is a Woman*, London: University of California Press.
Ricoeur, P. (1989) *Hermenutics and the Social Sciences*, Cambridge: CUP.
Unger, R. M. (1984) *Passion, an Essay on Personality*, London: The Free Press.

MATERNITY CONFINED – THE STRUGGLE FOR FERTILITY CONTROL (pp. 127–138)
Pauline Conroy

Bacik, Ivana (1996) *From Roe to X: A Comparison of Irish and US Law and Policy on Abortion*, Dublin: TCD Centre for Women's Studies, Working Paper no. 4.
Boston Women's Health Collective (1971) *Our Bodies Ourselves*, Mass.: New England Free Press; later editions (1976) New York: Simon and Schuster.
Commission on Emigration and other Population Problems 1948–1954 (1955), *Reports*, Dublin: Stationery Office.
Commission on the Status of Women (1972) *Report to the Minister for Finance*, Dublin: Stationery Office.
Conroy, Pauline (1987) *The Position of Women Workers in Overseas Manufacturing Plants in Ireland – A Social Policy Study*, Dublin: Doctoral Dissertation, Department of Social Policy and Social Work, UCD, unpublished.
– (1993) 'Managing the Mothers: the Case of Ireland' in Lewis, Jane (ed) *Women and Social Policies in Europe, Work, Family and the State*, Aldershot: Edward Elgar.
Cousins, M. (1995) *The Irish Social Welfare System: Law and Social Policy*, Dublin: Roundhall.

Eaton, P., Warnick, M. (1977) *Marie Stopes*, London: Croom Helm.

Eurostat (2000) *Statistics in Focus*, Luxembourg: Office of Official Publications of the European Community, no. 5.

Fahey, T. and Russell, H. (2001) *Family Formation in Ireland – Trends, Data Needs and Implications*, Policy Research Series no. 43, December 2001, Dublin: ESRI.

Gwynn Morgan, D. (2001) *A Judgement too Far? Judicial Activism and the Constitution*, Cork: Cork University Press.

ICCL, Irish Council for Civil Liberties (2002) *The Need for Abortion Law Reform in Ireland, The Case Against the Twenty-Fifth Amendment to the Constitution Bill, 2001 – a position paper*, Dublin: ICCL.

IFPA, Irish Family Planning Association (June 2001) *CQ – Special Reports*, Dublin: IFPA.

IFPA (2002) *see* website www.Ifpa.ie

Inglis, T. (1987) *Moral Monopoly – The Rise and Fall of the Catholic Church in Modern Ireland*, Dublin: UCD Press.

Jackson, P. (1983) *The Deadly Solution to an Irish Problem – Backstreet Abortion*, Dublin: Women's Right to Choose Campaign, July (pamphlet).

– (1984) 'Women in 19th Century Irish Emigration' in *International Migration Review*, vol. 18, winter, New York: Centre for Migration Studies of New York, Inc.

– (1992) 'Abortion Trials and Tribulations' in *Canadian Journal of Irish Studies*, vol. 18, no. 1, pp. 112–120, December, University of Saskatchewan.

Kennedy, F. (2001) *Cottage to Crèche – Family Change in Ireland*, Dublin: Institute of Public Administration.

Mahon, E., Conlon, C., Dillon, L. (1998) *Women and Crisis Pregnancy, A Report presented to the Department of Health and Children*, Dublin: Stationery Office.

McCafferty, N. (1985) *A Woman to Blame – The Kerry Babies Case*, Dublin: Attic Press.

McDonagh, S. (1992) *The Attorney General v X and Others, Judgements of the High Court and Supreme Court*, Dublin: Incorporated Council of Law Reporting for Ireland.

McGee v A.G.(1974) IR 284.

Murphy-Lawless, J., McCarthy, J. (1998) 'Social Policy and Fertility Change in Ireland' in *The European Journal of Women's Studies*, London, Thousand Oaks and New Delhi: Sage Publications, vol. 6, pp. 69–96.

NIALRO (Northern Ireland Abortion Law Reform Association) (1989) *Abortion in Northern Ireland*, Belfast: Beyond the Pale Publications.

Nic Ghiolla Phádraig, M., Clancy, P. (1995) 'Marital Fertility and Family Planning in Dublin' in Colgan, I. (ed) *Irish Family Studies, Selected Papers*, Dublin: Family Studies Centre, UCD.

O'Connell, D. (2001) 'Ireland' in Blackburn, R., Polakiewicz, Jörg (eds) *Fundamental Rights in Europe – the European Convention on Human Rights and its Member States, 1950–2000*, Oxford: Oxford UP.

O'Leary, O., Burke, H. (1998) *Mary Robinson – the Authorised Biography*, London: Hodder and Stoughton.

O'Reilly, E. (1988) *Masterminds of the Right*, Dublin: Attic Press.

Randall, V. (1992) 'The Politics of Abortion – Ireland in Comparative Perspective' in *The Canadian Journal of Irish Studies*, vol. 18, no. 1, pp. 121–128, December, University of Saskatchewan.

R. v Bourne (1939) 1 KB 687.

Referendums in Ireland 1937–1999 (2000) Dublin: Stationary Office.

Sanger, M. (1971) *An Autobiography*, New York: Dover Publications, Inc.

Saorstat Éireann Reports, August 1935.
Second Commission on the Status of Women (1993) *Report*, Dublin: Stationery Office.
Stopes, M. (1918) *Married Love, a New Contribution to the Solution of Sexual Difficulties*, London: A. C. Fifield.
Sweetman, R. (1979) *On Our Backs – Sexual Attitudes in a Changing Ireland*, London: Pan Books.

MOTHERHOOD, SEXUALITY AND THE CATHOLIC CHURCH (pp. 139–159)
Betty Hilliard

Foucault, M. (1976) *The Birth of the Clinic*, London: Tavistock.
Inglis, T. (1997) 'Foucault, Bourdieu and the Field of Irish Sexuality' in *Irish Journal of Sociology*, vol. 7, pp. 5–28.
– (1998) (rev. ed) *Moral Monopoly*, Dublin: UCD Press.
– (1998) *Lessons in Irish Sexuality*, Dublin: UCD Press.
Parsons, T. (1956) *Family: Socialisation and Interaction Process*, London: Routledge & Kegan Paul.

THE MAGDALENE EXPERIENCE (pp. 160–169)
Patricia Burke Brogan

Burke Brogan, P. (1994) *Above the Waves*, Clare: Salmon Publishing.
– (1994) *Calligraphy*, Clare: Salmon Publishing.
– (1994) *Eclipsed*, Clare: Salmon Publishing.
– *Stained Glass at Samhain* (a play for stage: in preparation).
Gates, A. (1999) 'Mothers for a Moment, Then Cloistered Forever' in *The New York Times*, 9 November.
Loynd, R. (1995) 'A Cruel Slice of Irish Life' in *The Los Angeles Times*, 21 April.
Luddy, M. and Murphy, C. (1989) *Women Surviving, Studies in Irish Women's History in the Nineteenth and Twentieth Centuries*, Dublin: Poolbeg.

INFANTICIDE: THE CRIME OF MOTHERHOOD (pp. 170–180)
Alexis Guilbride

Bunreacht na hÉireann (1937) Dublin: Government Publications.
Cassidy, J. (1924) *Women of the Gael*, Dublin: Talbot Press.
Inglis, T. (1987) *Moral Monopoly: The Catholic Church in Modern Irish Society*, Dublin: Gill & Macmillan.
Jackson, Pauline Conroy (1987) 'Outside the Jurisdiction – Irish Women Seeking Abortion' in Smyth, Ailbhe (ed) (1992) *The Abortion Papers*, Dublin: Attic Press, pp. 119–137.
Keogh, D. (1994) *Twentieth Century Ireland – Nation and State*, Dublin: Gill & Macmillan.
Lee, J. J. (1989) *Ireland 1912–1985 Politics and Society*, Cambridge: CUP.
Lyons, J. B. (1980) *Oliver St John Gogarty: The Man of Many Talents*, Dublin: Blackwater Press.
McCafferty, N. (1985) *A Woman to Blame: The Kerry Babies Case*, Dublin: Attic Press.
Prager, J. (1986) *Building Democracy in Ireland*, Cambridge: CUP.
Archive Material
Infanticide Act File (1949) from the Department of the Taoiseach
State Files in the Central Criminal Court, 1924–1956

The Irish Times, 1940s
The Irish Independent, 1940s
The Irish Press, 1940s
Trial Record Books in the Central Criminal Court: October 1924–December 1956

MOTHERHOOD INTERRUPTED: ADOPTION IN IRELAND (pp. 181–193)
Eileen Conway

Advisory Council on Childcare (1970) *A Guide to Adoption Practice*, London: HMSO.
Andrews, R. (1979) 'A Clinical Appraisal of Searching' in *Public Welfare*, vol. 37. no. 3, pp. 15–22, Summer.
Barrett, C. (1952) *Adoption*, Dublin: Clonmore & Reynolds.
Beret, M. K. (1976) *The Character of Adoption*, London: Jonathan Cape.
Berman, L., Bufferd, R. (1986) 'Family Treatment to Address Loss in Adoptive Families' in *Social Casework*, vol. 67, no. 1, pp. 3–11, January.
Bernard, V. (1945) 'First Sight of the Child by Prospective Parents as a Crucial Phase in Adoption' in *American Journal of Orthopsychiatry*, vol. 15, no. 2, pp. 230–237, April 1945.
Boswell, J. (1988) *The Kindness of Strangers*, Allen Lane: The Penguin Press.
Burke, H. (1987) *The People and the Poor Law in 19th Century Ireland*, Dublin: The Women's Education Bureau.
Burnell, G., Norfleet, M. A. (1979) 'Women Who Place their Infant up for Adoption: A Pilot Study' in *Patient Counselling and Health Education*, Summer/Fall, pp. 169–172.
Clancy, P. (1984) 'Demographic Changes and the Irish Family' in *The Changing Family* (Seminar Papers), Dublin: Family Studies Unit, UCD.
Clothier, F. (1943) 'Psychological Implications of Unmarried Parenthood' in *American Journal of Orthopsychiatry*, vol. 13, pp. 531–549.
Cole, E. (1986) 'Adoption: History, Policy and Program' in Ashmore, R. Brodzinsky, D. (eds) *Thinking about the Family*, New Jersey: Lawrence Erlbaum Associates, pp. 638–666
Combs-Orme, T. (1990) *Social Work Practice in Maternal and Child Health*, New York: Springer Publishing Co.
Condon, J. (1986) 'Psychological Disability in Women who Relinquish a Baby for Adoption' in *Medical Journal of Australia*, vol. 155, pp. 117, 3 February.
Conway, E. (2000) *Adoption Policy and Practice in Ireland in the 1980s*, PhD Thesis, Dublin: Department of Social Policy and Social Work, UCD.
Darling, V. (1977) *Adoption in Ireland* (Reprint of a CARE discussion paper, first published in 1974), Dublin: CARE.
Deykin, E., Campbell, L., Patti, P. (1984) 'The Post-Adoption Experience of Surrendering Parents' in *American Journal of Orthopsychiatry*, vol. 54, no. 2, pp. 271–280, April.
Dukette, R. (1984) 'Value Issues in Present-Day Adoption' in *Child Welfare*, vol. 63, no. 3, pp. 233–243, May/June.
Flanagan, N., Richardson, V. (1992) *Unmarried Mothers: A Social Profile*, Dublin: Department of Social Policy and Social Work, UCD.
Howe, D., Sawbridge, P., Hinings, D. (1992) *Half a Million Women: Mothers who Lose their Children by Adoption*, London: Penguin.
Humphrey, M. (1969) *The Hostage Seekers*, London: Longmans.
Kilkenny Social Services (1972) *The Unmarried Mother in the Irish Community – a Report on the National Conference on Community Services for the Unmarried Parent*, Kilkenny: Kilkenny Social Services.

Kirk, H. D. (1964) *Shared Fate: A Theory of Adoption and Mental Health*, New York: The Free Press.

– (1981) *Adoptive Kinship: A Modern Institution in Need of Reform*, Canada: Butterworth & Co.

Kirke, D. (1979) 'Unmarried Mothers: a Comparative Study' in *Economic and Social Review*, vol. 10, no. 2, pp. 157–167, January.

Koch, J. (1985) *Our Baby: A Birth and Adoption Story*, Indianapolis: Perspectives Press.

Kornitzer, M. (1973) *The Holywell Family*, London: The Body Politic.

Liben, F. (1969) 'Minority Group Clinic Patients Pregnant out of Wedlock' in *American Journal of Public Health*, vol. 50, pp. 1,868–1,881, October.

Lifton, B. J. (1978) *Lost and Found: The Adoption Experience*, New York: Dial Press.

Littner, N. (1956) 'The Natural Parents' in Schapiro, M. (ed) *A Study of Adoption Practice, Selected Papers from the National Conference on Adoption 1955* (vol. 2) New York: Child Welfare League of America.

McCormick, R. (1948) 'The Adopting Parent Sees the Child' in Meyer, G. (ed) *Studies of Children*, New York: King's Crown Press.

Millen, L., Roll, S. (1985) 'Solomon's Mothers: a Special Case of Pathological Bereavement' in *American Journal of Orthopsychiatry*, vol. 55, no. 3, pp. 411–418, July.

O'Hare, A., Dromey, M., O'Connor, A., Clarke, M., Kirwan, G. (1983) *Mothers Alone? A Study of Women who gave Birth outside Marriage*, Dublin: Federation of Services for Unmarried Parents and their Children.

Pasley, J. (1997) PACT. Interview with social worker. November, Dublin.

Plionis, B. M. (1975) 'Adolescent Pregnancy: Review of the Literature' in *Social Work*, vol. 20, no. 4, pp. 302–307, July.

Raphael-Leff, J. (1991) *Psychological Processes of Childbearing*, London: Chapman & Hall.

Report of the Review Committee on Adoption Services (1984) *Adoption*, Dublin: Government Publications.

Reports of An Bord Uchtála (The Adoption Board) 1985 and 2000, Dublin: The Stationery Office.

Robins, J. (1980) *The Lost Children: A Study of Charity Children in Ireland 1700–1900*, Dublin: Institute of Public Administration.

Rondell, F., Michaels, R. (1951) *The Family that Grew*, New York: Crown.

Rowe, J. (1991) 'An Historical Perspective on Adoption and the Role of Voluntary Agencies'. in Fratter, J., Rowe, J., Sapsford, D., Thoburn, J. (eds) *Permanent Family Placement: A Decade of Experience*, Research Series no. 8, pp. 7–17, London: British Agencies for Adoption and Fostering.

Rynearson, E. (1982) 'Relinquishment and its Maternal Complications: a Preliminary Study' in *American Journal of Psychiatry*, vol. 139, no. 3, pp. 338–340, March.

Sandelowski, M., Harris, B., Holditch-Davis, D. (1991) '"The Clock has been Ticking, the Calendar Pages Turning and we are still Waiting": Infertile Couples' Encounter with Time, in the Adoption Waiting Period' in *Qualitative Sociology*, vol. 14, no. 2, pp. 147–173.

Schofield, M. (1968) *The Sexual Behaviour of Young People*, cited by Kirke, D. (1979) in 'Unmarried Mothers: a Comparative Study' in *Economic & Social Review*, vol. 10, no. 2, pp. 157–167, January.

Shawyer, J. (1979) *Death by Adoption*, New Zealand: Cicada Press.

Small, J. (1987) 'Working with Adoptive Families' in *Public Welfare*, Summer, pp. 33–41.

Smith, C. R. (1984) *Adoption and Fostering*, London: Macmillan Publishers Ltd.

Smith, D., Sherwen, L. (1988) *Mothers and their Adopted Children – the Bonding Process*, New York City: The Tiresias Press, Inc.

Vincent, C. (1961) *Unmarried Mothers*, New York: Free Press of Glencoe.

Vital Statistics (1994) *Fourth Quarter and Yearly Summary 1993*, Dublin: Department of Health, Central Statistics Office.

Walsh, B. (1972) 'Ireland's Demographic Transformation 1958–70' in *Economic and Social Review*, vol. 3, no. 2, pp. 251–275.

Winkler, R., Brown, D., Van Keppel, M., Blanchard, A. (1988) *Clinical Practice in Adoption*, New York: Pergamon Press.

Winkler, R., Van Keppel, M. (1984) *Relinquishing Mothers in Adoption*, Monograph No. 3, May, Melbourne: Institute of Family Studies.

Young, L. (1954) *Out of Wedlock*, New York: McGraw Hill.

MOTHERING IN A DISABLING SOCIETY (pp. 194–206)
Goretti Horgan

Accardo, P. and Whitman, B. (1990), 'Children of Mentally Retarded Parents' in *American Journal of Diseases of Children*, vol. 144, pp. 69–70, Chicago: American Medical Association.

Asch, A. and Fine, M. (1997) 'Nurturance, Sexuality and Women with Disabilities' in Davis, L. J. (ed) *The Disability Reader*, New York, London: Routledge.

Beresford, B. (1995) *Expert Opinions: A National Survey of Parents Caring for a Severely Disabled Child*, Bristol: Policy Press

Booth, T., Booth, W. (1995) 'Unto us a Child is Born: the Trials and Rewards of Parenthood for People with Learning Difficulties' in *Australia and New Zealand Journal of Developmental Disabilities*, vol. 20, no. 1, pp. 25–39, Sydney: Taylor and Francis.

– (1997) 'Making Connections: A Narrative Study of Adult Children of Parents with Learning Difficulties' in Barnes, C., Mercer, G. (eds) *Doing Disability Research*, Leeds: The Disability Press

Byrne, A., Lentin, R. (2000) '(Re)searching Women: Feminist Research' in *Methodologies in the Social Sciences in Ireland*, Dublin: IPA.

Horgan, G. (2000) *A Sense of Purpose: the Views and Experiences of Young Mothers about Growing up in Northern Ireland*, Belfast: Joseph Rowntree Foundation/Save the Children.

Lloyd, M. (2001) 'The Politics of Disability and Feminism: Discord or Synthesis?' in *Sociology* vol. 35, no. 3, pp. 715–728, Cambridge: British Sociological Association.

Mason, M. (1982) 'Life: Whose Right to Choose?' in *Spare Rib*, no. 115.

Monteith, M., McCrystal, P., Iwaniec, D. (1997) *Children and Young People with Disabilities in Northern Ireland*, Belfast: Centre for Childcare Research, Queen's University.

Morris, J. (ed) (1989) *Able Lives*, London: The Women's Press.

– (1991) *Pride against Prejudice: A Personal Politics of Disability*, London: The Women's Press.

– (1992) *Alone Together: Voices of Single Mothers*, London: The Women's Press.

– (ed) (1996) *Encounters with Strangers: Feminism and Disability*, London: The Women's Press.

National Disability Authority (2002) *Disability Related Research in Ireland 1996–2001*, Dublin: NDA.

OPCS (1989) *Survey of Disability in Great Britain: The Prevalence of Disability among Children*, London: HMSO

Read, J. (2000) *Disability, The Family and Society: Listening to Mothers*, Buckingham: Open University Press.

Scally, B. (1973) 'Marriage and Mental Handicap: Some Observations in Northern Ireland' in De La Cruz, F., La Veck, G. (eds) *Human Sexuality and the Mentally Retarded*, New York: Brunner/Mazel.

Shakespeare, T. (1997) 'Researching Disabled Sexuality' in Barnes, C., Mercer, G. (eds) *Doing Disability Research*, Leeds: The Disability Press

MOTHERS AND POVERTY (pp. 207–217)
Anne Coakley

Bauman, Z. (1988) Work, Consumerism and the New Poor. Buckingham: Open University Press.

Brannen, J. and Wilson, G. (eds) (1987) Give and Take in Families: Studies in Resource in Distribution. London: Allen and Unwin.

Breathnach, P. (2002) 'Social Polarisation in the Post-Fordist Informational Economy; Ireland in International Context'. In Irish Journal of Sociology, 11:3–22.

Byrne, A. and Leonard M. (eds) (1997) *Women and Irish Society: A Sociological Reader*, Belfast: Beyond the Pale Publications.

Callan, T., Nolan, B., Whelan, B. J., Whelan, C. T., Williams, J. (1996) *Poverty in the 1990s: Evidence from the 1994 Living in Ireland Survey*, Dublin: Oak Tree Press.

Callan, T., Layte, R., Nolan, B., Watson, D., Whelan, C. T., Williams, J., Maitre, B. (1999) *Monitoring Poverty Trends; Data from the 1997 Living in Ireland Survey*, Dublin: Stationery Office.

Central Statistics Office, *Quarterly National Household Survey, Households and Family Units*, 28 November 2001.

Charles, N., Kerr, M. (1988) *Women, Food and Families*, Manchester: Manchester University Press.

Coakley, A. (1997) 'Gendered Citizenship: The Social Construction of Mothers in Ireland' in Byrne, A. Leonard, M. (eds) *Women and Irish Society; A Sociological Profile*, Belfast: Beyond the Pale Publications.

– (1998) *Poverty and Social Inclusion: The Management Strategies and Views of Mothers in Social Welfare Households*, PhD Thesis, Dublin: TCD.

– (2001) 'Healthy eating: food and diet in low-income households' in *Administration* vol. 49, no. 3, pp. 87–103.

Daly, M. (1992) 'Europe's Poor Women? Gender in Research on Poverty' in *European Sociological Review* vol. 8, no. 1, pp. 1–12.

DSCFA (Department of Social Community and Family Affairs) 1999 Annual Report.

De Vault, M. (1997) 'Conflict and Deference' in Counihan, C. Van Esterik, P. (eds) *Food and Culture; A Reader*, New York: Routledge.

Dobson, B., Beardsworth, A., Keil, T., Walker, R. (1994) *Diet, Choice and Poverty*, London: Family Studies Centre.

Glendinning, C., Millar, J. (1991) (eds) *Women and Poverty in Britain in the 1990s*, London: Harvester Wheatsheaf.

Goode, J., Callender, C., Lister, R. (1998) *Purse or Wallet? Gender Inequalities and Income Distribution within Families on Benefits*, Gateshead: Policy Studies Institute.

Graham, H. (1994) 'Breadline Motherhood: Trends and Experiences in Ireland' in *Administration*, vol. 42, no. 4, pp. 352–373.

Kennedy, P. (2002) *Maternity in Ireland; A Woman-Centred Perspective*, Dublin: The Liffey Press.

Kennedy, P., Murphy-Lawless, J. (2002) *The Maternity Care Needs of Refugee and Asylum-Seeking Women*, Dublin: The Women's Health Unit, Northern Area Health Board.

Land, H. (1989) 'The Construction of Dependency' in Bulmer, M. Lewis, J., Pichaud, D. (eds) *The Goals of Social Policy*, London: Unwin Hyman.

Leira, A. (1992) *Welfare States and Working Mothers*, New York: Cambridge University Press.

Lewis, J. (1992) 'Gender and the Development of Welfare Regimes' in *Journal of European Social Policy*, vol. 2, no. 31, pp. 159–173

Lee, P., Gibney, M. (1989) *Patterns of Food and Nutrient Intake in a Suburb of Dublin with Chronically High Unemployment*, Dublin: Combat Poverty Agency.

Lupton, D. (1996) *Food, the Body and the Self*, London: Sage.

Mahon, E. (1994) 'Ireland: a Private Patriarchy?' in *Environment and Planning* vol. 26, pp. 1277–1296.

McKeown, K., Sweeney, J. (2001) *Family Well-Being and Family Policy; a Review of Research on Benefits and Costs*, Dublin: Department of Health and Children.

Murcott, A., (1983) *The Sociology of Food and Eating*, London: Gower.

Murphy-Lawless, J. (2002) *Fighting Back: Women and the Impact of Drug Abuse on Families and Communities*, Dublin: The Liffey Press

Nolan, B., Whelan, C. T., Williams, J. (1998) *Where are Poor Households?* Dublin: Combat Poverty Agency.

Nolan, B., Maitre, B., O'Neill, B. D., Sweetman, O. (2000) *The Distribution of Income in Ireland*, Dublin: Combat Poverty Agency.

Nolan, B., Watson, D. (1998) *Women and Poverty in Ireland*, Dublin: Oak Tree Press.

O'Flaherty, L. (1984) *Famine*, Dublin: Wolfhound Press.

O'Neill, C. (1992) *Telling It Like It Is*, Dublin: Combat Poverty Agency.

Pahl, J. (1989) *Money and Marriage*, London: Macmillan

Ruspini, E. (2000) 'Women and Poverty; a New Research Methodology' in Gordon, D., Townsend, P., *Breadline Europe; the Measurement of Poverty*, Bristol: the Policy Press.

Social Inclusion Strategy (2001) *Annual Report of the Inter-Departmental Policy Committee*, Dublin: Stationery Office.

Sainsbury, D. (1996) *Gender, Equality and Welfare States*, Cambridge: CUP.

Vogler, C., Pahl, J. (1994) 'Money, Power and Inequality within Marriage' in *Sociological Review*, vol. 42, pp. 262–288.

Williams, F. (1999) 'Good-enough Principles for Welfare' in *Journal of Social Policy*, vol. 28, no. 4, pp. 667–668.

Wilson, G. (1987) *Money in the Family*, Hants: Avebury.

Yeates, N. (1997) 'Gender and the Development of the Irish Social Welfare System' in Byrne, A., Leonard, M. (eds) *Women and Irish Society: A Sociological Reader*, Belfast: Beyond the Pale Publications.

MOTHERHOOD ADJOURNED: THE EXPERIENCE OF MOTHERS IN PRISON (pp. 218–227)
Celesta McCann James

Caddle, D., Crisp, D. (1997) *Mothers in Prison, Research Findings No. 38, Research and Statistics Directorate*, Home Office: UK.

Carey, T. (2000) *Mountjoy: the Story of a Prison*, Cork: Collins Press.

Council of Europe (2000) *Mothers and Babies in Prison, Recommendation 1469*, Parliamentary Assembly, Council of Europe.

Department of Justice (1994) *Management of Offenders, A Five Year Plan*, Dublin: The Stationery Office.

– (1997) *Towards an Independent Prison Agency: Report of Expert Group*, Dublin: The Stationery Office.

Department of Justice, Equality and Law Reform (1998) *Annual Report*, Dublin: The Stationery Office.

Gabel, S., Schindledecker, R. (1993) 'Characteristics of Children whose Parents have been Incarcerated' in *Hospital and Community Psychiatry*, vol. 44, no. 7, pp. 656–660.

Keavey, M. E., Zausniewski, J. A. (1999) 'Life Events and Psychological Well-Being in Women Sentenced to Prison' in *Issues in Mental Health Nursing*, vol. 20, no. 1, pp. 73–89.

McCann James, C. (2001) *Recycled Women: Oppression and the Social World of Women Prisoners in the Irish Republic*, unpublished PhD dissertation, NUI, Galway.

Pennix, P. R. (1999) 'An Analysis of Mothers in the Federal Prison System' in *Corrections Compendium*, vol. 24, no. 12, pp. 4–6.

Young, D. S., Jefferson Smith, C. (2000) 'When Moms are Incarcerated: The Needs of Children, Mothers and Caregivers' in *Families in Society: The Journal of Contemporary Human Services*, vol. 81, no. 2, pp. 130–147.

MOTHERHOOD IN NORTHERN IRELAND (pp. 228–240)
Margaret Ward

Aretxaga, B. (1997) *Shattering Silence: Women, Nationalism and Political Subjectivity in Northern Ireland*, New Jersey: Princeton University Press.

Breen, R., Devine, P. (1999) 'Segmentation and the Social Structure' in Mitchell, P., Wilford, R. (eds) *Politics in Northern Ireland*, Colorado: Westview Press.

Edgerton, L. (1996) 'Public Protest, Domestic Acquiescence: Women in Northern Ireland' in Rid, Rosemary, Callaway, Helen (eds) *Women and Conflict*, London: Macmillan.

Fairweather, E., McDonough, R., McFadyean, M. (1984) *Only the Rivers Run Free, Northern Ireland: the Women's War*, London: Pluto Press.

Human Rights Watch (1998) *Report*.

Leonard, M. (1997) 'Women Caring and Sharing in Belfast' in Byrne, A. Leonard, M. (eds) *Women and Irish Society, a Sociological Reader*, Belfast: Beyond the Pale.

McLaughlin, E. (1993) 'Women and the Family in Northern Ireland: a review' in *Women's Studies International Forum* vol. 16, no. 6, pp. 553–568.

Meyer, M. K. (2000) 'Ulster's Red Hand: Gender, Identity and Sectarian Conflict in Northern Ireland' in Ranchod-Nilsson, S., Tetreault, M., *Women, States and Nationalism: at Home in the Nation?* London and New York: Routledge.

Mulholland, M. (2001) 'The Challenge to Inequality: Women, Discrimination and Decision-Making in Northern Ireland' in Moser, C., Clark, F., *Victims, Perpetrators or Actors? Gender, Armed Conflict and Political Violence*, London and New York: Zed Books.

North Belfast's Community Internet Site: www.northbelfast.org

Northern Ireland Life and Times Survey (Nov. 2001) *Young Life and Times, Research Update*, No. 8.

Sales, R. (1998) 'Women, the Peace Makers?' in Anderson, J. Goodman, J., (eds) Dis/agreeing Ireland, Contexts, Obstacles, Hopes, London: Pluto Press.

Sharoni, S. (2001) 'Rethinking Women's Struggles in Israel-Palestine and in the North of Ireland' in Moser, C., Clark, F., (eds) Victims, Perpetrators or Actors? Gender, Armed Conflict and Political Violence, London and New York: Zed Books.

Stringer, P., Robinson, G. (1993) (eds) Social Attitudes in Northern Ireland: the third report, 1992–1993, Belfast: Blackstaff Press.

The Observer, 25 November 2001.

YOUNG MOTHERS (pp. 241–254)
Valerie Richardson

Acton, M. (2002) 'The Teen Parents Support Project' in Childlinks Quarterly Journal of Barnardos' Resource Centre, Dublin, Spring 2002, pp. 15–18.

Alan Guttmacher Institute (1976) Eleven Million Teenagers: What can be Done about the Epidemic of Adolescent Pregnancies in the US? New York: Alan Guttmacher Institute.

– (1981) Teenage Pregnancy: One Problem That Has Not Gone Away, New York: Alan Guttmacher Institute.

– (1991) Teenage and Sexual Reproduction Behaviour (Facts in Brief) New York: Alan Guttmacher Institute.

An Bord Uchtála (1999 and 2000) Annual Reports of An Bord Uchtála, Dublin: Government Publications, Department of Health and Children.

Berthoud, R., Robson, K. (2001) The Outcomes of Teenage Motherhood in Europe Essex: Institute for Social and Economic Research, University of Essex.

Bloom, K. C. (1995) 'The Development of Attachment Behaviours in Pregnant Adolescents' in Nursing Research, vol. 44, no 5, pp. 284–289.

Cole, M., Cole, S. (1996) The Development of Children, New York: W. H. Freeman.

Commission on the Family (1998) Strengthening Families for Life, Dublin: Stationery Office.

Dempsey, M., Heslin, J., Bradley, C. (2002) The Experience of Teenage Pregnancy in the South East of Ireland, Report for the South Eastern Health Board, Cork: UCC.

Department of Health (2002) Vital Statistics: Fourth Quarter and Yearly Summary 2001, Dublin: Government Publications.

Fianna Fáil and the Progressive Democrats (2002) An Agreed Programme for Government between Fianna Fáil and the Progressive Democrats, Dublin: Stationery Office.

Fitzpatrick, C., Fitzpatrick, P. E., Turner, M. (1997) 'Profile of Patients Attending a Dublin Adolescent Antenatal Booking Clinic' in Irish Medical Journal, vol. 90, no .3, pp. 96–97, April/May.

Franklin, C., Corcoran, J. (2000) 'Preventing Adolescent Pregnancy: A Review of Programs and Practices' in Social Work, vol. 45, pp. 40–52.

Goulding, J. (1998) The Light in the Window, Dublin: Poolbeg.

Greene, S., Joy, M. T., Nugent, J. K., O'Mahoney, P. (1989) 'Contraceptive Practice of Irish Married and Single First-Time Mothers' in Journal of Biosocial Science, vol. 21, pp. 379–385.

Jorgensen, S. (1981) 'Sex Education and Reduction of Adolescent Pregnancies: Prospects for the 1980s' in Journal of Early Adolescence, vol. 1, pp. 38–52.

Konje, J. D., Palmer, A., Watson, A., Hay, D. M., Imrie, A. (1992) 'Early Teenage Pregnancies in Hull' in British Journal of Obstetrics and Gynaecology vol. 99, pp. 969–973

Lawson, A., Rhode, D. L. (1993) *The Politics of Pregnancy: Adolescent Sexuality and Public Policy*, New Haven: Yale University Press.

McAnarney, E. R., Schreider, C. (1984) 'Identifying Social and Psychological Antecedents of Adolescent Pregnancy' in *Contribution of Research to Concepts of Prevention*, New York: William T. Grant Foundation.

McCarthy, G., Cronin, C. (2000) *To Identify the Needs, Perceptions and Experiences of Young First-Time Mothers*, Cork: Department of Nursing Studies, National University of Ireland.

McCashin, A. (1993) *Lone Parents in the Republic of Ireland: Enumeration, Description and Implications for Social Security*, Dublin: Economic and Social Research Institute.

– (1996) *Lone Mothers in Ireland: A Local Study*, Dublin: Oak Tree Press.

– (1997) *Employment Aspects of Young Lone Parenthood in Ireland*, Dublin: Irish Youthwork Press.

Mahon, E., Conlon, C., Dillon, L. (1998) *Women & Crisis Pregnancy*, Dublin: Stationery Office.

Milotte, M. (1997) *Banished Babies: The Secret History of Ireland's Baby Export Business*, Dublin: New Island Books

Monahan, D. (2002) 'Teen Pregnancy Prevention Outcomes: Implications for Social Work Practice' in *Families in Society: Journal of Contemporary Human Services*, vol. 83, p.4.

Moving On: Young Mothers and Employment Project (2002) Dublin: Irish Youthwork Press.

Nic Ghiolla Phádraig, M. (1985) 'Social and Cultural Factors in Family Planning' in *The Changing Family*, Dublin: Family Studies Unit, UCD.

Phoenix, A. (1991) *Young Mothers?* Oxford: Polity Press/Basil Blackwell.

– (1993) 'The Social Construction of Teenage Motherhood – a Black and White Issue?' in Lawson, A. and Rhode, D. (eds) *The Politics of Pregnancy: Adolescent Sexuality and Public Policy*, New Haven: Yale University Press.

Richardson, V. (1991) 'Decision Making by Unmarried Mothers' in *The Irish Journal of Psychology*, vol. 12, no. 2, pp. 165–181.

– (1993) *Mothers Too Soon: A Study of The Decision Making Process of Unmarried Pregnant Adolescents*, unpublished PhD thesis, Dublin: National University of Ireland.

– (2001) *Young Mothers*, Dublin: Vincentian Partnership for Justice and Social Science Research Centre, UCD.

Ryan, L. (1998) *Participation in the Labour Force: Barriers to Employment as Identified by Young Mothers*, Dublin: Moving on Project, unpublished.

Scanlan, S. (1994) *This Mother and Baby Stayed at Home*, unpublished M.Soc.Sc (Social Policy) thesis, Dublin: UCD.

Simms, M., Simms, C. (1986) *Teenage Mothers and Their Partners*, Research Report Number 15, London: HMSO.

Vinovski M. A., (1988) *An Epidemic of Teenage Pregnancy? Some Historical and Policy Considerations*, Oxford: Oxford University Press.

Voydanoff, P., Donnelly, B. W. (1990) *Adolescent Sexuality and Pregnancy*, Sage: London.

Wiley, M., Merriman, B. (1996) *Women and Health Care in Ireland*, Dublin: Oak Tree Press/ESRI.

Wilson, C. (1999) *Young Single Mothers: A Research Document*, Sligo: Northside Community Partnership.

TRAVELLER MOTHERS (pp. 255–269)
Pavee Point Primary Health Care for Travellers Project and Patricia Kennedy

Barry, J., Herity B., Solan, J. (1989) *The Travellers' Health Status Study: Vital Statistics of Travelling People*, Dublin: Health Research Board.
Crowley, N. (1999) 'Travellers and Social Policy' in Quin, S., Kennedy, P., O'Donnell, A., Kiely, G. (eds) *Contemporary Irish Social Policy*, Dublin: UCD Press.
Department of Health and Children (2002) *Traveller Health: A National Strategy 2002–2005*, Dublin.
O'Reilly, N. (1997) *The Health of Traveller Women*, unpublished study conducted on behalf of Pavee Point Travellers' Centre
Pavee Point Travellers' Centre (2002) *Traveller Proofing – Within an Equality Framework*, Dublin: Pavee Point Travellers' Centre.

MOTHER COURAGE? IRISH MOTHERS AND
EMIGRATION TO NORTH AMERICA (pp. 270–292)
Grace Neville

Arensberg, C. M., Kimball, S. T. (1940) *Family and Community in Ireland*, Cambridge: Harvard University Press.
Bertaux, D. (1997) *Les Récits de Vie*, Paris: Nathan.
Boland, E. (1995) *Collected Poems*, Manchester: Carcanet.
de Certeau, M. (1984) *The Practice of Everyday Life*, Berkeley: The University of California Press.
Diner, H. (1983) *Erin's Daughters in America: Irish Immigrant Women in the Nineteenth Century*, Baltimore: Johns Hopkins University Press.
Dwyer, Ryle T. (1991) *De Valera: The Man and the Myths*, Dublin: Poolbeg
Foster, M. (2000) 'The Hurley Emigrant Letters: 1871–1938' in *The World of Hibernia*, vol. 5, no. 4, pp. 117–121, Spring 2000.
Geremek, B. (1987) *La Potence ou la Pitié: L'Europe et les Pauvres du Moyen Age à nos Jours*, Paris: Gallimard.
Gray, B. 'Breaking the Silence: Staying at Home in an Emigrant Society' (research team led by Dr Breda Gray) on http://migration.ucc.ie/oralarchive/
Healy, J. (1978) *Nineteen Acres*, Galway: Kenny.
Le Goff, J. (ed) (1978) *La Nouvelle Histoire*, Paris: Retz CEPL.
Matson, L. (1996) *Méiní: The Blasket Nurse*, Cork: Mercier.
McCann, C. (1995) *Songdogs*, New York: Picador.
McCourt, F. (1997) *Angela's Ashes*, London: HarperCollins.
Miller, Kerby A. (1985) *Emigrants and Exiles: Ireland and the Irish Exodus to North America*, Oxford: Oxford University Press.
Montague, J. (1984) *Dead Kingdom*, Portlaoise: Dolmen.
– (1991) *Born in Brooklyn: John Montague's America*, New York: White Pine Press.
Ní Shúilleabháin, E. (1978) *Letters from the Great Blasket*, Cork: Mercier.
Nolan, J. A. (1989) *Ourselves Alone: Women's Emigration from Ireland 1885–1920* Lexington: University Press of Kentucky.
Nora, P. (ed) (1984–1992) *Les Lieux de Mémoire*, Paris: Gallimard, 7 vols.
Ó Criomhtháin, T. (1978) *An tOileánach, The Islandman*, translated by Robin Flower, Oxford: Oxford University Press.
O'Brien, E. (1976) *Mother Ireland*, London: Weidenfeld and Nicolson.
O'Guiheen, M. (1982) *A Pity Youth Does Not Last*, Oxford: Oxford University Press
Rich, A. (1977) *Of Woman Born*, London: Virago.
Rossiaud, J. (1988) *La Prostitution Médiévale*, Paris: Flammarion.

Schrier, A. (1958) *Ireland and the American Emigration 1850–1900*, University of Minnesota Press.

Synge, J. M. (1979) *In West Kerry*, reprint Cork: Mercier.

– (1979 [1907]) *The Aran Islands*, Oxford: Oxford University Press.

The Hurley Papers, Cork Archives Institute, South Main Street, Cork.

Wall, E. (2000) 'Winds Blowing from a Million Directions: Colum McCann's Songdogs' in Fanning, Charles (ed) *New Perspectives on the Irish Diaspora* Carbondale: Southern Illinois University Press.

Ward, P. (2001) *Exile, Emigration and Irish Writing*, Dublin: Irish Academic Press.

Weekes, A. Owens (2000) 'Figuring the Mother in Contemporary Irish Fiction' in Harte, L., Parker, M. (eds) *Contemporary Irish Fiction: Themes, Tropes, Theories*, London: Macmillan.